D0139592

ILL EFFECTS

'... A refreshing guide to what has often been a stale, circular argument, batted between different shades of moral opportunism in the papers – most of whose pundits have never seen the "immorality" in question.'

Tom Dewe Mathews, *Independent on Sunday*

Ill Effects revisits the 'media effects' debate. It asks why, when a particularly high-profile crime of violence is committed, there are those who blame film, television, video, pop music and, more recently, the Internet.

Ill Effects considers how the 'media effects' controversy has developed and combines a discussion about the responses to the shootings at Columbine High School, an analysis of the 1998 Home Office report on video violence and an exploration of why the Internet is being demonised, along with an analysis of fans' responses to supposedly dangerous films such as *Reservoir Dogs*, *Natural Born Killers* and *Man Bites Dog*.

In this new edition, the authors question why the popular press continues to peddle a cruel caricature of the way in which the media supposedly affects behaviour. They argue that there needs to be a change in the very questions that are asked about the influence of the media; rather than fruitlessly searching for evidence of 'harm', there needs to be a better understanding of the ways in which people actually use and interact with so called 'violent' media. Exploring what 'violence' means to different audiences, *Ill Effects* includes a guide to the important new research which is beginning to make a difference to the arguments about the influence of the media.

Contributors: Martin Barker, Sara Bragg, David Buckingham, Thomas Craig, David Gauntlett, Annette Hill, Patricia Holland, Mark Kermode, Graham Murdock, Julian Petley, Sue Turnbull

Editors: **Martin Barker** is Professor of Film and Television Studies at the University of Aberystwyth. **Julian Petley** teaches Communications and Media Studies in the Department of Human Sciences at Brunel University.

COMMUNICATION AND SOCIETY
Series Editor: James Curran

GLASNOST, PERESTROIKA AND THE SOVIET MEDIA
Brian McNair

PLURALISM, POLITICS AND THE MARKETPLACE
The regulation of German Broadcasting
Vincent Porter and Suzanne Hasselbach

POTBOILERS
Methods, concepts and case studies in popular fiction
Jerry Palmer

COMMUNICATION AND CITIZENSHIP
Journalism and the public sphere
Edited by Peter Dahlgren and Colin Sparks

SEEING AND BELIEVING
The influence of television
Greg Philo

CRITICAL COMMUNICATION STUDIES
Communication, history and theory in America
Hanno Hardt

MEDIA MOGULS
Jeremy Tunstall and Michael Palmer

FIELDS IN VISION
Television sport and cultural transformation
Garry Whannel

GETTING THE MESSAGE
News, truth and power
The Glasgow Media Group

ADVERTISING, THE UNEASY PERSUASION
Its dubious impact on American society
Michael Schudson

NATION, CULTURE, TEXT
Australian cultural and media studies
Edited by Graeme Turner

TELEVISION PRODUCERS
Jeremy Tunstall

NEWS AND JOURNALISM IN THE UK
A textbook, second edition
Brian McNair

WHAT NEWS?
The market, politics and the local press
Bob Franklin and David Murphy

IN GARAGELAND
Rock, youth and modernity
Johan Fornäs, Ulf Lindberg and Ove Sernhede

THE CRISIS OF PUBLIC COMMUNICATION
Jay G. Blumler and Michael Gurevitch

GLASGOW MEDIA GROUP READER, VOLUME 1
News content, language and visuals
Edited by John Eldridge

GLASGOW MEDIA GROUP READER, VOLUME 2
Industry, economy, war and politics
Edited by Greg Philo

THE GLOBAL JUKEBOX
The international music industry
Robert Burnett

INSIDE PRIME TIME
Todd Gitlin

TALK ON TELEVISION
Audience participation and public debate
Sonia Livingston and Peter Lunt

AN INTRODUCTION TO POLITICAL COMMUNICATION
Brian McNair

MEDIA EFFECTS AND BEYOND
Culture, socialization and lifestyles
Edited by Karl Erik Rosengren

WE KEEP AMERICA ON TOP OF THE WORLD
Television journalism and the public sphere
Daniel C. Hallin

A JOURNALISM READER
Edited by Michael Bromley and Tom O'Malley

TABLOID TELEVISION
Popular journalism and the 'other news'
John Langer

INTERNATIONAL RADIO JOURNALISM
History, theory and practice
Tim Crook

MEDIA, RITUAL AND IDENTITY
Edited by Tamar Liebes and James Curran

DE-WESTERNIZING MEDIA STUDIES
Edited by James Curran and Myung-Jin Park

BRITISH CINEMA IN THE FIFTIES
Christine Geraghty

ILL EFFECTS
The media/violence debate, second edition
Edited by Martin Barker and Julian Petley

ILL EFFECTS

The media/violence debate

Second edition

*Edited by Martin Barker
and Julian Petley*

London and New York

PJC MIL CAMPUS LRC

First published 1997
Reprinted 1998

Second edition first published 2001
by Routledge
11 New Fetter Lane, London EC4P 4EE

Simultaneously published in the USA and Canada
by Routledge
29 West 35th Street, New York, NY 10001

Routledge is an imprint of the Taylor & Francis group

© 1997, 2001 Martin Barker and Julian Petley, for selection and editorial
matter

© 1997, 2001 Contributors, individual chapters

Typeset in Times by RefineCatch Ltd, Bungay, Suffolk
Printed and bound in Great Britain by
Biddles Ltd, Guildford and King's Lynn

All rights reserved. No part of this book may be reprinted or
reproduced or utilised in any form or by any electronic, mechanical, or
other means, now known or hereafter invented, including photocopying
and recording, or in any information storage or retrieval system,
without permission in writing from the publishers.

British Library Cataloguing in Publication Data
A catalogue record for this book is available from the British Library

Library of Congress Cataloging in Publication Data
Ill effects: the media/violence debate / [edited by] Martin Barker
and Julian Petley.–2nd ed.
p.   cm.
Includes bibliographical references and index.
1. Violence in mass media.   2. Mass media–Influence.   3. Mass
media–Social aspects.   I. Barker, Martin.   II. Petley, Julian.

P96.V5 I55 2001
303.6–dc21   00–045952

ISBN 0–415–22512–4 (hbk)
ISBN 0–415–22513–2 (pbk)

CONTENTS

List of contributors   vii

Introduction: from bad research to good – a guide for the perplexed   1
MARTIN BARKER AND JULIAN PETLEY

1   **The Newson Report: a case study in 'common sense'**   27
MARTIN BARKER

2   **The worrying influence of 'media effects' studies**   47
DAVID GAUNTLETT

3   **Electronic child abuse? Rethinking the media's effects on children**   63
DAVID BUCKINGHAM

4   **Living for libido; or, 'Child's Play IV': the imagery of childhood and the call for censorship**   78
PATRICIA HOLLAND

5   **Just what the doctors ordered? Media regulation, education and the 'problem' of media violence**   87
SARA BRAGG

6   **Once more with feeling: talking about the media violence debate in Australia**   111
SUE TURNBULL

CONTENTS

7 **I was a teenage horror fan: or, 'How I learned to stop worrying and love Linda Blair'**   126

MARK KERMODE

8 **'Looks like it hurts': women's responses to shocking entertainment**   135

ANNETTE HILL

9 **Reservoirs of dogma: an archaeology of popular anxieties**   150

GRAHAM MURDOCK

10 **Us and them**   170

JULIAN PETLEY

11 **Invasion of the Internet abusers: marketing fears about the information superhighway**   186

THOMAS CRAIG AND JULIAN PETLEY

12 **On the problems of being a 'trendy travesty'**   202

MARTIN BARKER (WITH JULIAN PETLEY)

Index   225

CONTRIBUTORS

Martin Barker is Professor of Film and Television Studies at the University of Wales, Aberystwyth. He has a long history of researching censorship campaigns, ranging from the 1950s campaigns against 'horror comics' to the video nasties campaign of 1984/5. Recently, he has been studying the audiences for attacked media, in particular investigating the reception of action-adventure movies (published with Kate Brooks as *Knowing Audiences:* Judge Dredd, *its Friends, Fans and Foes*, 1997) and of David Cronenberg's *Crash*, excoriated by among others the *Daily Mail* in 1996/7 (the findings of this are to be published in 2001). In 2000 he published (with a contribution from Thomas Austin) *From Antz To Titanic: Reinventing Film Analysis.*

Sara Bragg taught Media Studies to adults and to 16- to 19-year-olds for five years before beginning doctoral research on youth audiences, media violence and education, at the Institute of Education in London. She has published articles based on her research in teaching journals. 'It makes you feel like a man: teaching and watching horror' was reprinted in *Where we've been: articles from the ENGLISH AND MEDIA MAGAZINE* (1996).

David Buckingham is Professor of Education at the Institute of Education, University of London, where he directs the Centre for the Study of Children, Youth and Media (www.ccsonline.org.uk/mediacentre). He has undertaken several major research projects on young people's relationships with the media and on media education, and has lectured on these topics in more than 20 countries world-wide. He is the author of numerous books, including *Children Talking Television* (1993), *Moving Images* (1996), *The Making of Citizens* (2000) and *After the Death of Childhood* (2000). He is currently directing a project investigating the changing relationships between 'education' and 'entertainment', and continuing research into the role of media in informal learning.

Thomas Craig, after leaving university in 1995, began working as a manager for Britain's largest firm of video game retailers. One year later, in the light of growing public and media criticism of the games industry, he returned to education. He now teaches Media and Cultural Studies at Nottingham Trent University. His publications include *Four Gothic Tales* (The English Association, 1996) and, more recently, 'Ben Dover in cyberspace: British pornographic films on the Internet', which appeared as part of the third volume of *The Journal of Popular British Cinema* (2000). He is currently conducting research into moral panics surrounding the popularity of role-playing games, and will be publishing a critical guide to the works of Thomas Pynchon later this year.

David Gauntlett is Lecturer in Social Communications at the Institute of Communications Studies, University of Leeds. His interest in the social impact of communications is reflected in his books: *Moving Experiences* (1995), a detailed critique of media effects studies; *Video Critical* (1997), which presented a new audience research method; and *TV Living: Television, Culture and Everyday Life* (with Annette Hill, 1999), a study of diaries kept by 500 people over five years. He has recently edited an introduction to the Internet and society, *Web.Studies: Rewiring Media Studies for the Digital Age* (2000). His next book will be *Media, Gender and Identity: A New Introduction*. He produces the award-winning web-sites www.theory.org.uk and www.newmediastudies.com, both of which contain material on media influences.

Annette Hill is Reader in Mass Media at the University of Westminster. She is the author of *Shocking Entertainment: Viewer Response to Violent Movies* (1997), and the co-author (with David Gauntlett) of *TV Living: Television, Culture and Everyday Life* (1999) as well as several articles on media audiences and popular culture. She is also the editor of *Framework: The Journal of Cinema and Media*.

Patricia Holland is a freelance writer and lecturer. She is the author of *What is a Child?: Popular Images of Childhood* (1992) and *The Television Handbook* (2nd edition 2000) and has published many articles on media, childhood and popular imagery. She is currently researching television history at Bournemouth University.

Mark Kermode is a freelance film journalist and broadcaster. He has written and presented numerous television documentaries including *The Fear of God: 25 Years of The Exorcist* and *Poughkeepsie Shuffle: Tracing the French Connection* for BBC 2, and *On the Edge of Blade Runner* for Channel 4. He introduces the Extreme Cinema series on the FilmFour Channel and Channel 4, and his radio work includes writing and presenting Celluloid Jukebox for BBC Radio 2. He is the author of a BFI Modern Classics volume on *The Exorcist*.

Graham Murdock is Reader in the Sociology of Culture at Loughborough University and Professor of Communication at the University of Bergen.

Julian Petley teaches Communications and Media Studies in the Department of Human Sciences at Brunel University. He is currently writing a book on media censorship for Routledge, for whom he is also co-editing a book on the British horror film. He is Chair of the Campaign for Press and Broadcasting Freedom and is a regular contributor to *Index on Censorship*.

Sue Turnbull is a Senior Lecturer in the Department of Media Studies at La Trobe University in Melbourne, Australia. A former secondary school teacher, she has published a number of essays on the topic of media violence and censorship in Australia and has a particular interest in the history of audience research. She is currently working on a book about crime fiction readerships, entitled *Fatal Fascinations*, while plotting further investigations into the representation of crime on television and its reception.

INTRODUCTION

From bad research to good – a guide for the perplexed

Martin Barker and Julian Petley

When we brought together the essays that made up the first edition of this book, we hoped that it would become a resource: a resource for those worried by the continual stream of claims about 'copy-catting', about the 'corrupting effects' of the 'rising tide of violent media'. For those who sensed that there was something fundamentally wrong with all those claims, but who either felt isolated in their beliefs, or felt they were lacking in clear and accessible evidence and arguments with which to make a counter-case: this book was meant to be something to which they could turn. We believe that to some extent, at least, we succeeded. And all our authors' essays contributed to this. The book received the responses for which we'd hoped: friendly (mainly) from those we'd intended to reach; hostile from those whom we could never have hoped to persuade away from their prejudices. That was about right.

Then our publishers asked us to prepare this second edition. We were delighted to have the opportunity. We were proud to publish every essay that went into the first edition, but now we think we can see a new direction and use for the book, and therefore we've taken this opportunity to rethink its overall shape and to commission a significant number of new essays. Still, the position from which we began then remains the same. We therefore begin by restating the premises that underlay the first edition, and which still frame the second:

1   The claims about the possible 'effects of violent media' are not just false, they range from the daft to the mischievous. The reason for this is that those who insistently make these claims are asking the wrong question. Their question has the same status as those who, for centuries, insistently asked if human illnesses, the death of pigs, thunderstorms, and crop failures were the result of witchcraft. The fallacy is that you have to have

a 'thing' called 'witchcraft' for the question to make sense in the first place.

2   The central reason, then, why the insistent question is so wrong is because *there is no such thing as 'violence' in the media which can have harmful – or beneficial – effects.* Of course, different kinds of media use different kinds of 'violence' for many different purposes – just as they use music, colour, stock characters, deep-focus photography, rhythmic editing and scenes from the countryside, among many others. But in exactly the same way as it is daft to ask 'what are the effects of rhythmic editing or the use of countryside scenes?' without at the same time asking where, when, and in what context these are used, so, we insist, it is stupid simply to ask 'what are the effects of violence?'

3   Sadly, the bogus question won't be disposed of that easily. For however mistaken the initial question, the endless subsequent claims about 'media violence' *perform crucial social and political functions,* just as accusations of witchcraft did in earlier times.

Our tasks, as critics of these contemporary witch-hunters and their pursuits, remain several and the same. We have to continue to demonstrate the fallacies on which their claims rest. Predictably, each new claim comes with an imprimatur of 'this time we've done it, this time we've finally proved it' – but never does an admission follow, when their claims fall apart yet again (as they invariably do), that they were simply wrong in the first place. We have to uncover and hold up to bright daylight the unstated assumptions that come camouflaged within these claims.

We have to show the ill effects of the campaigns run by the 'effects' campaigners – including their effects on those whom the campaigners frequently insult and denigrate as morally debased: the people who enjoy and enthusiastically participate in the movies, TV programmes, video games or whatever that the moralists are so certain are 'harmful'.

And we have, of course, to help to make available an alternative account of the relationship between the media and their audiences. And here we come to the main purpose of this new introduction. We devoted our first introduction to summarising the broad failings of the 'effects' tradition. We've decided to reverse priorities this time and to point you towards the *good* work that has become available. There has been a flush of important research in recent years, but it has been scattered in many places, not all of them easily accessible. We cannot cover all the research which has been done. Nor can we even offer a fully detailed account of these researches. But we can point up their main findings, and try to say why they are relevant to this book. What follows is an introduction to a selection of those which we find most challenging.

You will see that we give preference to a tradition of qualitative research. This isn't at all out of hostility to quantitative research *per se.* We do so first because this tradition is much less known – moral campaigners love a nice-looking statistic, even if that statistic is meaningless or unreliable (and of course the most meaningless of all is that assumption that 'violence' is an abstractable unit whose presence can be counted and whose 'influence' can be studied). The complications that come with real knowledge don't fit banner headlines, therefore tend to get ignored. But more importantly, this tradition of research begins by acknowledging that people who watch TV, or go to the cinema, or play video games, or whatever, do so because these activities *mean* something to them. 'Violent' media produce different kinds of pleasure. They are used and, yes, sometimes even abused, but always within the ordinary contexts of people's lives. If we don't notice, and study, these media and their uses with respect for their patterned complexities, it is a dead cert that we will end up understanding nothing. Fortunately, an array of methods of investigation has been developed in recent years which has been proving its usefulness, and offering insights and explanatory models which can transform our picture of these media, their audiences and their social, cultural and political implications.

Undoing the category 'violence'

We begin at the heart of the beast. A small but growing number of studies has begun to question the status of that central term 'violence', each in different ways showing that for real viewers, as against 'effects' researchers and moral campaigners, 'violence' is not some singular 'thing' which might grow cumulatively like poison inside people.

One of the earliest studies to explore the dimensions of 'violence' was Schlesinger *et al.*'s *Women Viewing Violence* (1992), which was undertaken for the Broadcasting Standards Council. The research focused on women's responses to four very different kinds of programme. One was *Crimewatch UK*, the BBC programme in which viewers are invited to call in with information to help solve current cases, focusing on an episode dealing with the rape and murder of a young hitchhiker. Second was *EastEnders*, the popular soap opera, and in particular a story-line about domestic violence. Third was a hard-hitting drama, *Closing Ranks*, also dealing directly with violence in the home, this time centred on a policeman's family. Finally, the 1989 feature film *The Accused*, which explored the difficulties of proving rape in a case in which men claimed that a woman had been behaving provocatively; the film ends by showing the rape. Schlesinger *et al.*'s research is particularly useful for the range of women interviewed, and its mix of research methods. They recruited women across a wide range of class, age and ethnic backgrounds, and distinguished those with and without personal experience of violence. Their research combined questionnaires giving a picture of the social positions of their respondents, and close interviewing of the women in order to gain access to the detailed patterns of their responses.

Their findings reveal many things. They show, for instance, that for many women there is an important distinction between finding something *disturbing* and nonetheless *wanting it to be shown*. The responses to *EastEnders* proved complicated, in that the violence involved a white man and a black woman, and the black women in the research tended to assess the events in terms of their *racial* significance rather than in terms of domestic violence. Again, in the responses to the *Crimewatch* hitchhiker story, wider cultural attitudes concerning women going out on their own cut across women's assessment of the programme. *The Accused* aroused strong feelings across almost all participants, with close identification with Jodie Foster's victim-character. But only in a few cases did these strong feelings result in demands for censorship. Rather, it brought forth discussion of 'men' as viewers, and of what might be done to control their ways of watching programmes containing violence against women. Here is perhaps their most important conclusion:

> The issue is not whether depictions of violence increase the likelihood of similar violence among potential perpetrators, but the feelings and reactions that it creates among those who are the actual or potential victims of violence. Are women likely to feel more vulnerable, less safe or less valued members of our society if, as a category, they are with some frequency depicted as those who are subjected to abuse? If so, the portrayal of violence against women may be seen as negative, even if women viewers have never experienced such violence and/or its likelihood is not increased.
>
> (Schlesinger *et al.*, 1992: 170)

These are not comfortable findings, and they challenge us all to a proper democratic debate about these issues. But comfortable or not, they change the terms in which that debate will need to take place. For it is not the sheer fact of the presence of violence that is the issue: it is its purpose and meanings, both within individual media items and the wider circuits and currents of feelings and ideas that accompany it, that have to be examined.

In 1998 Schlesinger *et al.* followed up this first investigation with a study of the ways in which groups of men perceived, understood and judged different kinds of media violence. They recognise that they are explicitly challenging the traditional 'effects' agenda: '[T]he present study, like its predecessor, is not a simplistic "effects" or "no effects" piece of research. Both studies represent attempts to move the research agenda away from this narrow debate onto more productive and relevant ground.' (1998: 4)

The study used 88 men aged between 18 and 75, with a deliberate mix of class, ethnic memberships and sexual preferences, and showed them various combinations of: an episode of *EastEnders* featuring alcoholism leading to domestic violence; *Trip Trap*, a quality TV drama addressing issues of sexual violence; a documentary about street fighting; and two Hollywood box office successes, *Basic Instinct* and *Under Siege*. There was as much variety in the specific responses as there had been among their women interviewees, but even more strongly than the women, the men's perceptions and judgements of violent media were based on the *rules and standards of the groups and communities to which they belonged*. So, the street-fighting was judged 'ordinary' and in fact exciting by those men whose lives included the kinds of relationships and risks that fairly easily lead to such fights.

But even more strongly than in the case of the women, a line was drawn between 'realistic' violence – which could make you stop and think – and 'unrealistic' violence such as the two Hollywood films. These were assessed not against 'life' but against other movies – their meaning for men such as these was in terms of a world of entertainment.

Yet again, therefore, research that listens to the operative ideas of people, rather than encasing them in psychologistic language, finds people always responding to 'violent media' through their social and historical worlds, through shared understandings, and with (whether we like or approve of them or not) complicated moral codes.[1]

Finally, in this section, we want to draw attention to *Defining Violence* (1999), by David Morrison. This research, which was commissioned by all the major broadcasters and carried out at Leeds University, set out to discover 'the subjective meaning of violence. How, in other words, did people classify acts as violent and other acts, although ostensibly violent, as not really violent? Did people, furthermore, have a common definition of violence, or were there many different definitions?' (1999: vii). To answer these questions, the researchers recruited a wide range of people who might be expected to have different experiences of and attitudes to violence both in real life and on screen: policemen; young men and women drawn from cultural groups familiar with violence; women who had a heightened fear, but no personal experience, of violence; women with small children; men with small children, and so on. The groups were shown a wide variety of visual material and, in a significant methodological move, were given the chance during discussions actually to re-edit the footage as a means of clarifying what they meant by 'violence'.

What the research showed was that it is not particular acts which make a programme seem violent, but the context in which they occur, a finding which clearly backs up the work of Schlesinger *et al.* (1992, 1998). The Leeds researchers were able to distinguish several different kinds of fictional screen violence:

> *Playful violence* is clearly acted violence, and is seen as unreal. The violence looks staged, and has little significance beyond its entertainment value. It is invariably seen as violence with a little v. A lot of

violent action may be involved, but it is not graphic and does not assault the sensibilities.

Depicted violence is violence that is characterised by 'realism'. It attempts to depict violence as it would appear in real life. It often includes close-up shots of injury, and is very graphic. This can indeed assault the sensibilities, and is invariably defined as violence with a big V.

Authentic violence is violence set in a world that the viewer can recognise. A classic case would be domestic violence. Violence in a pub or shopping precinct might be other examples. It is closer to the life of the viewer than other forms of violence. It might be seen as violence with a little v, depending on how the scene is played, although it does have the potential to be big V, and even massive V. In other words, it has the possibility of assaulting the senses very strongly indeed.

(Morrison, 1999: 4–5)

These categories helped them to determine how their group members distinguished between violent scenes, but they still left a central question: what causes something to be perceived as violent? Group discussions revealed two determining factors: the *nature and quality* of the violence portrayed, which is a moral factor, and the *way in which* it was portrayed, which is an aesthetic one. The elements which make up the first factor the researchers called the *primary definers* of violence, those which contribute to the second factor the *secondary definers*. Together these determine the definition of violence. The primary definers are 'drawn from real life, and what is deemed violent on screen is the same as what is deemed violent in real life. An act is defined as violent in real life if it breaks a recognised and mutually agreed code of conduct' (ibid.: 6). Thus, for example, for some groups a punch thrown in a pub is not judged to be violent in any serious sense, whereas 'glassing' somebody in the same situation would universally be regarded as a violent act. The researchers also found that the most prevalent general rule seems to be that behaviour which is judged to be appropriate, fair and justified – even when overtly violent – is not usually seen to be seriously or 'really' violent.

Once the primary definers have come into play, the secondary ones establish and grade the *degree* of violence perceived by the viewer:

The secondary definers categorise a scene of violence if it looks 'real' – as the viewer imagines it would if witnessed in real life. Close-up shots of an injury, and splattering blood, both make violence look 'real'. So does the manner in which an injury is delivered, and how it is portrayed. Each of these elements helps to produce a greater sense of violence once the primary definers have established the scene to be violent in the first place.

(ibid.: 7)

From their work with these groups, the researchers finally arrived at the following definition of violence:

> Screen violence is any act that is seen or unequivocally signalled which would be considered an act of violence in real life, because the violence was considered unjustified either in the degree or nature of the force used, or that the injured party was undeserving of the violence. The degree of violence is defined by how realistic the violence is considered to be, and made even stronger if the violence inflicted is considered unfair.
>
> (ibid.: 9)

This is valuable research with a great deal to teach, but here we simply draw attention to one of their central propositions, namely that in order to understand the meaning of 'violence' in the media, you have to understand the moral codes that different audiences bring to bear as they watch.

Positive pleasures

One central problem of the 'effects' tradition is its treatment of those who dare to enjoy or even admit to being users of the kinds of materials condemned by the moral campaigners. Because the materials (films, videos, games, whatever) are 'known' to be harmful, their audiences *must* be at best blind, at worst already thoroughly corrupted. So the only question, in truth, that 'effects' research knows to ask is: what signs are there that audiences for 'harmful media' have been adversely affected? Again, this is a question that the new qualitative research has sought to supplant. A few, too few, studies have done so by learning how to listen to the real enthusiasts, and in doing so have come up with some real surprises.[2]

One limitation of Schlesinger *et al.*'s first study was that many of its women respondents would not normally have watched, or certainly not watched with enjoyment, some of the materials about which they were asked to comment. In this, in fact, the research fits a little too comfortably with a stereotypical image that 'violent programming' is enjoyed only by men, not women.[3] Annette Hill's (1997) research has begun to unpick this. Hill's study investigates in detail the kinds of pleasure that both men and women have taken in the crop of films that, post-Tarantino and *Pulp Fiction*, have generally been regarded by the media as upping the stakes in 'levels of violence'. Most interestingly, Hill found a great deal of overlap between the responses of male and female fans of these films. For both, the most important element in the films was not the violence *per se* but the ways in which they found them mentally challenging and boundary-testing. According to Hill, consumers of violent movies possess 'portfolios of interpretation', a concept which she uses to catch hold of the ways people become

7

experienced and *knowledgeable* in their ways of understanding violent movies. These 'portfolios' include:

- a conscious awareness that violent movies test viewers in various ways.
- anticipation and preparation as an essential aspect of the enjoyment of viewing violent movies.
- building relationships and engaging with certain screen characters, whilst establishing a safe distance from others.
- bringing into play a variety of methods to self-censor violence.
- utilising violent images as a means of testing personal boundaries and as a safe way (within a clearly fictional setting) of interpreting and thinking about violence.
- actively differentiating between real-life violence and fictional violence.

Hill also draws attention to the fact that the process of viewing violent films is very much a social activity, arguing that 'part of the enjoyment of viewing violence is to monitor audience reactions, as the films themselves provoke reaction. Individual response is part of a much wider awareness of the variety of responses available to consumers of violent movies' (Hill, 1997: 105–6).

Understanding how its actual audiences respond to a film all too easily dismissed as simply 'violent' was part of a project into the reception of action-adventure movies by Martin Barker and Kate Brooks (1998). In particular, they were interested in the ways in which fans talked about how they used and enjoyed the film, which led them to analyse what they called the fans' 'vocabularies of involvement and pleasure'. These revealed a series of practices of pleasure which included: physical satisfaction; being part of a crowd; creating imaginative worlds; game-playing and role-playing; taking risks; rule-breaking and defying convention; confirming membership of communities of response; and critical appreciation. A key point about these practices of pleasure is that they all

> involve some kind of preparation, and therefore have a pattern of involvement which extends beyond the moments of pleasure, on which in significant ways the pleasures depend. Crudely, there are things we have to do, and to know, and to prepare for in advance if any of these pleasures are to be gained.
>
> (Barker and Brooks, 1998: 145)

In relation to their target film *Judge Dredd*, Barker and Brooks identified a number of distinct patterns of expectation revealed by their interviewees, each expressing in its own 'language' a particular relation to the film and cinema-going, and providing a basis for distinct ways of being involved. According to Barker and Brooks, each vocabulary of involvement and pleasure represents a culturally-generated SPACE (standing for Site for the Production of Active Cinematic Experiences) into which an individual can move. There were six such SPACES:

- The Action-Adventure SPACE, for those aiming to become involved in the film at a sensuous, physical level, treating it as a roller-coaster experience.
- The Future-Fantastic SPACE, for those anticipating a physical experience too, but also getting ready to respond to spectacular technologies and demonstrations of new cinematic skills.
- The 2000 AD-Follower SPACE, for those already familiar with the Judge Dredd world and who are hoping to see a huge character made as big and as public as he deserves and requires.
- The Film-Follower SPACE, for those committed to cinema as a medium and wanting the film to contribute to some aspect of 'cinematic magic'.
- The Stallone-Follower SPACE, for those wanting to see what the film adds to Stallone's career and his screen persona.
- The Culture-Belonging SPACE, for those who choose to raid a film for information, jokes, stories, catch-phrases which can contribute to their on-going membership of local groups.

Barker and Brooks are particularly interested in those respondents who combine two SPACES: Action-Adventure and Future-Fantastic. What they point to is an intriguing parallel between the filmic pleasures sought by young working class audiences – just the kind of young males who feature strongly in scares about 'dangerous' media – and the world view of those early Utopians, the medieval Chiliasts described by Karl Mannheim in *Ideology and Utopia* (1960). The Chiliasts, who tended to be drawn from the 'oppressed strata of society', sought their Utopia not in some far distant future, rather:

> The Chiliast expects a union with the immediate present. Hence he is not preoccupied in his daily life with optimistic hopes for the future or romantic reminiscences . . . He is not actually concerned with the millennium that is to come; what is important for him is that it has happened here and now, and that it arose from mundane existence, as a sudden swing over into another kind of existence.
>
> (Mannheim, 1960: 195)

In other words, what Chiliasm offered was a way of experiencing *in the present* the qualities of a transformed world, a process in which 'spiritual fermentation and physical excitement' (ibid.: 192) played its part and in which 'sensual experience is present in all its robustness' (ibid.: 194). In short: 'for the real Chiliast, the present becomes the breach through which what was previously inward bursts out suddenly, takes hold of the outer world and transforms it' (ibid.: 193).

The parallels with action movie fans' love of cinema's sensuous qualities, its orgiastic excess and its possibilities for envisioning other worlds are thought-provoking. Furthermore, just as Mannheim points out that 'the utopian vision aroused a contrary vision' (ibid.: 192), so action films such as *Judge Dredd* have been misrepresented and condemned as 'gratuitously violent' and so on. Barker and Brooks are at pains not to over-emphasise the parallel, but at the same time they do insist that it is a significant and meaningful one:

> To understand their participation in this way is not to romanticise their love of film as some kind of political opposition. It is simply to consider the particular ways in which their love of Action films is embroidered into the rest of their lives, and to see in it the incipient signs of an awareness of disjunctions: between present and future, between the celebration and the dread of the impact of technology in and on their lives; between heroic rescue of the world and the oppressiveness of 'heroes'; between the wealth that is possible, that is put daily on display in front of them, and the actual lot of 'the common people'. And that, paradoxically, means that the other world which can be glimpsed is not pretty. It is not the 'peaceful, other' world of the hippies. It can only operate as a utopia by simultaneously celebrating and excoriating the dumb brutalities of new technologies, their business lords and their oppressive systems.
>
> (Barker and Brooks, 1998: 290–1)

If they are right, the significance of Barker and Brooks' findings is that what is condemned as 'gratuitous' and 'immoral' is actually experienced by its key fans as *political*.

One other piece of research acknowledges its small scale but still points up some important issues for us. John Fiske and Robert Dawson (1996) report on the way a group of homeless American men watch violent movies, in particular *Die Hard*. As part of a much wider ethnographic investigation of the world of the homeless, centred on a church shelter, they gained the chance to observe how a group of men responded as they watched this film which they had selected on video. The findings, albeit based on one group, are very suggestive.

They observed, for instance, that the men shifted in who they favoured as the movie progressed. At the start, they cheered and commented on the terrorists who invade and seize a corporate building and kill its chief executive. But when the film's hero begins his lone action against the terrorists, the fact that he does it alone, outside the law and at some cost to himself made him also attractive to these viewers. But once he began to side overtly with the police, and to become in effect their agent, they not only lost interest in him, they went so far as to turn the video off. Fiske and Dawson interpret their actions as an expression of their alienation and anger:

> Another favoured scene was that in which the terrorists easily repelled the police's attempt to retake the building. The climax of the scene occurred when an armoured car attempting to batter its way in was disabled by a rocket launched by the terrorists. The hero, from his hidden vantage point, can see them preparing to fire another rocket, whose purpose is not to save the building from attack, but to complete the tactically unnecessary destruction of the machine and the men in it. In voice-over he begs them not to. They do, and as the camera lingers on the apparently pointless destruction and death, the homeless men cheer enthusiastically.
>
> (Fiske and Dawson, 1996: 306)

The men refused the 'lawful' positioning, and enjoyed their own refusal, Fiske and Dawson argue. What is interesting here is not just the demonstration of a political way of relating to the film, but that to make sense of it, Fiske and Dawson have to relate the men's behaviour to the detailed narrative workings of the film – something which moral campaigners simply don't understand how to do.

Children and the media

At the heart of the 'effects' tradition stands the figure of the 'child': innocent, vulnerable, corruptible. A small but growing group of researchers have undertaken the difficult task of learning how to investigate children's own views and understandings of the media. The results have been distinctly productive.

A good early example of such productive and challenging work is Robert Hodge and David Tripp's Australian study of children's responses to a television mock-horror cartoon *Fangface*. With an eye directly on the kinds of claim made about children and cartoons (too much violence, anti-educational because too undemanding, perhaps leading to confusions between fantasy and reality), Hodge and Tripp carried out a series of experiments with children aged 10 to 14. The experiments were aimed at opening up children's own understandings of such cartoons. Beginning with a careful semiotic examination of the episode of *Fangface* which they used centrally in their research, and showing through this its *potential* for raising complex issues such as the nature of good and evil, they go on to explore how children make sense of characters, action and narrative. All this is done by using a careful and semi-structured set of ways of listening symptomatically to the way the children talk, drawing out the categories they are implicitly using, the distinctions they are drawing and the connections they are making.

Among their findings are some directly relevant to the issues this book is trying to raise. Crucially, they show that a series of changes take place, as children are growing up, in the ways in which they learn to 'manage' the distinction between fantasy and reality, or how they learn how to make 'modality-judgements'. Children, they show, have a very complicated understanding, in which their judgements of 'reality' will for instance make distinctions between their parents (who is more 'real' can depend on who buys your clothes for you), and their friends and pets. So, 'reality' is not some simple category of 'true things versus fictional things'. But children learn over time to make sophisticated judgements – and one of the ways in which they learn this is precisely by engaging with story-forms. Cartoons and such equivalent materials are important to children *because* they simplify. They enable children to try out and develop complex conceptual connections, at the same time as they move from seeing stories as just composed of elements in a ('paratactic') series to perceiving and operating with the idea of a ('hypotactic') story-structure.

This recognition of the complexity of modality-systems is a great advance, and leads to one conclusion that is particularly apt to our arguments. Hodge and Tripp say:

> Young children do distinguish between fantasy and reality, but they do not know what is needed to distinguish with the precision and subtlety assumed for adult television. So their response to adult programming is typically skewed, and they have distinct needs of their own. Their modality judgements tend to be polarised, contradictory and unstable. They are likely to under-read modality cues, and respond with an intensity that seems inappropriate and disturbing to adults, especially if the modality of the programme is ambiguous or disguised. Paradoxically, it follows that children do in fact need a diet rich in explicit fantasy – including cartoons – in order to develop a confident and discriminating modality system. They also need, and crave, an understanding of the processes of media production. In sum, children's modality systems are developing throughout childhood: their grasp of reality, or the reality of television is not a simple matter. During this process of growth, children will often make modality 'mistakes', but it seems that their concepts of reality must sometimes be put at risk if they are to develop a complex and fruitful modality system.
>
> (1986: 130)

Far from being 'harmful', Hodge and Tripp have shown ways in which these kinds of frequently damned materials are *necessary* to full human development.

Some of the most valuable work on children and television to have emerged in recent years has been carried out by David Buckingham, most notably in *Children Talking Television* (1993) and *Moving Images* (1996). Buckingham's work is concerned not with television's 'effects' in the conventional sense of the term, but rather with how children and young people actually perceive, define and understand television programmes. His research brief has been wide, much wider than this book's. In particular he has become concerned with the ways in which children become citizens of their society (see Buckingham (2000)), and the role of the media in these processes. As Buckingham points out, one of the many problems of traditional research into children's relationship with television is that 'it has paid very little attention to the diverse ways in which they make sense of what they watch; to the kinds of knowledge they bring to television, and the critical skills they develop in relation to it; or to the social contexts in which the medium is used and talked about' (1996: 7). Buckingham's focus, on the other hand, is precisely upon the development of television literacy in children. His own qualitative researches lead him to this conclusion:

> Children respond to and make sense of television in the light of what they know about its formal codes and conventions, about genre and narrative, and about the production process. In these respects, they are much more active and sophisticated users of the medium than they are often assumed to be.
>
> (1996: 7)

Buckingham's work is too wide to be adequately summarised here, but among his more specific conclusions are the following:

- most parents and children challenged the view that television on its own was a sufficient cause of violent behaviour. Parents were more likely to express concern about the possible 'effects' of television on other people's children than on their own, whilst the children themselves displaced such concerns onto younger children. Parents were more concerned that their children might be frightened or traumatised by violence on television than that they might try to imitate it.
- children had negative responses, such as fright, disgust, sadness or worry, not only to the more predictable genres such as horror, but also to a surprisingly wide and apparently innocuous range of programmes, including those specifically aimed at children. Negative responses are common amongst children, though they are rarely severe or long-lasting.
- children clearly distinguished between factual and fictional material on television, and found it easier to distance themselves from the latter than

from the former. However, even where factual material, such as news coverage of wars and disasters, was described as upsetting it was also regarded by many as being important to watch, in that it provided necessary information about the real world.

- the main concern of children who watched horror films or true crime programmes was that they might become victims of violence. There was little sense of vicarious 'identification' with the monster or the perpetrator of violence.

- children had a wide range of strategies to protect themselves from or deal with negative responses. These ran the gamut from partial or total avoidance of potentially upsetting programmes to actively denying their reality status ('it's only a movie').

- children who watched fictional violence might become habituated to watching more fictional violence, but this did not 'desensitise' their perceptions of real-life violence, whether mediated by television or not.

Buckingham's work on children as media audiences is among the very best, in our view. He has shown with commendable clarity how research on children and the media should be conducted. And his work challenges in detail many of the assumptions that underpin the 'figure' of the child which is so essential to media moral scares. But it does much more than this. It shows the ways in which even young children are already making complex moral decisions about what they should watch, and for whom particular kinds of materials are appropriate. It also shows that children themselves know about, and indeed are influenced by, those scares – a point of greater weight than has so far been acknowledged.[4]

Symbolic politics

One of the themes of our book is that there is a strong tendency for press, politicians and pundits to 'name' something as 'violence', to judge it in simplistic moral terms, and thus to warrant searches for simple 'causes' (such as 'violent media') of events which happen for a whole variety of complex social and political reasons. An important example of just this kind is explored in Darnell Hunt's (1997) study of responses to the television coverage of the 1992 Los Angeles 'riots', which followed the initial Not Guilty verdict for the police who had been filmed beating up black motorist Rodney King. An important study in much wider ways than concern this book, Hunt's work has much to say that is relevant to our argument. Hunt investigated the responses to the television coverage of white, Latino and black LA viewers, and shows the different ways in which these audiences understood the events, the key players, and the 'violent acts' committed according not simply to their 'colour' but to their sense of the communities to which they belong.

Hunt argues that people responded to the TV coverage in the light of their 'raced subjectivity', that is, their sense of who they are and what groups they belong to in the wider world. This strongly affected not only their responses to the particular coverage, but also their wider sense of which media and which spokespeople they will trust. But perhaps most interestingly for our purposes, Hunt uncovered the way people acknowledged or denied a 'racial' component:

> When one surveys intergroup patterns . . . evidence begins to mount for what I have referred to as 'raced ways of seeing'. Black-raced and Latino-raced study groups were quite animated during the screening of the KTTV text, while white-raced study groups watched quietly. For black-raced informants, in particular, raced subjectivity was clearly an important lens through which the events and the text were viewed . . . [W]hile white-raced and Latino-raced informants were *less* likely than their black-raced counterparts to talk about themselves in raced terms, they were *more* likely than black-raced informants to condemn the looting and fires and to support the arrests.
>
> (Hunt, 1997: 141)

Hunt is arguing that *everyone* responded via their sense of their 'racial' community, but that this was most clearly *acknowledged* in the case of black viewers. For white and Latino viewers, in ducking this, represented their responses through the seemingly 'neutral' categories of 'violence' and 'law and order'. The echoes for our own experiences of attitudes towards 'violence' are clear and audible.

In this connection, it is also worth considering the research reported in an essay by John Gabriel (1996), who explored the ways in which the film *Falling Down* was received in Britain. As with Fiske and Dawson, Gabriel starts by recognising the complicated meanings of this film, which tracks a white middle class defence worker (played by Michael Douglas), known mainly through his car plates 'tag', D-Fens, who, finding his world going to pieces as he loses his job and is mugged and cheated by various ethnic groups, fights back violently, and is eventually killed. When the film was released in America, a series of press stories reported that white male audiences had cheered on Douglas' character, apparently identifying with his assertion that 'whiteness' has become minority in contemporary America.

Gabriel explores in detail the responses of 16 viewers, of whom a number were non-white. He found some real complexities in their responses, based on people at times giving and at others withholding their assent to his actions and values. So, his black interviewees could join in and cheer when D-Fens confronts, as they felt on the basis of class, some rich golfers who seek to exclude him. But when he faces down a group of Latino muggers, they recognise a racist potential in him which leads them to distance themselves from him. So, although Gabriel's reading of the film indicates that it is centrally organised around ideas of 'whiteness', he concludes that 'whiteness' is not a singular thing, but something conveyed and understood in complicated ways:

> Ironically, D-Fens was arguably at his most popular with his audience not in the Korean shop or the wasteland with the Latino gang members, but on the golf course when he confronted another version of white masculinity. In this scene, the golfers were more conspicuously white than D-Fens himself, not just because their whiter-than-white outfits outshone D-Fens' battle-dress, but also because their whiteness was associated with the affluence and exclusivity of the golf-course setting.
>
> (Gabriel, 1996: 150)

But D-Fens' seeming racism could be 'written out' by audiences who could see him as flawed and driven to extremes by his frustrations – and who could thus see his death as redeeming him. As with Fiske and Dawson, Gabriel reveals complexities of both attention and symbolic response which can be grasped only by methods of research which hear their audiences in complex ways. Both pieces of research, crucially, remind us that 'violence' too easily becomes a coded term hiding all sorts of political factors and preferences.

Video games

In this second edition, we have tried to keep abreast of recent developments in the arguments about 'media violence'. One of the striking new features has been the emergence of fears about computers and, especially, video games. Currently, to our knowledge, there has been very little research into the players of video games of a kind that escapes the clutches of the 'harm' brigade.[5] The best example we can find comes within Sue Howard's *Wired-Up* (1998), itself generally a collection of thoughtful essays on various aspects and periods of young people's relations with different electronic media, from TV through telephones to video players, cameras and games. Video games are touched on in one particular essay. It reports on the findings of two small pieces of research, using interviews and group activities with players, some of them very young. The essay, although slight, provides useful evidence that children do not get 'lost' in their games, as is sometimes claimed. They are certainly committed to them, but are articulate about their games' forms and strategies. But the essay is essentially defensive – video games don't do the 'harm' that is claimed. So, the authors talk about the 'reassurance to be found' (Howard, 1998: 37) in the fact that the boys they interviewed were well able to take control both of the games they played and of their interview – at the same time! But they put their finger on the nub when they write that future researchers have to learn, however hard it is, to see the games *'from the standpoint of the child'* (ibid.: 36).

Aside from these, the most useful writings on this still quite new area are a small number of books written by games fans, who are able to describe with insider-acuity the different natures of the games, and the kinds of skill and involvement that they offer to readers. Two in particular stand out: J C Herz's (1997) *Joystick Nation*, and Steven Poole's (2000a) *Trigger Happy*. Herz's book is a wonderfully informed history of the rise of video gaming, offering a host of insights into what these games mean to their committed players. But for our purposes, Poole's book is the more relevant.

Poole runs his gamer's experienced eye over the various main genres. For instance, the world-builders (*SimCity*, for instance); the racing games ('every increase in technological power enhances the genre's unique pleasure, the feeling of hurling a vehicle around a realistic environment at suicidal velocities' (Poole 2000a: 39)); the shoot-'em-ups (from *Space Invaders* onwards, whose premise is that there are always more enemies than you are ever likely to be able to survive . . . so, how long can you keep firing?); the crazy worlds (*Mario Bros* exemplifies its fundamental principle – if it moves towards you, jump!); and so on. What Poole is particularly good at is demonstrating the *logics* of games, and how they call up complicated combinations of know-ledges, skills and daft decisions. Talking, for example, of the beat-'em-ups – one genre that has regularly been greeted with opprobrium – he smiles over the weirdly 'politically inclusive' way in which we have first to adopt a role. You can, by playing various games, be 'a blonde, sandal-wearing Greek woman in a miniskirt . . . a Hawaiian Sumo wrestler . . . Bruce Lee in a gold lamé leotard, a pogo-happy alien cyborg or a tiny, annoying dragon . . .' (ibid.: 46). Once committed, you then have to make sure you know the rules. Far from being uncontrolled mayhem, it is necessarily constrained. This is their Achilles' Heel; every possible move a character can make *has* to be pre-planned:

> Not only is it (understandably) impossible to perform a move for which there is no animation, but motion-capture techniques mean that once an animation has started, it *must* finish before the next one can start. You can't change tactics mid-move. That rules out true feints, which are critical in real fighting sports such as fencing.
>
> (ibid.: 47)

Poole is also very good at demonstrating the many ways in which games depend upon science fiction conventions and trade continuously with other filmic genres. For instance, space is very noisy, lasers are extremely visible, even in a vacuum – and slow enough to duck and avoid. This is highly relevant to the obsessively repeated worry about games becoming more 'realistic'. But 'realism' in games is of a different order from scientific laws, and performs different functions. Where games do obey physical laws, it is because a game without predictability would be unplayable: 'a critical requirement is that a game's system remains consistent, that it is internally coherent' (ibid.: 64). So, *Tomb Raider III* has a problem with its rocket launcher. This 'blows up one's enemies into pleasingly gory, fleshy chunks, but does no damage to a simple wooden door, for which one simply has to find a rusty old key' (ibid.: 65). The more experienced a player, Poole is arguing, the more s/he assesses games by how well they provide an adequate and internally-logical game-world.

This is the real strength of Poole's book. It does not report any audience research, but it lays down a sufficiently clear picture of how games actually work to make it relatively easy to see what would be worth knowing, and even how it might come to be known. His intelligent account of the logics and pleasures of games gives no comfort at all to the moralists' critiques, and Poole himself published a brilliant demolition of one much-vaunted piece of 'research' in the *Guardian* (2000b).

'Effects' and beyond

It should by now be abundantly clear that a good deal of work on how audiences respond to media portrayals of violence of one kind or another has moved far beyond the crudities of the 'effects' paradigm. However, as David Buckingham points out:

> There are, of course, other effects which have been addressed within media research – effects which might broadly be termed 'ideological'. For example, the extensive debates about media representations of women or of ethnic minority groups are clearly premised on assumptions about their potential influence on public attitudes.
>
> (Buckingham, 1996: 310)

We agree. Anyone with half an eye on the recent *News of the World* campaign to 'name and shame' paedophiles couldn't help but see real 'effects' of media output. Vigilantism, attacks on innocent people, at times escalating to near-riots: all fed by the ways in which the media, and especially the tabloid press, covered the murder of Sarah Payne, 'informed' their readers and gave vent to the most brutish of feelings in their editorial columns. But the example is apposite. No one 'copied'. No direct 'message' was involved. There was no 'cumulative' influence. The issue of *how* the media can be influential must now move centre-stage. The trouble is, the word 'effects' has come to be burdened with such a mighty load of negative, judgmental and censorious connotations that we need virtually a new language in order to delineate the impacts which Buckingham rightly calls 'ideological'.

Some particularly useful work in this area has emerged from the Glasgow University Media Group, and we highlight two studies in particular. The first is *Seeing and Believing* (1990) by Greg Philo, which is based on a study of responses to television coverage of the 1984–5 coal dispute. Here, foreshadowing the study by Morrison (1999) described earlier, groups of people were asked not simply to comment on the news broadcasts which the researchers showed them, but also to write their own. As Philo explains:

> This would show what they thought the content of the news to be on a given issue. It might then be possible to compare this with what they actually believed to be true and to examine why they either accepted or rejected the media account. The approach made members of the public temporarily into journalists and became the basis for the study.
>
> (1990: 8)

Philo was interested in the differences within the audience (including gender, regional location, class position, political culture and so on), and the consequences these might have for the way in which information from the media is received. Investigation of the complex interactions of media messages and their readers thus enabled the researchers to investigate 'long-term processes of belief, understanding and memory'.

What the researchers found was that in many cases there were 'extraordinary similarities' between the actual news programmes which their groups had watched and the news reports which they themselves subsequently wrote. In particular the groups tended strongly to reproduce the themes of the 'drift back to work' and of 'escalating violence' (especially by striking miners) which so heavily dominated media coverage of the dispute. To quote Philo: 'it was remarkable how closely some of the group stories reflected not only the thematic content of the news but also the structure of actual headlines. One of the surprises in this research was the clarity with which the groups were able to reproduce themes from the news. It also surprised group members' (ibid.: 260).

The researchers also found remarkable the number of people who believed that the violent images of picketing which they saw on television accurately represented the everyday reality of picketing during the dispute. In all, 54 per cent of the general sample believed that the picketing was mostly violent, and the source for these beliefs was overwhelmingly given as the media, with the emphasis on television because of its immediate quality. However, Philo warns:

> It would be wrong to see people as being totally dependent on such messages, as if they were simply empty vessels which are being filled

19

up by *News at Ten*. To accept and believe what is seen on television is as much a cultural act as the rejection of it. Both acceptance and rejection are conditioned by our beliefs, history and experience.

(ibid.: 260)

What emerged here was that beliefs about how much violence occurred on picket lines, and about how accurately television reflected actual daily life on the lines, differed greatly according to how much specialist knowledge and direct experience of the strike group members possessed. In short, the more knowledge they possessed the less likely they were to believe that the picketing was mostly violent and that the television pictures of violence accurately represented the daily reality of the strike. But perhaps the most interesting finding came from a 'wild card' in the research. Respondents had been given a set of stills from news broadcasts which they were asked to put in order and then to write an accompanying news commentary. Among the stills was a shot of a gun (in fact, from a news item about a working miner threatening to defend himself). Such was the force of the news 'template' of picket line violence that even those who were most suspicious of the television coverage tended to associate the gun with the strikers or with 'militant outsiders'. Either way, even a year after the events, critics of the coverage and supporters of the striking miners still had to *defend themselves* against the perceived force of the news' claims.

Philo's work on television coverage of the coal dispute is particularly useful in that it clearly demonstrates that the interpretation of images is an extremely complex affair involving culture, logic and experience in a negotiation process that can lead to either acceptance or rejection of media messages, or even to a qualified mixture of both. A similar project was also undertaken by other members of the group (Miller *et al.* (1998)) which, in the words of the book's subtitle, examines 'media strategies, representation and audience reception in the AIDS crisis'. Although the subject is outside the range of this present book, the research does nonetheless open up some important lines of thought which we believe readers will find useful.

In order to try to understand audience reception of media messages about AIDS, the researchers posed the following questions:

What factors influence the acceptance or rejection of a specific message? Why do some media messages mobilise public action and others do not? What do people bring to their understandings of AIDS? How are audience responses to AIDS media messages related to the broader cultural context and to people's socio-demographic positions and political identities?

(Miller *et al.*, 1998: 168)

In order to try to answer these questions, over 350 people in 52 focus-groups took part in group discussions, completed questionnaires, and were involved with script-writing exercises in which they were presented with stills from television news bulletins and asked to reproduce a news report about AIDS. What they found was

> widespread similarities in how people understood the coverage of AIDS, and we identified systematic patterns in the information and impressions recalled by the research participants. It was also clear that aspects of the media coverage helped to inform, sustain and shape attitudes to the epidemic.
>
> (ibid.: 171)

On the other hand, the researchers show how people do not indiscriminately absorb every media message, rather they interpret what they hear and see in the context both of what they already know and what they learn from other sources:

> The 'power' of any media report or advertisement is not embedded solely in the individual message itself. Each image or item of information enters a world already populated by a multitude of other sources of information ... Mass media messages intersect with moral judgements and broader cultural assumptions and compete with, or reinforce, messages from other non-media sources, such as the attitudes and behaviour of friends, pervasive sexism, racism or heterosexism, and the practicalities of their daily lives. Each message thus interacts with people's personal experiences and structural positions.
>
> (ibid.: 190)

It is these wider factors which enable, on occasions, media messages to be challenged, resisted or rejected, and which thus help to explain the diversity of audience response to such messages. For example, whilst for some the saturation coverage of AIDS and the status of the sources carried great weight, for others these had precisely the opposite effect. Some started from the position that the media sensationalise issues, distort the facts and mislead the public, and such misgivings were greatly increased by actual personal experience of events that had received media coverage. Others were sceptical of anything, even healthcare information, emanating from a Conservative government. Not surprisingly, such mistrust was often related to political affiliation and sexual and ethnic identity. In some cases, scepticism about official information was reinforced by uncertainty over expert knowledge, much of this reinforced by contradictory or changing reports of the state of expert opinion. However, the researchers concluded that:

> Scepticism did not operate in isolation as an explanation for people's responses. Other factors came into play; factors such as their personal 'stake' in the message, socio-demographic and structural position, political perspective, personal experience and their access to other sources of information.
>
> (ibid.: 199)

But even personal experience is socially patterned and not necessarily a media-free zone. Personal experience may be shaped by media constructions of reality, and is anyway a shaky basis for challenging powerful prevalent cultural definitions. Furthermore, the researchers add that although 'logic, scepticism, personal experience and critical thinking can enable people to resist media messages' it is also the case that 'such resistance cannot be guaranteed' (ibid.: 207). Thus, for example, some impressions gained from the media remained stubbornly in place even though they overrode logic (such as the idea that lesbians must be intrinsically 'high risk'). The research also demonstrated that cynicism about the media does not necessarily immunise against media influence – especially if no alternative sources of information are available. Nor were people necessarily able to resist all the messages which they might consciously wish to reject, and some expressed surprise at the ease with which, during discussions, they used words and phrases that, on reflection, did not accord with their preferred political position. For these and other reasons the researchers conclude that personal experience and critical thinking do indeed have their limits, and that 'television and newspaper texts are still, for many people, the lens through which they view AIDS. It is this lens which shapes how they perceive events and interpret personal encounters' (ibid.: 209).

This kind of subtle research can give no comfort to 'effects' theorising. Even though it works with the most direct form of media materials – news, and public information – it still recognises a complexity of symbolic forces which disallows crude discovery of 'messages' by moral campaigners.[6] Like the rest of the research reviewed in this introduction, it gives full force to the ways in which people have wider access to other sources of information and understanding. It understands the importance of the groups to which people belong, and of their political outlooks. The great strength of the recent rise of qualitative media audience research has been in the impetus which it has given to replacing figures of 'the audience' with detailed pictures of different kinds of audiences. This research, utilising increasingly sophisticated methodology, works from how those audiences themselves talk about or in other ways express their feelings about, responses to and relationships with different media.

This kind of research is not easy to conduct, but its findings are like gold dust amid the false glint of 'effects' findings (where, we are tempted to say, the brightest glitter comes from the tempting spectacle of seemingly wide open coffers of public money poured for over seventy years into asking stupid questions in unanswerable ways). We badly need more such research, because now we are beginning to understand a number of important processes in the ways that the media can persuade particular groups of readers and viewers under particular circumstances.

There is an urgency in all this. Anyone who has followed the horrific events at Columbine High School in Littleton, Colorado will have seen the fingers pointing at all the traditional targets. Rock music, because the two boys seemed to enjoy it – although the fact that one of them appears to have played opera at full volume as he prepared to shoot his father raised no spectres. *The Basketball Diaries*, because characters in that wore trenchcoats, and newspapers had dubbed the boys members of a 'trenchcoat mafia'. Video games, because they sometimes played them. And so on and on. Dave Cullen, a local journalist in Littleton, has documented the myths which almost immediately sprang up around the killings, not least the myth that one girl was shot for refusing to renounce Jesus.[7] What his work demonstrates is that the media are *indeed* powerful. Here is the awful paradox: whilst one section of the media (the news media) blame events such as Columbine on the 'effects' of other sections of the media (films, music, video games and the Internet), it is the news media themselves, and especially those in thrall to the religious Right, which have really had the marked and measurable influence – on populist politicians, and on an increasingly confused and alarmed public desperate for explanations of deeply disturbing events such as Columbine – or, for that matter, the disappearance and death of Sarah Payne But that is another kind of influence altogether, and one which, because of its very nature and because they themselves are so thoroughly implicated in the process, press and politicians are simply not willing to discuss. Which is why we do so.

NOTES

1 An interesting small test. Schlesinger *et al.* (1998) include the following sentence from one man, reporting his feelings about films such as *Under Siege*: 'you do desensitise from it . . . 'cos you know it's not real'. The complexities of categorisation, self-evaluation and recognition of social discourses indicated in this one sentence are beyond understanding by the crudities of traditional psychological theory.

2 There is, of course, a substantial and important body of work on fans of other kinds of material, most famously on science fiction fans (see, for instance, Tulloch and Jenkins (1995)). Only more rarely have researchers examined fans of more controversial materials. For instance we still await, as far as we know, a single published study of horror fans.

3 Aside from the studies of audiences we are reporting on here, there is an altogether other kind of work which is still interesting and useful. This is a kind of advanced 'textual' work carried out in the cultural studies tradition. Essentially, it asks the

question: what kinds of use do things such as horror films, or slasher movies, *allow* or *support*? Are the films constructed in such a way as to allow or sustain sympathy with the aggressors, for instance? Carol Clover's (1992) justly well-known study of slasher movies is a prime example of this kind of work, where she demonstrates the narrative significance of the 'final girl' who so often defeats the monstrous assailant. More recently Isabel Pinedo (1997) has looked in particular at the possibilities for female (including her own) pleasure generated by the way horror movies are constructed. Particularly worthy of note in this respect is Brigid Cherry's essay in Stokes and Maltby (1999) which usefully challenges the notion that 'horror' is a genre for young males. Cherry crosses the line between textual work and audience studies. First, she gathers together overwhelming quantitative evidence to show that women, and in particular young women, have long been among the prime audiences for horror films, and take great pleasure in them (as against being 'dragged along' by boyfriends). She then interviewed a number of women in order to find out just what those pleasures actually are. What she reveals is that women fans are critical and selective, and that many contemporary young women reject the older 'screamer' representation of women in horror films as sexist. As ever, the category 'horror' therefore contains good and bad examples, from their point of view ('boring and predictable' films being scorned). Furthermore, in recent films they frequently delight in the sexual possibilities raised by the figure of the vampire, an involvement which Cherry calls a 'subversive affinity' with the monsters who threaten the women in the films (along with a pleasure in the gothic romanticisation of the past carried by costume and setting). At the same time, the small but significant crop of recent films with strong female leads (the *Alien* series being the most obvious example) has offered, for some women, a more straightforward involvement in the pleasures of horror.

4   A forthcoming book (Wallflower Press, 2001) byBarker *et al.* will report on the findings of a research project into the reception in Britain of David Cronenberg's *Crash*. The research demonstrates the powerful, misleading, and intrusive effects of the campaign against the film on viewers who mainly 'wanted to see for themselves' what the film was like.

5   For a useful and quite critical overview of traditional research into video games, see Barrie Gunter (1998). There clearly is a good deal of research on users of digital media, in particular the Internet. Some of it is very good. To take one significant example, Sherry Turkle (1996) has done some very important research into the complex ways in which different kinds of users of digital media understand the technology, and understand their own roles on-line as, for instance, they adopt different personae in on-line communities. But although such research is clearly simply incompatible with the crude claims of 'effects' theorists, the issues of 'violence' and 'pornography' on-line do not play a large role in such researches.

6   The transition from the direct, information-led character of news to the imaginative universes of fiction inevitably brings in many new layers of complexity, if one wants to think about 'media messages'. Unfortunately some among the Glasgow Group have not proceeded into the realm of fiction with the requisite caution. In a desperately weak report (which nonetheless received a good deal of uncritical press coverage) Greg Philo investigated the responses of ten 12-year-old children to *Pulp Fiction*. His report laid great stress on the fact that many of the children could accurately remember and reproduce large chunks of the film's dialogue. But Philo then jumps in an account which attaches a pre-known significance to this, that the film 'invites a vicarious pleasure in the actions of central characters who are gangsters. In their world, killing and torture can be enjoyed; the total power which they exercise is "cool" and can even be a "laugh" at the expense of the victims'

(Philo, 1999: 37). On the basis of this reading, the children were then asked a number of questions which revolved around the notion of 'coolness', such as 'Who is the "coolest" person in it?', 'Why is he/she "cool"?', 'Who is the next "coolest"? – Why?', and 'Who is "uncool" in the film? – Why?' Hardly surprisingly then (and this is what the press inevitably picked up on), the violence in the film, and the related issues of power and control, are discussed by the children almost entirely in terms of 'coolness', although it's interesting to note that, even given the discursive limits within which the film was discussed, 'six children saw coolness in terms of values of power/control, four had reservations about the violence, and two of these made it clear that, for them, being cool was about having different values from the enjoyment of interpersonal power and "jumping down people's throats"' (ibid.: 48). Perhaps, though, the most interesting comment came from a girl who wanted pictures on her bedroom wall of the John Travolta character carrying a gun: 'the point of the film is to make them look cool and you just go along with it. If the point of the film had been to make them look violent and horrible you'd have gone along with that' (ibid.: 49). This comment, to us, reveals quite a sophisticated understanding of one of the ways in which fictional universes work and how we relate to them – and what it immediately acknowledges is that the film could have been different, and so could her response. In Philo's monocular vision, however, it is 'an extraordinary testament to the power of the film' and demonstrates 'how the images, style and excitement generated by the film could overwhelm other possible responses to cruelty and killing' (ibid.: 49). Once again, the search for some simple account of the 'power of the media' has interrupted any chance of any sustained analysis of these children's responses to the world of *Pulp Fiction*, which they clearly recognised as indeed fiction, and its relations to the real world in which they lived.

7   We had hoped to include an essay by Dave Cullen in this second edition. Sadly this proved impossible. Some of his existing work is still available at www.salon.com. A book of his writings about Columbine is to be published in 2001.

REFERENCES

Barker, Martin and Kate Brooks (1998), *Knowing Audiences:* Judge Dredd*, Its Friends, Fans and Foes*, Luton: University of Luton Press.

Barker, Martin, Jane Arthurs and Ramaswami Harindranath (forthcoming 2001), *The 'Crash' Controversy*, London: Wallflower Press.

Buckingham, David (1993), *Children Talking Television: the Making of Television Literacy*, London: Falmer Press.

Buckingham, David (1996), *Moving Images: Understanding Children's Emotional Responses to Television*, Manchester: Manchester University Press.

Buckingham, David (2000), *The Making of Citizens: Young People, News and Politics*, London: Routledge.

Cherry, Brigid (1999), 'Refusing to refuse to look; female viewers of the horror film', in Stokes, Melvyn and Richard Maltby, eds, *Identifying Hollywood's Audiences: Cultural Identity and the Movies*, London: British Film Institute.

Clover, Carol J. (1992), *Men, Women and Chainsaws: Gender in the Modern Horror Film*, London: B.F.I.

Fiske, John and Robert Dawson (1996), 'Audiencing violence: watching homeless men watch *Die Hard*', in Grossberg, Lawrence and Ellen Wartella, eds, *The Audience and its Landscape*, Boulder, Co.: Westview Press.

Gabriel, John (1996), 'What do you do when minority means you? *Falling Down* and the construction of "whiteness"', *Screen*, 37:2, 129–51.

Glasgow University Media Group, John Eldridge (ed.) (1993), *Getting the Message: News, Truth and Power*, London: Routledge.

Glasgow University Media Group, Greg Philo (ed.) (1999), *Message Received*, Harlow: Addison Wesley Longman.

Gunter, Barrie (1998), *The Effects of Video Games on Children: the Myth Unmasked*, Sheffield: Sheffield Academic Press.

Herz, J.C. (1997), *Joystick Nation*, NY: Abacus.

Hill, Annette (1997), *Shocking Entertainment: Viewer Response to Violent Movies*, Luton: University of Luton Press.

Hodge, Robert and David Tripp (1986), *Children and Television: A Semiotic Approach*, Cambridge: Polity Press.

Howard, Sue, ed. (1998), *Wired-Up: Young People and Electronic Media*, London: UCL Press.

Hunt, Darnell M (1997), *Screening the Los Angeles 'Riots'*, New York: Cambridge University Press.

Mannheim, Karl (1960), *Ideology and Utopia*, London: Routledge and Kegan Paul.

Miller, David, Jenny Kitzinger, Kevin Williams and Peter Beharrell (1998), *The Circuit of Mass Communications*, London: Sage.

Morrison, David E. (1999), *Defining Violence: The Search for Understanding*, Luton: University of Luton Press.

Philo, Greg (1990), *Seeing and Believing: The Influence of Television*, London: Routledge.

Philo, Greg (1999), 'Children and film/video/TV violence', in Greg Philo, ed., *Message Received*, Harlow: Addison Wesley Longman.

Pinedo, Isabel Cristina (1997), *Recreational Terror: Women and the Pleasures of Horror Film Viewing*, NY: SUNY Press.

Poole, Steven (2000a), *Trigger Happy: The Inner Life of Video Games*, London: Fourth Estate.

Poole, Steven (2000b), 'Healthy living', in the *Guardian G2*, 26 April, 16.

Schlesinger, Philip, R. Emerson Dobash, Russell P. Dobash and Kay C. Weaver (1992), *Women Viewing Violence*, London: British Film Institute (in association with the Broadcasting Standards Council).

Schlesinger, Philip, Richard Haynes, Raymond Boyle, Brian McNair, R. Emerson Dobash and Russell P. Dobash (1998), *Men Viewing Violence*, London: Broadcasting Standards Council.

Tulloch, John and Henry Jenkins (1995), Science Fiction Audiences: Watching *Doctor Who* and *Star Trek*, London: Routledge.

Turkle, Sherry (1996), *Life on the Screen: Identity in the Age of the Internet*, London: Weidenfeld & Nicolson.

1

THE NEWSON REPORT

A case study in 'common sense'

Martin Barker

In June 1994, the *Christian Democrat* celebrated a famous victory. It had forced the Home Secretary, Michael Howard, to amend his Criminal Justice Bill to make the British Board of Film Classification much more stringent about what was allowed on to video. Howard hadn't adopted their amendment – one which had been drafted at a meeting of the Movement for Christian Democracy in March – outright. But its main thrust, without question, was accepted.

How had they done this? By a combination of arguing and lobbying. They had talked of the need to protect children. They had spoken of gratuitously violent films and videos, and how bad they are for the young. And they had played on memories of recent cases where young people, even children, had so obviously gone to the bad. And they got their argument into every news-paper in the land, and on to many radio and television programmes. The effect, as their Parliamentary sponsor David Alton himself put it, was that they had 'changed the terms of reference' in which 'films of this kind' would henceforth be discussed.

That was no small achievement. And it owed much to one thing: a report by Professor Elizabeth Newson published in April 1994, just two weeks before the 'Alton Amendment' reached the floor of the House of Commons – a report which, as this essay aims to demonstrate, was wildly misleading (Newson, 1994). But the most important thing to note is not just its appall-ing quality of evidence and argument, but that, *because of the nature of what it was arguing, those weaknesses went wholly unnoticed.* What we have, in the Newson Report, is a classic case of 'common sense writ large'. By this I mean that its claims have the same status as medieval witchcraft accusations. When a 'witch' was denounced, a whole array of evidences and proofs could be adduced; but these could only ever convince because those hearing them were already completely persuaded that these were the only likely explanations. You can only believe someone to be a witch if you believe there are 'witch-events'. The facts adduced only look like evidence and arguments if you are already within that frame of reference. So the Newson Report.

In this chapter, I aim to demonstrate just how bad the Newson Report was. But my broader aim is to push to the centre of our attention the question: why don't we spot this more easily? And I focus on the Newson Report because it is so symptomatic. There, condensed within a few pages, are all the marks of a contemporary witch-craze. Few will now remember the details of what Newson wrote. And yet look how the same framework of ideas was so easily reactivated in more recent attacks: on magazines for young girls (for 'encouraging young girls to experiment sexually'); on *The X-Files* (for 'encouraging young people to play with the supernatural'); on any photography of naked children (for 'pandering to child pornographers'); on 'porn on the Internet' (for giving access to a 'vast array of corrupting materials'); and so on and on. Newson's report allows us to see in miniature all these processes.

How does 'common sense' operate?

The aftermath of the murder of James Bulger in Liverpool gave a huge fillip to the prosecution case against TV, film and video. At the trial, the judge speculated on what might have prompted the killing. He wondered if there wasn't a connection with violent videos. He didn't mention any particular films, but the press had been primed, and one film, *Child's Play III*, became their target. However, it soon became clear that, despite police efforts, there was not a scrap of evidence that the boys had watched the film. Did this failure produce retractions of the claim? Did any of the newspapers, or Alton, or the other campaigners, admit they had been wrong? Not one. So urgent is the wish to find such a link, it seems, that when an exemplar like this falls apart the response is simply to carry on.

In fact, several things happen. Some retreat to the position 'Well, they certainly had/could have had access to films of this sort; after all, we all know children will find ways . . .', or: 'Of course, there is an evil climate that surrounds children from films like this, whether they actually see them or not.' (This apparently weaker position is in fact rhetorically stronger. For what would count as a test of it?) Others escape by arguing 'Well, maybe not that time – but here's another . . .', and cite another new case, in its turn difficult to check.

These strategies were all at play in the Granada TV programme, *TV Violence – Will It Change Your Life?* on 1 May 1994, intended as television's riposte to the threatening resonances of the Bulger case. Granada had arranged for one of the Merseyside police investigators to be present, to 'give the facts'. And he did so, briefly acknowledging that they had found no link. But he continued: no, they hadn't seen that film, but they had grown up in a 'violent video culture'. And, to see the harm that could do, look at the case of Suzanne Capper in Manchester, a young woman brutally murdered in a drugs case. Inevitably a warm round of applause greeted this rebuttal. The trouble is, the claimed link in the Capper case was just as bogus, but no one was there to show it. The story most people remember is the story as the press told it – as the Liverpool policeman retold it, having heard it from the press.

Most of us have no chance to check claims in cases like this. We are therefore dependent on how the facts are presented to us by the media. In fact, if we want an example of media effects, this is probably the clearest we can get! And it is very tempting to welcome and accept quick-fix explanations that seem to 'make sense'. They speak in a vocabulary that we recognise. So, even when refuted, such cases don't go away. They linger like ghosts, always half-alive to 'explain' the next 'inexplicable'. Long after the link in the Bulger and Capper cases had been thoroughly disproved, journalists and others were happily repeating them as if they were established truths.

This isn't something new, though it currently has a new vigour. In the 1950s, for example, when there was a scare about the possible effects of horror comics on the young, a story hit the press which seemed to prove the point perfectly. A young Borstal absconder, Alan Poole, was killed in a police shoot-out. The press story was that when the police broke into his hideout they found him surrounded by hundreds of crime and horror comics.

Or did they? Some months later the Home Secretary had to make a statement to Parliament:

> Take the case of Alan Poole the Borstal absconder who shot a policeman and was himself then killed resisting arrest. In that case it was reported in the press that he had a library of 50 of these comics. Indeed a social worker said that he had a collection of over 300 . . . [I]n spite of all the publicity, we found that this particular lad had one 'Western' comic in his possession, and that not a very alarming one.
>
> (cited in Barker, 1984a, p. 30)

Yet, despite this official refutation, the case of Alan Poole was cited as proof for a long time after. It suggests that these claims are not part of a rational debate.

But we need to take this further: these arguments have a very particular nature and structure. There are many horrible events 'out there', but only certain very specific kinds of explanation are mobilised to account for them. In the Bulger case, it seemed to 'make sense' to explain their behaviour by saying they had been 'corrupted' by watching videos – and never mind that they hadn't actually watched them at all. They could have, might have; it could all make sense if they had.

Then, what about this?

FATHER STABBED BABY TO DEATH 'AS SACRIFICE TO WARD OFF EVIL': A father who thought he was Joseph, his wife was Mary and they and their children were on the way to the Garden of Eden killed his 17-month-old daughter as a sacrifice, an Old Bailey court was told yesterday ... Before the attack in June, he had ... watched the film *King of Kings*, about the life of Christ.

(*Guardian*, 21 December 1994)

Not one newspaper which recounted this sad story thought it worth suggesting that *King of Kings* is a potential cause of murder. Why not? Actually there is probably more evidence to sustain such a link, because of the tendency for certain very disturbed violent offenders to adopt a 'killer-missionary' role; they explain their violence as a command from God. The reason why such a link wouldn't be proposed is because it doesn't seem 'obvious' – and that is the problem we must explore.

Newson's assumptions

David Alton may have used the good offices of the Movement for Christian Democracy to prepare and promote his case, but he also apparently had science on his side, in the form of Elizabeth Newson's Report, co-signed by twenty-four other child professionals. I want to put that 'science' to the test. One of the problems has been the disparity between its size and scope, and its impact. Here is a short report, making no claim to present new evidence. It mainly tells of a supposed change of heart by twenty-five people. Its tone is certainly thoughtful and concerned. It makes no obviously wild claims. Follow, then, its narrative, to see where steps are taken that might give us cause to question.

Newson begins with the Bulger case. She is careful not to assert that the two boys really did see *Child's Play III* or other equivalent films. Rather, the boys are depicted as exemplars of a new cruelty in children. Something exceptional must explain this new viciousness. And here Newson acts as spokesperson for a group who have been growing increasingly worried: the child professionals. It is their view that there are now new kinds of film, and that these films have disturbing 'messages'. To confirm this, we are referred to two films as examples, and to a large body of research evidence which (we are assured) now concludes that these messages are doing harm. The conclusion is inevitable: professionals must forego their traditional liberalism. The problems are just too over whelming.

We need to get behind this narrative. For it is built on a series of claims, all of which have to be true for her argument to hold up. There are eight such claims:

1   the murder of James Bulger was so special as to require special explanation;

2   such an explanation has to be some singular change. The most singular recent change is the easy availability of sadistic images within films;

3   these films offer a distinctive message which can be traced and correlated with the attitudes and/or behaviour of James's killers. *Child's Play III* might well be an example of such a film;

4   there is also now a new kind of film, in which 'the viewer is made to identify with the *perpetrator* of the act, not the victim';

5   these four propositions are linked to a general claim: 'The principle that what is experienced vicariously will have *some* effect on *some* people is an established one, and is the reason why industry finds it worth while to spend millions of pounds on advertising';

6   this new kind of film is the start of a worsening curve, as film-makers, video games writers and the like exploit the growing potential of their technologies. Therefore their effects are almost certain to get worse;

7   a great deal of research has already been done, with consistent conclusions: 'media violence' is linked via 'heavy viewing' to 'aggressive behaviour';

8   there is now a vast world literature on this topic, which consistently supports this link.

Eight claims, then, so common to debates on these issues they could be endlessly reproduced. Unfortunately not one of them can be justified. Not one of these claims can be supported by either evidence or logic, as I aim to demonstrate. Yet each one looked disturbingly obvious and persuasive. So persuasive in fact that only a fool or a villain would ignore that obviousness. I will tackle them through four key themes around which they are organised: How do we tell what the 'message' of a film is? . . . How can we understand 'media influence' . . . Is there, as claimed, an overwhelming body of evidence for 'harm' . . . And just what is 'media violence'?

How can we tell what the 'message' of a film is?

There have been claims about 'new, bad media images' for a very long time. An example:

> Granted, my dear sir, that your young Jack, or my twelve year old Robert, have minds too pure either to seek after or to crave after literature of the sort in question, but not infrequently it is found without seeking. It is a contagious disease, just as cholera and typhus and the plague are contagious, and, as everybody is aware, it needs not personal contact with a body stricken to convey either of these frightful maladies to the hale and hearty. A tainted scrap of rag has been known to spread plague and death through an entire village,

just as a stray leaf of *Panther Bill* or *Tyburn Tree* may sow the seeds of immorality amongst as many boys as a town may produce.

(see Barker, 1989, p. 102)

Thus a nineteenth-century campaigner against 'penny dreadfuls'.
Or again:

Before these children's greedy eyes with heartless indiscrimination horrors unimaginable are . . . presented night after night . . . Terrific massacres, horrible catastrophes, motor-car smashes, public hangings, lynchings . . . All who care for the moral well-being and education of the child will set their faces like flint against this new form of excitement.

Thus *The Times*, eighty years ago (see Pearson, in Barker, 1984b, p. 88).
Or again:

I find that many parents and teachers are blissfully ignorant of the contents of comics and they would be wise when the opportunity occurs to examine them in detail. They will not be impressed by the printing, colouring, drawing or literary contents, and they will soon see that the comics can be broadly divided into two classes, harmful and harmless.

Thus one of the 1950s campaigners (see Barker, 1984a, p. 81).

If we look carefully at these three quotations we can discern the core of critics' claims. There are 'bad materials' out there, and we only have to look to know that they are bad. One contact can be enough (if in the nineteenth century the favourite metaphor for this was disease, today it is drug addiction), so the dangers when we are 'bombarded' with 'floods' of these things are incalculable. So how do we tell 'bad' materials from 'good'? Let us take Newson's examples head-on.

Child's Play III is not a very good film. But the point is: what *kind* of film is it, and what could reasonably be claimed about it? Not many people will have seen it, and therefore it is interesting to ask readers to fill out a mental image of what it must be like. After all, the film was widely claimed to be the possible trigger for the murder of James Bulger. What sort of a film is it in your imagination?

The most remarkable thing about this film is that a great majority of the film is devoted to a desperate attempt to save a small child from being killed. It is a horror film, no question. In part it is scary, sometimes a bit bloody. But judge for yourselves whether it fits your mental image. Here is a synopsis:

The story is the third in a series in which teenager Andy Barclay is forced to do battle with a 'Good Guy' doll which has been possessed by the mind of a former murderer. The title sequence shows a doll forming out of plastic contaminated with the blood of the murderer: evil is returning. The opening scene shows the chairman of the doll-making company resolving to resume production of the doll. He is a cynical man – 'Let's face it,' he sneers at one of his executives, 'what are children, after all, but consumer trainees?' For that he will get his comeuppance. That night, he takes home the first doll off the production line, and it comes alive and kills him gleefully. 'Don't fuck with the Chuck', it rudely pronounces.

The remainder of the film takes place around a military academy for the young, where Andy Barclay has been sent to help him 'grow up'. From the start, he is viewed as a troublemaker, and is victimised, especially by a sadistic Sergeant who cuts all their hair, and by the young Lieutenant Shelton. On his first parade, he is saved from the worst of the bullying by the intervention of da Silva, a tough-cookie girl who doesn't mind standing up to Shelton. Barclay and da Silva are attracted to each other. Soon Andy sees on television an advertisement for the newly released Good Guy dolls, and knows trouble is brewing. A parcel delivered for him is opened by Tyler, a tiny wide-eyed black boy who only loves to play. In it is Chucky.

We see Chucky attempting to take over Tyler's body. Interrupted, it reverts to its 'lifeless' form, and is thrown out as rubbish. Chucky uses a ruse to escape from the garbage truck, killing the driver in the process. On the parade ground, Andy guesses what has happened.

There follows a series of episodes as Andy discovers that Chucky is targeting little Tyler; he again and again tries to capture Chucky to destroy him, only to find himself misunderstood and humiliated by Shelton, who sees him just as a wimp. Chucky's level of mayhem rises. Finally, the Colonel dies of a heart attack when confronted with a talking doll.

The next day is a War Game, and it will go ahead in honour of the dead Colonel. Tyler is separated from Andy and da Silva. Andy absconds to try to save him. Chucky meantime has substituted live bullets in one team's guns, and lures Shelton to his death. In the final showdown at a nearby fairground, da Silva is wounded and has to leave Andy Barclay to stop Chucky alone. As Chucky once more begins the chant to transfer his soul into Tyler, an injured Andy manages to throw him off the top of a 'ghost mountain'. Chucky falls into the blades of a wind machine, and is destroyed. The film ends with Andy saying goodbye to da Silva as she is taken away by ambulance – and as he is once more taken into care . . .

Even this short synopsis demonstrates that *Child's Play III* is the *exact opposite* of everything that was said about it; this is in fact one of a thousand films which show a sort of rite of passage of adolescence: a misunderstood, essentially gentle boy gains courage and a girlfriend through the need to confront evil. Misunderstood and maltreated by the adults around him, he does the right thing, no matter what the cost to himself. This is a very *moral* tale.

Of course that is not all there is to say about this film. Any horror film has to *show* evil to make sense of the hero's struggle. And Chucky is a curious form of evil: the idea of an animated doll, a cuddlesome thing that might turn on you, is 'risky'. But, then, a horror film can only work because it deals in notions which are potentially frightening. Interestingly, the film also displays a most cynical view of big business, and its attitude to children – and it would not be the first time that a political strain in a film has led to attacks on it in the name of 'protecting children'.

If Newson and so many others can be so wrong about *Child's Play III*, let us check the other film she obliquely references as especially dangerous because of that issue of 'identification':

> A parallel in a recently released film is where we witness in lit silhouette the multiple rape of a woman by a queue of men, and hear her agonised screams, all in the context of an intent to punish her.

What film is this? It proved very hard to track down. Even Professor Newson herself, when I asked her, was not sure of its title – an odd situation for someone quoting it in a published report. Finally, I identified the film as Peter Greenaway's *The Baby of Macon*. Once again, what kind of film was this, and can it carry the reading that Newson makes of it?

The Baby of Macon is, like all Greenaway films, a highly stylised art-house product. Every scene is filmed at slow speed, lit and set like classical oil-paintings. The film deals with social power, symbolised in the conflicts between the Church and a young woman whose baby brother has miraculous powers. Who will control his powers? But there is also a play-within-the-film; we see that the story of the Church, the woman and the baby is being acted to an audience; and below stage we see the actors also living out various conflicts. The scene to which Newson refers comes right at the end of the film. Her account of it is seriously misleading. We do not see the woman being raped in lit silhouette in the way she suggests. An enclosed four-poster bed is just about visible. It is hidden from us by the Church representatives who, having won control over the baby, calmly ignore the woman's screams while discussing their new power over women. Even this meaning is complicated by the fact that at this point the gap between the story and the actors is breaking down. The 'rape' is meant to be simulated, but the male actors have decided to take revenge for being up-staged by the young actress. They will *really* rape her, but no one will notice, because they will assume her screams are simulated. In no sense at all will this narrative, and this scene within it, support a claim of 'getting the viewers to identify with the attackers'. The whole film is about male domination, and the forms through which it is enforced. It is precisely these ambiguities, and the deliberate breakdown of the narrative, which make this scene so meaningful, and so powerful.

The reason for spending so much time on this is because it throws into relief the question: *how can we know what the 'message' of a film is?* There is now a body of research into film and all other kinds of media, into how they work to produce meanings, and how audiences receive and make sense of those meanings. This is a developing field, and a great deal is still being explored and debated. But two things are clear: neither Elizabeth Newson or any of her co-signatories has any expertise in this field. And the possible 'effects' they imputed to these films, and their audiences, contradict every-thing practitioners in the field do know – but which nobody wanted to hear.

All this inevitably provokes the question: how do people like Newson get away with making unsubstantiated and insupportable claims about films, on the basis of unblemished ignorance of all such matters? Imagine the situ-ation where a bunch of amateurs published claims about the way 'chemicals' affect the body, claiming that sulphur affects our 'humours', and that if we ingest it in particular ways it is guaranteed to make us hum . . . imagine the scorn that would fall on them. The scorn which is regularly visited on those who do have expertise in these matters looks remarkably like that visited on those who questioned the claims of the witch-finders.

What can we say more generally about the kinds of media material that get labelled in this way? In fact there is a growing body of research which suggests that the labelling of media materials as 'bad influences' is not the innocent process it proffers itself as being. Histories of censorship, for instance, show how repeatedly the censors act in self-serving ways to limit or bar materials which might embarrass them. Yet, in attacking them, they always do so by calling them 'harmful'. Examples are legion. In the nine-teenth century, critics of the 'penny dreadfuls' reserved their worst hatred for the 1866 publication *Wild Boys of London.* Yet, when examined (something made difficult by the fact that the police were persuaded to break into the printers, and smash the printing plates), it turns out not to be the catalogue of gang warfare and delinquency that the title might seem to suggest. In fact, the story connects closely with a deep-running sore of the time: the problem of orphans and the urban poor.[1] Annette Kuhn has shown how censorship of early films was predicated on the concerns of Empire, and in particular on the imposition of a definition of proper female sexuality (Kuhn, 1988). Between the two world wars, film censorship was used to prevent embarrassment in foreign affairs (Mathews, 1994).

My own work on the 1950s horror comics campaign showed how particu-lar comics were targeted which dealt with strongly political issues, including anti-McCarthyite stories (Barker, 1984a). In the 1970s, the film *Scum* was barred from television for a long time; in fact it is a powerful critique of the brutality of the Borstal system, and the way it can make its inmates more desperate and violent. And it raised embarrassing questions at a time when the Conservative Party was pressing the introduction of 'short, sharp shock' schemes for young offenders. Again it was banned on grounds of being 'vio-lent'. In fact it seems that the word 'violence' frequently acts as a code-word

35

for objections made to materials on quite other, often political, grounds. We need to bear this in mind when we come to the final part of this chapter. For it raises acutely the question: Is it meaningful to research into such a question at all?

How can we understand 'media influence'?

In Elizabeth Newson's report, there is one classic sentence which has been heard so often, if in different words, it has become like a mantra. 'The principle that what is experienced vicariously will have *some* effect on *some* people is an established one, and is the reason why industry finds it worth while to spend millions of pounds on advertising.' What does this amount to? One very typical problem faced by those who reject the rhetorics of the anti-media campaigners is the challenge: then, are you saying that television has no influence at all? If that was the case, then advertisers wouldn't be willing to spend all that money, would they? Isn't that sufficient proof that TV must have *some* effect? Given that, what is the problem with admitting that TV violence might cause people to go out and commit real-life violence?

This is, I suspect, the most commonly repeated move by anti-violence campaigners. It was certainly there in 1984 at the height of the campaign against video nasties. The evangelical Christian Action, Research and Education (the equivalent then of David Alton's Movement for Christian Democracy) urged:

> Organisations spend around £1.6bn in advertising each year. They must believe that by seeing an advertisement on TV, on a poster etc., the consumer will be persuaded to purchase a product, make a donation or change their behaviour. The Government itself has used advertising to portray messages about safe sex, drinking and driving, and firework safety in an attempt to change the behaviour of the public. All the political parties make broadcasts before elections to persuade voters to cast their vote in a particular direction. There must be instances when each of us can recall seeing a product that had been recently advertised, and deciding just to 'try it out'. It would be trite to stretch the argument and say that after seeing one episode of violence, an individual is going to commit a crime. But the point is illustrated: what we see *does* affect our behaviour.
>
> (CARE, 1994, p. 29)

This argument is evidently felt to be a clincher. Yet even a cursory examination shows it to be palpable nonsense. The simple error the campaigners make is to assume that, if TV, or film, or whatever, has *some* influence, it must have the kinds of influence they want to ascribe to it. It would be a very stupid person who denied that television had any influence at all – but only if 'influence' includes all the following and many more (add your own examples to our list):

1 interesting us in things we didn't previously know about;
2 making us stay up too late;
3 giving us a sense of our place in the world, through its ability to take us to events as they are happening;
4 making us smile, laugh, be sad, cry, feel nostalgic, patriotic, disturbed, uneasy, want to join in, bored, disenchanted, and disaffected with our own lives;
5 making us think about things, shaking our assumptions, making us complacent, talking to us in languages we feel comfortable or uncomfortable with;
6 and so on.

All these are effects, no question. They are a very small part of any list of possible effects. So, why so firmly dismiss the analogy with advertising, and challenge the idea that television violence might cause violence? There are a number of strands to this argument which must be disentangled in turn.

Consider the following (real) cases:

1 A man takes a gun and shoots his entire family after watching the news. Arrested and tried, he explains his actions on the basis that the world news was so bad there seemed no point anyone going on living.
2 A paedophile is convicted of molesting a young boy. In his house, the police reported, he has a collection of newspaper cuttings about court cases involving paedophiles.
3 An elderly woman commits suicide after watching *Schindler's List.* In a note, she expresses an overwhelming sense of guilt at being a survivor of the Nazi camps.

What is the difference between cases like these and putative cases of television causing violence? In the first case, any explanation would have to refer to the man's mental state (he must have been already depressed, perhaps there were already signs of disturbance or family breakdown, etc.). So it could not be put down simply to the 'effects of the news'; the man's reaction was non-normal, unpredictable, and therefore could not provide us with grounds for judging the suitability or rightness of the news. It was he who was aberrant, not the news.

The second case poses an interesting problem. We are well used to hearing of claims that sexual attackers possessed pornographic materials – with the implication that this provides a causal factor. But we know that the press materials this man collected will have been condemnatory of paedophilia. Yet somehow the man 'used' them. What judgement could be based on this –

that we should ban even the word 'paedophilia', lest it stimulate the desires?

In the third case, a woman is 'induced' to suicide by a film. Not by the violence of the film (of which there is some, and very disturbing it is, too), but by a sense of deep shame when she relates the film to her own and other Jewish people's lives. Yet curiously my suspicion is that, however sad her death, the judgement would be that this only proves the *worth* and *quality* of the film.

This is not what the anti-media campaigners mean. In each of these cases, they will argue that while TV or press or films were factors they can't be blamed as causes. But when they make claims about TV or films causing violence they change the way the explanation works.

There is something very strange about the way they argue this, as I have argued before (see Barker, 1984b). Their claim is that the materials they judge to be 'harmful' can only influence us by trying to make us be the same as them. So horrible things will make us horrible – not horrified. Terrifying things will make us terrifying – not terrified. To see something aggressive makes us feel aggressive – not aggressed against. And the nastier it is, the nastier it is likely to make us. This idea is so odd, it is hard to know where to begin, in challenging it. Let me start, then, by saying that if it were true, then their own whole analogy with advertising breaks down, and collapses even more completely if we add in that notion of 'vicarious viewing'. This is why.

Mass advertising began in the 1880s, with the arrival of brand names. Research to make that advertising more effective developed in the 1920s. Since then, the overwhelming tendency of advertisers has been towards more and more targeted advertising, precisely because they know that advertising that depends on 'vicarious contact' – that is, on our happening to see an advertisement which isn't really aimed at us, which we haven't selected for any reason – is singularly ineffective.

Advertisers have also learnt another principle, and that concerns the difficulties of negative advertising. From the 1950s at least, advertisers have understood that products associated with negative images are unlikely to be acceptable. The most notorious example of this is the cigarette campaign with the slogan 'You're never alone with a Strand'. The assumption that you might be alone but for the cigarette did no good for its sales, and it bombed. The kinds of film which the campaigners attack are, on this principle, the *least likely to be influential*, since they depend on the construction of feelings of negativity: fear, anxiety, shock, horror, and so on.

Advertisers work from the premise that vicarious contact with their materials is the least likely to be effective, and that if it has any 'effect' at all it is likely to be the opposite of what they are seeking. The only advertising materials which use negative images are *educational* materials, which are *intended to make us think critically* – anti-drink/driving campaigns, for instance. So everything we know about the way advertisements work conflicts with the notion that filmic violence is likely to promote audience copying.

Is there a consistent and overwhelming body of evidence in favour of the proposition that 'media violence causes violence'?

It is now common to hear that 'more than 70 per cent of published studies support this conclusion'. A current publisher's catalogue asserts without qualification that

> the consensus among the psychologists, media theorists, sociologists and educators presented is that there is a direct, causal link between the excessive viewing of violence, or the playing of video games, to becoming stimulated to acting violently or to becoming desensitised to violence.

It is certainly true that endless experiments have been conducted. Since the 1930s, in particular in America, vast sums of money have been obtained to test this relationship. But curiously, and with hardly an exception, researchers in this field have hardly ever set up what are called 'critical experiments'.

In any branch of science, not all experiments are of equal worth – and not just because some are better designed or conducted than others. An experiment is useful to the extent that it can add to our knowledge, not just by confirming what we think we know, but by clarifying aspects which are not yet clear. As knowledge accumulates, it becomes necessary to develop theories and models that can make sense of what we think we know. Without theories, information is dry and uninformative. But theories always and of necessity go wider and involve more than the evidence on which they claim to be based. Theories involve generalisations, they assert patterns and causal links, they even perhaps allow predictions. So, a critical test is one which focuses on some particular feature of a theory or model, and asks: are we sure that it really works like that? Designing experiments that really do this is especially hard – because very often theories point towards hidden, non-obvious processes.

Take, then, a simple example. Many claims about media influence talk about viewers 'identifying' with a film character. This is a *theoretical* claim. It amounts to arguing that a viewer may become persuaded by a film *because* (causal linkage) they have identified with a character. There is nothing wrong with claims of this kind. Any theory has to make them. And the theory of media/violence connections frequently depends on it, because it offers an explanation as to how and why people are linked to elements in a film.[2] But note: 'identification' is not something you can see happening. An observer can't look at someone, and say: 'Look, s/he is identifying!' Still less can an observer look at four people, and see one as more prone to identification than the others.

So what can researchers do in this situation? They have to develop *models* of what might be going on in 'identification', and then design *tests* to see if things happen according to the predictions of the model. For example, they will have to have measures for who is an 'identifier' (making as sure as possible that there is something there to be measured, of course). Suppose they do this, how will they know if they have done it well? The trouble is, since no one can *see* an identifier – it is not an observable act – there are only limited ways to be sure they have really located the process. Researchers can use *consistency* – using several tests that ought, if they are right, to come up with the same results. They can use *repeatability* – doing the same test several times, while varying supposedly irrelevant conditions. They can test for *critical links* – that is, taking two measures, and seeing if the predicted link is as expected between them. What good science does, then, is to carry out experiments that can help guard against 'experimental artefacts', that is, results that only mean something because of the way the experiment was set up.

In the field of media effects work researchers are extraordinarily careless about such basic requirements of theory as these. In another work, for example, I re-examined the basic research which has been seen as providing the justification for the concept of 'identification'. It had two problems. First, the research was virtually non-existent – concepts such as 'identification' have been so much taken for granted that it has not been felt necessary to test them directly at all. Instead, research has been carried out that *assumes* its presence. Second, the research was grossly self-contradictory – but no one had bothered to check. On only two occasions had research been conducted to see whether the claimed process of 'identification' could be discovered at all – and on both occasions the answer was negative (see Barker, 1989, Chapter 6).[3]

This carelessness about critical tests then links with the other unexplored problem, which we might call the 'problem of accumulated results'. Essentially, it has been assumed that if two studies of media-effects both come up positive, then they can be added together – eventually to generate that '70 per cent of all studies'. Guy Cumberbatch addresses this issue (Cumberbatch and Howitt, 1989). What he shows is that published studies contradict each other on a whole range of dimensions: on which groups are most 'vulnerable'; on the kinds of stimulus that might trigger responses; on whether films make us prone to copy directly, or just generally raise aggressive levels; and on the contexts most conducive to effects. To take just two of his examples: he shows that William Belson's much-cited work in fact conflicts with many others:

> Belson . . . finds no evidence that high exposure to television reduces boys' respect for authority, or that it desensitises them, makes them

less considerate for others, produces sleep disturbance or (in an earlier study . . .) is associated with stealing. Belson's findings contradict many previous studies.

(p. 48)

Cumberbatch also draws attention to the awkward fact that research has shown that 'aggression can be raised by *humorous* films as much as by aggressive ones' (p. 38). In other words, the studies simply don't support each other. Indeed, to the extent that some of them might be right, then others have to be counted as wrong. It is once again only a grim determination not to ask difficult questions that allows claims like this to go unchallenged.

This tendency can be illustrated in another way. Earlier, I used three quotations drawn from a wide historical period. It is commonplace to researchers that such objections to 'dangerous media' go back a very long way. In the nineteenth century, when such objections first reached full flood, the charges were brought against 'penny dreadfuls' (in Britain) and dime novels (in America). By the turn of the century, music hall (Britain) and vaudeville (America) were the objects of dismay. Then cinema. Then radio. Then comic books. Then television, video, video games, computers, and most recently the Internet. The litany of threats is remarkable for the way each new medium was cited as marking a virtual collapse of civilisation.

But not only did no one think to check or research these claims, or wonder at their extravagance when they could pass so regularly into history; but in fact the claims are mutually contradictory. When 'penny dreadfuls' were attacked, a major part of their danger was the fact that they were found 'on the streets' – they were the street literature of their time. That being so, you might have thought that the security of cinema would make it less dangerous. Not so – here, it was the 'moral dangers of darkness' which appalled critics. But, then, television, which is mostly viewed with the light on, must be less dangerous. Not so – now a new danger emerged, the 'invasion of the home' (though of course that would imply the relative safety of cinema, wouldn't it?).

But cinema and film did, so it was said, have the shared risk that they scroll past you uncontrollably. But, then, in that case, video should have been seen as an improvement because viewers can stop and start it. Ah, not so – now the dangers were that viewers would obsessively rerun their 'favourite bad bits'. But, in that case, film and TV must have been safer than we first thought. Not so, because . . . and so the game goes on. These claims cannot all be true. If one medium is damned, the others must be excused. But the most important point is that all these are made as *ad hoc* assertions, with no attempt to prove or disprove them. Simply, no one has bothered to ask, because it is all so obvious – the witches are out there, aren't they?

What exactly is 'media violence'?

Everything I have been arguing comes together at this point. The expression 'media violence' has to be one of the most commonly repeated, and one of the most ill-informed, of all time. It is supposed to encompass everything from cartoons (ten-ton blocks dropped on Tom's head by Jerry, Wily Coyote plummeting down yet another mile-deep canyon); children's action adventure films (the dinosaurs of *Jurassic Park* alongside playground scuffles in *Grange Hill* and last-reel shootouts in westerns); news footage from Rwanda and Bosnia; documentary footage showing the police attacking Rodney King in Los Angeles; horror films from Hammer to cult gore movies; the range from Clint Eastwood as the voiceless hard man of *Dirty Harry* to Arnie as the violent humorist of almost any of his films, etc., etc.

And therein lies the point: no single ground has ever been given for us to suppose that such a list has any single property in common other than that certain critics don't like them. It is a useless conflation of wholly different things. Yet somehow that conflation endlessly continues. And whenever the phrase 'media violence' is used it conjures up one image above all else: an image of motiveless mayhem, to which words such as 'gratuitous' easily attach themselves. A trip to America intervened in the drafting of this chapter. While I was there, President Clinton put his signature to a Bill requiring TV manufacturers to fit 'V-Chips' in TVs; and with immaculate timing a 'new report' on TV violence simultaneously came out. Among its findings was the assertion that over 73 per cent of violence in programmes went unpunished. That sounds worrying. It is the kind of datum that seems to require a concerned response – until we note, as an acid commentary in an American magazine did, that this figure related to punishment of the perpetrator *in that scene*. It went on:

> But to do the opposite, a violent program would have to create a scene in which, let's say, a man is shot, a cop sees it happen, and the criminal is arrested on the spot. US television chooses to do things the old fashioned way. There's something called a *plot*.
>
> (*Electronic Media*, 1996)

This is not a point of detail. The moment 'plot' is allowed in, the whole category 'media violence' dissolves into meaninglessness. And that is precisely what needs to be asserted. *There simply is no category 'media violence' which can be researched; that is why over seventy years of research into this supposed topic have produced nothing worthy of note.* 'Media violence' is the witchcraft of our society. This is such an important point, yet its significance seems constantly to get lost. Imagine that medical researchers were to propose a classification of drugs according to whether they taste nice or nasty. Not only that, but they add that they are going to research – and be funded for more than seventy years for the purpose – into the claim that nasty-tasting drugs do you harm, whereas nice-tasting drugs do you good. What would we say? Quite apart from folksy responses, the scientific response would have to be that there is no reason to suppose that 'nasty-tasting drugs' can be a research object at all. Not everyone finds the same drugs unpleasant. Taste may be a wholly incidental aspect of a chemical's behaviour. Finding them unpleasant may equally be a function of being told that you have to 'take your medicine'. And so on. In other words, *it wouldn't be worth doing the research at all, because there is nothing there worth researching.*

Hard though it may be to accept that an entire research tradition is based on thin air, this is my case. I challenge the research tradition to show a single reason why we should treat cartoons, news, horror, documentaries, police series, westerns, violent pornography and action adventure as having anything in common. Let it be noted: for any one of these that is withdrawn from the list, that '70 per cent of all studies' must be instantly reduced, because some of the studies have (usually without telling us) used just such a mix of genres as their research-objects. And every single 'count' of 'acts of violence' will have to be redone, to eliminate those no longer included.

Pending a reply to my challenge, I end this chapter by proposing a different research agenda.

1 Many opinion polls show wide public concern for limiting 'violence' on television and film. Yet the same people, when asked, have much greater trouble naming the films and programmes which they think have too much. My proposal is that we need to research *how different segments of the public develop their category 'media violence', and what they mean by it.*

2 In a study of children's responses to violence, a Dutch researcher found that children simply do not think of cartoons as violent at all – though they agree generally with adults' concerns and estimates about violence (see Morrison, 1993 for details; see also Buckingham, 1996). While media researchers tend to count 'incidents of violence', it seems that the children follow the *story-lines*, and are always aware of the *kind* of film or programme they are watching. My proposal is that we need to study *how children develop a 'sense of story', and how does this relate to their liking for the kinds of material that the critics worry about?*

3 The languages employed to describe how much people use the media are loaded: from 'heavy viewing' to 'excessive'. These judgemental terms distort research. There has recently been a body of research on 'fans', including fans of supposedly problematic materials such as horror (see Kermode in Chapter 4 of this book; also Penley, 1992; Bacon-Smith, 1992; Sconce, 1996; and Sanjek, 1990). My proposal is that we need to study *how viewers who choose to commit themselves to a medium, genre or series differ in their understandings of them from those whose relationship with them is more casual.*

4 We need to deepen our investigation of the moral campaigners, and their relationship to the research community, in a number of ways. The first

is the problem of language. One of the disturbing aspects of the anti-media campaigners' way of arguing is their tendency to hyperbole and emotional talk. This infects the researchers who start to talk of people being 'bombarded' with images of violence, of an 'incessant menu' of 'particularly damaging' and 'gratuitous' materials. Even when no damaging consequences are being implied, this kind of language is still used. So reports of the girl who had a fascination (no doubt long since ended) with *Silence of the Lambs* always talked of her as 'addicted' to the film – whereas a man who went to see *The Flintstones* forty times was called a 'fan'. Quite different images of the people and their reasons for seeing the film are conjured up by the two expressions. We need to research *the invasion of 'effects research' by these languages.*

5 Then there is the talisman against which to test everything: the protection of children. This is the cornerstone of common sense thinking on this topic. Replying to a letter from me, Elizabeth Newson said this:

> I have throughout been careful to stick to my last, which is the protection of children, despite the fact that many correspondents have made the point that adults too might be vulnerable to such images, however presented or wrapped up . . . I hope that any arguments you wish to present will acknowledge that my case is about children, not adults.

Why does Professor Newson think this makes the argument stronger? Because 'children' in our culture are seen as specially in need of care and protection. Now that really is a hard one to get past – but we have to try. We have to get past it because the argument is making quite illegitimate use of our feelings for our individual children to make a case for something quite different, called 'childhood'. *We need to research the way the lives of actual children have been affected by the predominant image of themselves as incompetent.*

6 What can we positively say about the media preferences of those who become involved in delinquency and crime? As yet, not much. But the little we do know contradicts all the claims of the campaigners. The ignored study by the Policy Studies Institute (Hagell and Newburn 1994) may have been limited, but it provided at least a genuine starting point. It was ignored because its findings didn't 'fit'. For they found that the only slightly significant differences between delinquent and non-delinquent boys were in the former's liking for *The Bill* and for the *Sun*! Actually, it wouldn't be difficult to offer an explanation of these preferences: *The Bill* as a police procedural, helping them to prepare for what would happen if they get caught; and the *Sun* for its melodramatic view of the world. The trouble is that this *kind* of explanation is not at all what the campaigners want to hear. It treats the delinquents as normal people, using the media in exactly the same

complicated ways as everyone else. *We need further research not only into what media preferences delinquents have, but also into how they understand and use them.*

7 Finally, there are the anti-media campaigns themselves. From much that is shown in this book, it should be clear that these campaigns are not the innocent things they manage to appear. At best, they are blind and ignorant forms of protectiveness, at worst disguised political campaigns. *We need urgently to research and gather together a historical picture of such campaigns.*

I am not meaning to imply that none of this research has been done – it has, in fragments. But there is now an urgent need to counter-attack; and our part as critical researchers and academics is to pull together what is known, and to press this agenda that will cut away the ground from under them. They hide their nonsense in a fog of their making, but also of our unquestioning.

NOTES

1 *Wild Boys of London* was published in complete form in 1866, and began republication in 1873, until the police action prevented its completion. At the time of suppression, two parallel stories were running. One concerned a group of boys who had stowed away to the West Indies, where they were captured by pirates. But this was no simple adventure, for the pirates were all escaped slaves roaming the Caribbean looking for slaving ships, in order to free the slaves and kill their captains. The boys debate the morality of such killings, and conclude that they are indeed justified. The second story-line involved the arrival in London of a group of foreigners to pursue their political cause: Fenians. There can be little doubt that the act of suppression was a political act. But what is just as important is that it was passed off as an act of morality, for the 'protection of children'.

2 It is of course not the only one. Another commonly claimed candidate is 'desensitisation'. Lack of space prevents me dealing with all such claims equally, but it must be noted that the two are not compatible with each other. If media influence worked via 'identification', then we would have to concern ourselves with different kinds of film, and different kinds of audience, than if it worked via 'desensitisation'. They are not simply alternatives we can shift between, or add together.

3 This fact may be uncomfortable to many working within the media studies field itself, where also that assumption has largely gone unquestioned.

REFERENCES

Bacon-Smith, Camille (1992), *Enterprising Women: Television Fandom and the Creation of Popular Myth*, Philadelphia, PA: University of Pennsylvania Press.

Barker, Martin (1984a), *A Haunt of Fears: The Strange History of the British Horror Comics Campaign*, London: Pluto Press.

Barker, Martin (1984b), *The Video Nasties: Freedom and Censorship in the Arts*, London: Pluto Press.

Barker, Martin (1989), *Comics: Ideology, Power and the Critics*, Manchester: Manchester University Press.

Buckingham, David (1996), *Moving Images: Children's Emotional Responses to Television*, Manchester: Manchester University Press.

CARE (Christian Action, Research and Education) (1994), *Evidence to the Home Affairs Committee*, London: HMSO, pp. 27–33.

Cumberbatch, Guy and Howitt, Dennis (1989), *A Measure of Uncertainty: the Effects of the Media*, London: John Libbey.

Electronic Media (1996), 'Getting moving on violence', 12 February, p. 12.

Hagell, A. and Newburn, T. (1994), *Young Offenders and the Media: Viewing Habits and Preferences*, London: Policy Studies Institute.

Kuhn, Annette (1988), *Cinema, Censorship and Sexuality, 1909–1925*, London: Routledge.

Mathews, Tom Dewe (1994), *Censored!: The Story of Film Censorship in Britain*, London: Chatto & Windus.

Morrison, David (1993), 'The idea of violence', in Andrea Millwood-Hargrave, ed., *Violence in Factual Television*, London: John Libbey, pp. 124–8.

Newson, Elizabeth (1994), *Video Violence and the Protection of Children*, Report of the Home Affairs Committee, London: HMSO, 29 June, pp. 45–9.

Penley, Constance (1992), 'Feminism, psychoanalysis, and the study of popular culture', in L. Grossberg *et al.*, eds, *Cultural Studies*, London: Routledge, pp. 479–500.

Sanjek, David (1990), 'Fans notes: the horror film magazine', *Literature/Film Quarterly*, 18:3, pp. 150–60.

Sconce, Jeffrey (1996), 'Trashing the academy: taste, excess and the emerging politics of cinematic style', *Screen*, 36:4, pp. 371–93.

2

THE WORRYING INFLUENCE OF 'MEDIA EFFECTS' STUDIES

David Gauntlett

On 8 January 1998, the *Guardian*, the liberal UK newspaper, prominently featured a story with the headline 'Film violence link to teenage crime' and the sub-head '"Vulnerable" young people may be influenced by screen killings'. A new study, the article stated, had shown that violent films could encourage certain people to commit crime. On the same day, readers of headlines in two other newspapers learned of the same study in rather different terms: 'Research fails to link crime with video violence' (*The Times*) and 'Research fails to link crime with video violence' (*Daily Telegraph*). These articles explained that this study had found no evidence that violent films provoked real-life violence. *Telegraph* readers, though, would also have seen a feature article by Theodore Dalrymple, inspired by the new research, whose sub-head stated in large letters that 'the admission that screen violence and the real thing are linked is long overdue'.

Over in the *Daily Express*, meanwhile, a menacing piece headed 'The Rambo culture' revealed in its sub-head that 'Violent videos are linked to real-life brutality'. It then went on to explain that 'A disturbing report . . . shows that screen violence reinforces violent behaviour'. Confused newshounds may have turned for a more balanced analysis to the *Independent*. There, however, the issue was further muddied by an article which reported that a study had shown that 'violent videos do not make people violent' but which, bizarrely, carried the headline 'Video link in violence chain'!

The study which promoted this feast of contradictory reporting had been commissioned by the Home Office in 1995 from Kevin Browne and Amanda Pennell, members of the Forensic Psychology Group at the University of Birmingham. It was intended to meet the inevitable calls for 'further research' in the wake of speculation about the possible influence of violent videos on the two schoolboys who murdered toddler James Bulger in 1993. The research that was actually carried out, however, focused on which videos young offenders preferred to watch, and on what they could remember about 'violent' videos which the researchers had shown them. Although it was pointlessly and misleadingly entitled *Effects of Video Violence on Young Offenders*, it was in no way a study of the influence of those videos.

That this research provoked the appearance of a number of completely contradictory articles in British newspapers on a couple of days in 1998 might at first sight seem insignificant, but the research appears to have made an impact on people in positions of power in the area of media regulation. For example, in an article published in the *Independent* on 14 June 1999, after Browne had given a public lecture about the same material (Browne, 1999), Andreas Whittam Smith, the recently appointed President of the British Board of Film Classification (BBFC), wrote that his organisation would be following Browne's work closely. This immediately struck many commentators as odd, since Browne's work – on the viewing interests of young offenders – would surely have very little of interest to say to the Board. The BBFC announcing that it is taking a professional interest in studies of what videos young offenders prefer is like a body of criminologists announcing that they have decided to subscribe to *Sight and Sound*: there's no reason why they shouldn't but, equally, it's not clear why they should, and even less clear why it should be thought significant enough to be reported in a national newspaper. It has always been the case that adults who have committed crimes are allowed to view the same material as other adults, and if the BBFC was wondering whether to suggest that young offenders should have their choice of videos curtailed, or whether for classification purposes it should simply treat all adults like criminals, these would surely be matters for rather more substantial debate.[1] Unfortunately, Whittam Smith seems to have completely misunderstood the very nature of the research, describing it as 'a study of the effects of video violence on young offenders' (*Independent*, 14 June 1999), which it explicitly is not.

In order to gain any understanding of what was going on beyond the extremely confusing coverage of Browne and Pennell's report, we must, of course, turn to the original study itself. However, the full report has never been published or even made available to other academics and researchers in this area who have requested copies directly from the authors or their sponsors. To put it mildly, this is pretty odd. Research which is not made available in full for the scrutiny of scholarly peers or the general public, is usually regarded with a large dose of suspicion, and we have little reason to break with that tradition in this particular case.

The only way in which we can hope to understand this research is via a publicly-available four-page *summary* document produced by the Home Office. Whilst the availability of this summary is welcome (it is even on the Internet, at http://www.homeoffice.gov.uk/rds/publf.htm), it does not alter the fact that public money was spent on a two-year research project on a matter of public and academic concern, the details of which remain largely secret for no obvious reason.

The Home Office summary indicates that this was a relatively straightforward piece of research, and one that makes no grand claims for itself. It does not show that violent films make people violent, nor the opposite. It is not the kind of study which could claim to do so, as the summary (which was circulated to journalists) makes quite clear. 'The research cannot prove whether video violence causes crime', it states, quite unequivocally (1998: 4). One wonders, then, why the title of the summary (*Effects of Video Violence* . . .) suggests otherwise, and why Browne told the *Guardian* that 'violent films have the potential to cause crime', a view which his own study did not actually support. No wonder the journalists were confused!

What the study 'suggests', to use its own words, is that 'the well established link between poor social background and delinquent behaviour may extend to the development of a preference for violent film' (1998: 4). The research findings, whilst not able to make any claims about 'effects', do attempt to make some links regarding possible influences upon offenders, but ultimately the study has to admit that it 'provides little evidence that offenders were more influenced by the experimental film than non-offenders' (1998: 3). Instead, the researchers clearly emphasise that they may have found that people with violent backgrounds, who go on to engage in violence themselves, may also develop a taste for films which contain violence. And that's all. The study was not able to trace a path from violent screen images out into the real world; instead, we learn simply that some violent people might want to come in from the mean streets to watch, well, *Mean Streets*. However, research by Hagell and Newburn (1994) which investigated the *already-existing* viewing habits of young offenders – unlike Browne and Pennell, who interfered with the situation by sitting their participants down in front of violent films – found compelling evidence that the offenders actually had *less* interest in TV and films (whether violent or not) than ordinary viewers.

Not much there, then. But if the BBFC is going to treat the study as if it has something to tell us about how we might patrol the availability of violent films in our society, then it is worth taking it seriously for just a bit longer, while we note the following:

• The study is quantitative in its methods, but uses a total of only 122 young men – 54 'violent young offenders', 28 'non-violent young offenders', and 40 students as a 'control group' (see below). It is not clear whether the spread of ages (from 15 to 21) was the same in each group – which it would need to be in order to deal with age differences in viewing preferences. In any case, these samples are much too small for quantitative research.

• The offenders were compared with what the authors call a 'control sample'. However, rather than being a cross-section of ordinary people matching the demographics of the other groups, these were 40 students. This would be a major error in any serious study: every researcher knows that students are a unique group who are unrepresentative of the general population, even within their age band.

- The summary gives us very little idea which 'violent video films' were used. The films it mentions in passing are *ID* (1995), a seriously-intentioned film about football violence, and *Last Gasp* (1995), an unsuccessful supernatural thriller. The rationale for these selections is not given.

- Only one in five of the offenders said that they liked a movie character 'because they were violent'. (Even fewer of the other participants in the study said this.) Browne uses this small bit of data, which is only about what the subject likes to see in a movie anyway, as a significant building-block in his argument suggesting that movies might be a worrying influence.

- Browne seems to be more interested in some statistics than others. For example, his data shows that non-offenders were just as likely as violent offenders to state that a violent part of the film shown excited them the most, but he does not take this to be troubling in the way that he finds other bits of data troubling.

- Since the offenders were incarcerated in 'secure institutions', comparisons cannot really be made between their and other's TV viewing preferences. Prisoners are unlikely to be able to choose freely what they watch, and will also be more likely to maintain routines (like following soaps) than those on the outside. The report finds that offenders watch more TV than others, but since they are confined this is hardly surprising.

In the public lecture which apparently so impressed the BBFC President, Browne (1999) classified violent films into 'three broad categories: violent drama films, violent action films, and violent horror films'. Although it is not actually central to his argument, it is worth looking at this way of considering movies because we can thereby gain a useful insight into the way in which psychologists view popular entertainment, and also because this way of looking at 'violent films' was admiringly regurgitated in Andreas Whittam Smith's 1999 article.

The first of Browne's categories, 'violent drama films', quite rightly allows for the possibility of there being movies which contain violence but which are not simply celebrations of fighting and gore. These are films where 'the violence portrayed is necessary to tell the story'. The examples given, predictably enough, are *Schindler's List* (1993) and *Platoon* (1986). (In the mid-1990s, whenever the Home Office became publicly concerned about the spectre of 'violent films', there would always be a modicum of concern amongst right-thinking people that we would end up banning Spielberg's *List*, which everyone seemed to agree represented the epitome of justifiable screen violence.) These unimaginative examples suggest that filmmakers who are thinking about making a realistic war film about a conflict that has actually taken place, and who also can remember to make it clear that wars are not nice, will be guaranteed protection from the criticisms made of other kinds of films which contain violence. But what should we make, for example, of *Starship Troopers* (1997), a simultaneously entertaining *and* serious, semi-realistic war film about a fictional war, which satirises the notion (suggested by the right-wing novel upon which it is based) that having a heavily disciplined society which sends off its young people to kill or be killed by space bugs is a really neat idea?

Perhaps one of Browne's other categories has the answer. 'Violent action films', we are told, are designed 'to excite and stimulate the viewer rather than concentrate on the story to be told.' The examples given are *Rambo* (1987) and *Out for Justice* (1991). Both films, in fact, have a clear story and contain some scenes of violence, scenes in which the audience is clearly called upon to support one or more characters who are trying to stop another character from committing cruel acts of violence. Hmm.

The third category is 'violent horror films' (single example: *Cannibal Holocaust* (1979), banned in the UK on both film and video), which are those where viewers are invited 'to share in the degradation, humiliation, physical harm and death of people as a form of entertainment'. This category may, at first sight, appear to be the most straightforward, covering a particular kind of 'nasty' which is far from the mainstream of even '18' rated film and video: until, that is, you wonder whether any of the James Bond films could seriously claim to fall outside this description.

In general, the category of 'violent action films' would seem to cover the majority of popular Hollywood action movies. But the producers of any of these could easily argue that 'the violence portrayed is necessary to tell the story': this will *obviously* be the case if you have a violent story to tell! All Browne's examples of individual films make it look as if his system of categorising films is more unproblematic than it actually is. Even the example of a 'violent action film', *Rambo*, is carefully selected as one of the few well-known movies which many of those who haven't actually seen it will imagine is all violence and no story. In most cases it would in fact be very difficult to decide whether a film is a story-led 'violent drama', which Browne seems to feel is OK, or a 'violent action film' centrally concerned with excitement, which Browne equates (negatively) with pornography.

As noted above, Whittam Smith's *Independent* article cites these categories positively, although admittedly with certain reservations. To his credit, he notes that 'in practice, violent films do not always fit easily into Professor Browne's categories', since violence can be represented in more or less serious or realistic contexts. He also notes that horror films are a genre with unique conventions, and that of these films 'only a minority' fit Browne's 'violent horror' category. Nevertheless, Whittam Smith repeats the silly point that 'violent action films . . . are designed primarily to excite and stimulate the viewer, and are thus a form of exploitation'. However, it remains entirely unclear just why a successfully enthralling action film has to be labelled 'exploitative'. Are we to understand from Whittam Smith's remarks that *anything* which excites and stimulates us is *necessarily* exploitative?

Browne's argument concerning how certain young people with violent family backgrounds *might* read certain videos in a particular way which *might* lead to violent responses is certainly unusually qualified and cautious. However, it has in common with the worst of effects studies that it goes beyond the data: as we have seen, Browne's study was absolutely unable to show that videos would influence anything or anybody. At best, his argument can be summed up as consisting of quite well-informed, but ultimately perhaps misguided, speculation.

Although Browne's study was refreshingly different, in that it took offenders rather than screen violence as its starting-point, it still went awry because the researchers imposed a media-centred approach onto the data. This is one of the most common flaws of studies which think that they are studies of media effects. Indeed, these studies have quite consistently taken the wrong approach to popular media, to its audiences, and indeed to society in general. For the remainder of this chapter, rather than considering the flaws of individual pieces of research, I will consider the mountain of studies – and the associated claims about media effects made by commentators – as a whole, and outline ten fundamental flaws in their approach.

Ten things wrong with the 'effects model'

This analysis contains very few references to specific studies because these arguments apply to *so many* studies. The author hopes that the intelligent student of media effects studies will apply these ideas to whatever research they read about elsewhere. The book *Moving Experiences* (Gauntlett, 1995) was a close examination of numerous individual studies; the criticisms below are deliberately much more general.[2]

The effects model tackles social problems 'backwards'

To understand the causes of violence, or other human behaviour, research should logically begin with the people who engage in those actions. By studying what motivates and prompts their behaviour, by understanding their background and their goals, we might hope to be able to explain the roots of such acts.

Media effects researchers, however, have typically started at the wrong end of this question: informed only by speculation (and, often, a certain disregard for both young people and popular media), they begin with the idea that the media is to blame, and then try to make links back to the world of actual violence. This 'backwards' approach to a perceived problem makes little sense. To illustrate this point by way of a different example: if it had been suggested that the most successful entrepreneurs were people who had listened to a great of classical music when younger, the first step in any investigation of a causal link would be to interview a number of successful entrepreneurs and ask them whether they had heard much classical music and, if so, whether (and how) they felt it had affected their development. Only then, if this provided encouraging results, would we proceed to the second stage, which would be focused upon classical music itself: for example, we might try to identify 'inspirational' chords or harmonies and engage in studies which explored how people seemed to be affected by the music. The problem with much media effects research, however, is that researchers have jumped straight to the second stage – investigating the media and its possible 'effects' – without even bothering with the first one, namely checking whether any notable suspects have in fact been affected.

To understand violent people, I recommend studying violent people.

To their credit, Browne and Pennell are unusual in this respect, in that they do begin their study with offenders – although they unfortunately impose a degree of media-centrism on the project through both their methods (in showing videos to the offenders) and their analysis (in which they go beyond the data and implicate the media). In the well-designed piece of research mentioned above, which did not contain the flaws in Browne's methods, Hagell and Newburn (1994) studied 78 teenage offenders (who had histories of violence and other serious offences), and compared them with a group of over 500 non-offending young people of the same age. They found that the young offenders, when not incarcerated, actually watched *less* television and video than their other teenage counterparts, and even had less access to the technology in the first place. They were found to have no particular interest in specifically violent programmes, and either enjoyed the same material as non-offending teenagers or were simply uninterested in it. In particular, most of the young offenders were simply not sufficiently engaged with television to be able to answer a question about identifying with television characters, which they generally seemed to think would be a pretty stupid thing to do anyway.

Both these studies, by Browne and Pennell, and by Hagell and Newburn, are unusual and helpful in that they start with the perpetrators of violence. But both studies fail to show a strong connection between young offenders and media influences.

The effects model treats children as inadequate

Much of the discourse about children and the media positions children as potential victims, and as little else. Furthermore, media effects research usually employs methods which will not allow children to challenge this assumption. The studies give no voice to young people and no opportunity for them to demonstrate their independence, intelligence or free will. The hundreds of shallow quantitative studies, often conducted by 'psychologists', have often been little more than traps for their subjects. The methods used – most obviously in numerous misguided laboratory and field experiments – allow, paradoxically, no scope for developing any psychological insights. The young participants may or may not fall into the trap of giving the response which is then read as evidence of a media effect, but, since the researchers record only this binary result, the subjects are unable to provide their observers with any evidence at all of their skills or critical abilities. In addition, whilst the responses of children in experiments are generally interpreted as being unique to this age group, comparison studies of adults are rarely performed. The researchers, we have to presume, are simply not bothered by such matters.

Research which has sought to establish what children can and do understand about the media have exposed the deficiencies of previous research. Such projects have shown that children can and do talk intelligently, and indeed cynically, about the media (Buckingham, 1993, 1996), and that children as young as seven can make thoughtful, critical and 'media literate' video productions themselves (Gauntlett, 1997).

Assumptions within the effects model are characterised by barely-concealed conservative ideology

Media effects research is good news for conservatives and right-wing 'moralists'. Whilst not all of the researchers engaged in effects research have a particular interest in advancing right-wing and moralistic causes, that is nevertheless their definite function, since the studies heavily reinforce the idea that violence in society can be explained by looking to the media.

Conservatives have traditionally liked to blame popular culture for the ailments of society, not only because they fear new and innovative forms of media, but also because it allows them to divert attention away from other and, for them, more awkward social questions such as levels of welfare provision and (in the States) the easy availability of guns.

Media effects researchers often talk about the *amount* of violence in the media, encouraging the view that it is not important to consider the *meaning* of the scenes involving violence which appear on screen. Again, this makes life easy for people who wish to turn public attention away from the real social causes of violence and to blame the media instead.

Critics of screen violence often reveal themselves to be worried about the challenges to the status quo which they feel that some violent movies present (even though most European and many American film critics see most popular films as being ridiculously status quo-friendly). For example, Michael Medved, author of the successful *Hollywood vs. America: Popular Culture and the War on Traditional Values* (1992) finds worrying and potentially influential displays of 'disrespect for authority' and 'anti-patriotic attitudes' in films like *Top Gun* – a movie which many other commentators find embarrassingly jingoistic. This opportunistic mixing of concerns about the media roots of violence with a political critique of the content of violent films represents a particularly distasteful trend in 'social concern' commentary. Media effects studies and TV violence content analyses help only to sustain such an approach by maintaining the notion that 'antisocial behaviour' is an objective category which can be measured, which is common to numerous programmes, and which will negatively affect those children who see it portrayed on screen.

The effects model inadequately defines its own objects of study

Media effects studies are usually extremely undiscriminating about how they identify worrying bits of media content, or subsequent behaviour by viewers. An act of 'violence', for example, might be smashing cages to set animals free or using force to disable a nuclear-armed plane. It might be kicking a chair in frustration or a cruel and horrible murder. In many studies, 'verbal aggression' is included as a form of aggression, which means that studies which are interpreted by most people as being about the representation of physical violence may actually be more concerned with the use of swear words. Once processed by effects research, all of these various depictions or actions simply emerge as a 'level of aggression', but without a more selective and discriminating way of compiling these numbers, the results can be at best deceptive and at worst virtually meaningless.

In the Browne and Pennell study, 'violence' seems to be understood in a vague, 'common sense' way. Typically, there is no discussion of the meanings associated with the violent acts shown in the videos (indeed, as we have seen, it is a study concerning violent videos which barely mentions violent videos). Browne's attempt to categorise violent films into different types shows a refreshing willingness to accept that 'violent film' is a term so broad as to be meaningless, but his three categories are themselves so simplistic that no real progress is made.

The effects model is often based on artificial studies

Since careful sociological studies of media influences require considerable amounts of time and money, they are heavily outnumbered by simpler studies which often put their subjects into artificial and contrived situations (but then pretend that they are studying the everyday world). Laboratory and field experiments involve forcing participants to watch a particular programme or set of programmes which they would not have chosen if left to their own devices and – just as artificially – observing them in a particular setting afterwards. In these settings, the behaviour of the children towards an inanimate object is often taken to represent how they would behave towards a real person. Furthermore, this all rests on the mistaken belief that children's behaviour will not be affected by the fact that they know that they are being manipulated, tested and/or observed. (Studies by researchers such as Borden (1975) have shown that this is quite erroneous: participation in an experiment, and even the appearance of the adults involved in the study, can radically affect children's behaviour.)

The effects model is often based on studies with misapplied methodology

Many of the studies which do not rely on the experimental method, and so may evade the flaws mentioned above, fall down instead by wrongly applying a methodological procedure or by drawing inappropriate conclusions from particular methods. For example, the widely-cited longitudinal panel study[3] by Huesmann et al. (Lefkowitz et al., 1972, 1977) has been slated, less famously, for failing to keep to the proper procedures, such as assessing aggressivity or levels of TV viewing with the same measures at different times, procedures which are obviously necessary if the study's statistical findings are to have any validity (Chaffee, 1972; Kenny, 1972). The same researchers have also failed to account adequately for the fact that the findings of this study and of another of their own (Huesmann et al., 1984) completely contradict each other, with the former concluding that the media has a marginal effect on boys but no effect on girls, and the latter arguing the exact opposite! They also seem to ignore the fact that their own follow-up of their original set of subjects twenty-two years later suggested that a number of biological, developmental and environmental factors contributed to levels of aggression, whilst the media was not even mentioned (Huesmann et al., 1984). These astounding inconsistencies, unapologetically presented by perhaps the best-known researchers in this area, must surely be cause for considerable unease about the effects model. More careful use of similar methods, as in the three-year panel study involving over 3,000 young people conducted by Milavsky et al. (1982a, 1982b), has indicated only that significant media effects are not to be found.

Perhaps the most frequent and misleading abuse of research methodology occurs when studies which are simply *unable* to show that one thing causes another are treated as if they have done so. Such is the case with correlation studies, which can easily find that a particular personality type is also the kind of person who enjoys certain kinds of media – for example, that violent people like to watch 'violent films' – but are quite unable to show that media use has *produced* that character. Nevertheless, psychologists such as Van Evra (1990) and, as we have seen, Browne and Amanda (1998) and Browne (1998) have assumed that this is probably the case. There is a logical coherence to the idea that children whose behaviour is antisocial and disruptive will also have a greater interest in the more violent and noisy television programmes, whereas the idea that their behaviour is a *consequence* of these programmes lacks both rational consistency and empirical support.

The effects model is selective in its criticisms of media depictions of violence

As suggested earlier, effects studies may involve distinctly ideological interpretations of what constitutes 'antisocial' action. Furthermore, researchers tend to refer only to violence in *fictional* TV programmes and films. Violence shown in news and factual programming is generally exempt from researchers' criticisms – although they typically fail to account for this. The point here, of course, is not to argue for serious coverage of serious violent events to be subjected to the same simplistic, blinkered criticisms that are aimed at fictional portrayals. However, there is a substantial problem with an approach which suggests that on-screen violence is bad if it does not extend this to cover news and factual violence, which is often cruel and has no visible negative consequences for the perpetrator. That it is mainly popular fictional programmes which are singled out for criticism suggests (again) that many researchers have in fact an ideological objection to this particular area of television, and that their concerns about violence in this area are but an aspect of their negative attitude towards popular television forms in general.

The effects model assumes superiority to the 'masses'

An obvious point which can be made about all media effects studies is that whilst the researchers consider that other people might be affected by media content, they assume that their own approach is objective and that the media will have no effect on *them*. In fact, surveys show that almost everybody feels this way: whilst varying percentages of the population say they are concerned about media effects on others, almost nobody says that they have ever been affected *themselves*. Sometimes the researchers excuse their approach by saying that they are mature adults, whereas their concerns lie with *children*, but, as already noted, one of the many flaws of the effects model is that it treats children as inadequate. In cases in which this is not possible, because the researchers have used young adults in their study, it is traditional to invoke the menacing spectre of the unruly 'Other' (the undiscriminating 'heavy viewer', the 'uneducated', the working class, and so on) as the victim of 'effects', thus allowing the researchers over-enthusiastically to interpret their weak or flawed data in such a way as to suggest that somebody other than them will be negatively affected by the media.

The effects model makes no attempt to understand meanings of the media

A further fundamental flaw, already hinted at above, is that the effects model necessarily rests on a base of reductive assumptions about and unjustified stereotypes of media content. To assert that, say, 'media violence' will bring about negative consequences is not only to presume that depictions of violence in the media always promote antisocial behaviour, and that such a category actually exists and makes sense, but it also assumes that whatever medium is being studied by the researchers holds a singular message which will be carried unproblematically to the audience. The effects model, therefore, performs the double deception of presuming (a) that the media presents one singular and clear-cut 'message', and (b) that the proponents of the effects model are in a position to identify just what that message is.

The assumption that similar acts of violence in different programmes or films will all have the same power and 'message' ignores the all-important *meanings* of media content: for example, seeing a woman cut in two in a violent thriller would be quite different to seeing Darth Maul chopped in half at the climax of *Star Wars: The Phantom Menace* (1999). Equally seriously, different viewers will respond to the *same* scene quite differently (some people will be delighted when Obi-Wan slices Darth Maul, others will be disappointed, others will wish that Queen Amidala had killed him, and so on). In-depth qualitative studies have, entirely unsurprisingly, given strong support to the view that media audiences routinely arrive at their own, often heterogeneous, interpretations of everyday media texts (see for example Buckingham, 1993, 1996; Hill, 1997; Gauntlett and Hill, 1999; Schlesinger *et al.*, 1992; Gray, 1992; Palmer, 1986). The effects model can really only make sense to people who consider popular entertainment to be a set of very basic propaganda messages flashed at the audience in the simplest possible terms.

The effects model is not grounded in theory

How does seeing an action depicted by the media translate into a motive which actually prompts an individual to behave in the same way? The lack of convincing explanations (let alone anything which we could call a 'theory') of how this process might occur is perhaps the most important and worrying problem with effects research. There is the idea that violence is 'glamorised' in some films and TV shows, which sometimes seems relevant; however, the more horrifyingly violent a production is, the less the violence tends to be glamorised. On these terms, effects researchers' arguments that children must be protected from the most violent media depictions, doesn't quite make sense. As with the model as a whole, it just isn't subtle enough.

Even in the case of a film in which serious violence looks rather stylish, such as in the virtual reality world of *The Matrix* (1999), there is no good explanation of why anyone would simply copy those actions; and we do *need* an explanation if the effects hypothesis is to rise above the status of 'not very convincing suggestion'.

This lack of firm theory has led to the effects model basing itself on the variety of assumptions outlined above – that the media (rather than people) is an unproblematic starting-point for research; that children are unable to 'cope' with the media; that the categories of 'violence' or 'antisocial behaviour' are clear-cut and self-evident; that the model's predictions can be verified by scientific research; that screen fictions are of concern, whilst news pictures are not; that researchers have the unique capacity to observe and classify social behaviour and its meanings, but that those researchers themselves need not attend to the various possible meanings which media content may have for its audiences. Each of these very substantial problems has its roots in the failure of media effects commentators to found their model in any coherent theory at all.

So is media effects research finished?

Depressingly, the media effects model remains quite popular, as the study by Browne and Pennell (1998) quite clearly demonstrates: a largely quantitative study using a laughably small number of participants and an inappropriate 'control sample' which produced a few entirely unsurprising correlations and then embroidered on these results with some reasonable-sounding but ultimately unfounded and meaningless speculation about media influences . . . is hailed as a valuable contribution to the debate. It could be said that there is little point in trying to question the methodology of those people working within the effects model, because, by our own definition of that work, they are much more concerned with creating an illusion of empiricism to support their prejudged conclusions than in designing methodologically sound research. In other words, they're not going to stop. The solution must be two-fold: to raise awareness of the flaws in that research in the hope that this will make it more difficult for the press to report their findings uncritically and, perhaps more importantly, to produce new kinds of research which will tell us more subtle and interesting things about possible media influences than anything which the effects researchers can provide.

In conclusion, it is both bemusing and somewhat frightening to note the numbers of psychologists (and others) who conduct research according to prescribed recipes, despite the many well-known flaws with those procedures, when it is in fact so easy to imagine alternative research methods and processes. For example, I usefully tried out a method which encouraged children to make videos *themselves* as a way of exploring what they had got from the mass media (Gauntlett, 1997), and nor is it exactly hard to think of different and probably superior alternative methods – see also, for example, Philo

(1990, 1996). The discourses about 'media effects' from politicians and the popular press are already quite laughably simplistic enough: academics shouldn't encourage them in their delusions.

NOTES

1 Interestingly, in 1999 the BBFC was also arguing that it should refuse to give some videos 'R18' certificates because children might see and be harmed by them. This classification is for sex videos which can be purchased only by adults in licensed sex shops. The BBFC had previously refused to award certificates to certain videos destined for this strictly adults-only category, but only on the grounds of obscenity, never on the basis that children might view them in the home – the whole point of the R18 category, the very reason that it was created in the first place, being that children aren't supposed to see videos with this classification. The BBFC would appear thus to be undermining the entirety of its own classification system by suggesting that the age-based restrictions on its certificates are in fact irrelevant. (For further details see Petley (2000) and the relevant pages at *http://www.melonfarmers.co.uk.*)

2 For a previous discussion of this topic, see also Gauntlett (1998).

3 A longitudinal panel study is one in which the same group of people (the panel) is surveyed and/or observed at a number of points over a period of time.

REFERENCES

Barker, Martin (ed.) (1984), *The Video Nasties: Freedom and Censorship in the Media*, London: Pluto.

Barker, Martin (1989), *Comics: Ideology, Power and the Critics*, Manchester: Manchester University Press.

Barker, Martin (1993), 'Sex, violence and videotape', in *Sight and Sound*, 3:5, pp. 10–12.

Borden, Richard J. (1975), 'Witnessed aggression: influence of an observer's sex and values on aggressive responding', in *Journal of Personality and Social Psychology*, 31: 3, pp. 567–73.

Browne, Kevin (1999), 'Violence in the media causes crime: myth or reality', Inaugural Lecture, 3 June 1999, University of Birmingham.

Browne, Kevin and Pennell, Amanda (1998), 'Effects of video violence on young offenders', *Home Office Research and Statistics Directorate Research Findings*, No. 65.

Buckingham, David (1993), *Children Talking Television: The Making of Television Literacy*, London: Falmer Press.

Buckingham, David (1996), *Moving Images: Understanding Children's Emotional Responses to Television*, Manchester: Manchester University Press.

Chaffee, Steven H. (1972), 'Television and adolescent aggressiveness (overview)', in Comstock, George A., and Rubenstein, Eli A., eds, *Television and Social Behaviour: Reports and Papers, Volume III: Television and Adolescent Agressiveness*, National Institute of Mental Health, Maryland.

Cumberbatch, Guy and Howitt, Dennis (1989), *A Measure of Uncertainty: The Effects of the Mass Media*, John Libbey, London: Broadcasting Standards Council Research Monograph.

Gauntlett, David (1995), *Moving Experiences: Understanding Television's Influences and Effects*, London: John Libbey.

Gauntlett, David (1997), *Video Critical: Children, the Environment and Media Power*, Luton: John Libbey Media.

Gauntlett, David (1998), 'Ten things wrong with the "effects model"', in Dickinson, Roger, Harindranath, Ramaswani, and Linne, Olga, eds, *Approaches to Audiences* London: Edward Arnold, pp.120–30.

Gauntlett, David, and Hill, Annette (1999), *TV Living: Television, Culture and Everyday Life*, London: Routledge.

Gray, Ann (1992), *Video Playtime: The Gendering of a Leisure Technology*, London: Routledge.

Hagell, Ann and Newburn, Tim (1994), *Young Offenders and the Media: Viewing Habits and Preferences*, London: Policy Studies Institute.

Hill, Annette (1997), *Shocking Entertainment: Viewer Response to Violent Movies*, Luton: John Libbey Media.

Huesmann, L. Rowell, Eron, Leonard D., Lefkowitz, Monroe M. and Walder, Leopold O. (1984), 'Stability of aggression over time and generations', in *Developmental Psychology*, 20:6, pp. 1120–34.

Huesmann, L. Rowell, Lagerspetz, Kirsti and Eron, Leonard D. (1984), 'Interviewing variables in the TV violence – aggression relation: evidence from two countries', in *Developmental Psychology*, vol. 20, no. 5, pp. 746–75.

Kenny, David A. (1972), 'Two comments on cross-lagged correlation: threats to the internal validity of cross-lagged panel inference as related to "Television violence and child aggression: a follow-up study",' in Comstock and Rubenstein, eds, *Television and Social Behavior: Reports and Papers, Volume III: Television and Adolescent Aggressiveness*, Maryland: National Institute of Mental Health.

Lefkowitz, Monroe M., Eron Leonard D., Walder, Leopold O. and Huesmann, L. Rowell (1972), 'Television violence and child aggression: a follow-up study', in Comstock, George A. and Rubinstein, Eli A., eds, *Television and Social Behavior: Reports and Papers, Volume III: Television and Adolescent Aggressiveness*, Maryland: National Institute of Mental Health.

Lefkowitz, Monroe M., Eron, Leonard D., Walder, Leopold O. and Huesmann, L. Rowell (1977), *Growing Up To Be Violent: A Longitudinal Study of the Development of Aggression*, New York: Pergamon Press.

Medved, Michael (1992), *Hollywood vs. America: Popular Culture and the War on Traditional Values*, London: HarperCollins.

Milavsky, J. Ronald, Kessler, Ronald C., Stipp, Horst and Rubens, William S. (1982a), *Television and Aggression: A Panel Study*, New York: Academic Press.

Milavsky, J. Ronald, Kessler, Ronald, Stipp, Horst and Rubens, William S. (1982b), 'Television and aggression: results of a panel study', in Pearl, David, Bouthilet, Lorraine and Lazar, Joyce, eds, *Television and Behavior: Ten Years of Scientific Progress and Implications for the Eighties, Volume 2: Technical Reviews*, Maryland: National Institute of Mental Health.

Miller, David and Philo, Greg (1996), 'The media do influence us', in *Sight and Sound*, 6:12, pp. 18–20.

Palmer, Patricia (1986), *The Lively Audience: A Study of Children Around the TV Set*, Sydney: Allen and Unwin.

Petley, Julian (2000), 'The censor and the state: or why *Horny Catbabe* matters', in *Journal of Popular British Cinema*, no.3, pp. 93–103.

Philo, Greg (1990), *Seeing and Believing: The Influence of Television*, London: Routledge.

Philo, Greg (ed.) (1996), *Media and Mental Distress*, London: Longman.

Schlesinger, Philip, Dobash, R. Emerson, Dobash, Russell P. and Weaver, C. Kay (1992), *Women Viewing Violence*, London: British Film Institute.

Van Evra, Judith (1990), *Television and Child Development*, Hillsdale, New Jersey: Lawrence Erlbaum Associates.

3

ELECTRONIC CHILD ABUSE?

Rethinking the media's effects on children

David Buckingham

The figure of the child is at the heart of the majority of debates about media effects. To some extent, this may be inevitable. Since ancient times, the idea of childhood has been invested with far-reaching hopes and anxieties about the future; and, as a highly visible manifestation of modern technology and modern culture, the same is true of the electronic media. The combination of the two is therefore bound to invoke profound concerns about the continuity of the social order and of fundamental human values. It is only natural that we should care about what our children will become.

What remains striking here, however, is that this combination is so often perceived in such negative terms. Children are seen here, not as confident adventurers in an age of new challenges and possibilities, but as passive victims of media manipulation; and the media not as potential agents of enlightenment or of democratic citizenship, but as causes of moral degradation and social decline. Children, it would seem, are unable to help themselves; and it is our responsibility as adults to prevent them from gaining access to that which would harm and corrupt them.

Among the enormous range of material which the media make available to children, it is the category of 'violence' which has, of course, remained the obsessive focus of adult concern. Media violence is seen, not only to encourage children to commit acts of violence, but as itself a form of violence *against* children, committed by adults whose only motivation is that of financial greed. In Elizabeth Newson's terms, media violence represents a form of electronic 'child abuse', which we must have the courage to regulate and resist.[1]

Children as 'others'

Debates about the negative effects of the media are almost always debates about *other* people. Elite discourses about popular culture have traditionally been suffused with patronising assumptions about the audience, based largely on a contempt for women and other members of the 'lower orders'.[2] Yet it is also children who are often defined as quintessentially 'other', and who have historically been seen to be most at risk from the media. As other contributors to this book will argue, this in turn reflects dominant ideological assumptions about childhood itself.

Children are largely defined here in terms of what they lack – that is, in terms of their inability (or unwillingness) to conform to adult norms. While this lack can be perceived in 'positive' terms – as a form of innocence, an absence of guile or artifice, a child-like charm – such formulations are often merely patronising. Relative to adults, children are seen to lack the knowledge, the experience and the intellectual capacities that would entitle them to social power. Vulnerability, ignorance and irrationality are regarded as part of the inherent condition of childhood.

Thus imitative violence, which has remained the central focus of anxiety in such debates, is largely seen as arising from the inability to distinguish between fiction and reality. Children copy what they see on television because they lack the experience and the intellectual capacities that might enable them to see through the illusion of reality which the medium provides. They take what they watch as an accurate reflection of the world, and as a trustworthy guide to behaviour, because they are simply too immature to know any better. And, of course, in expressing our concern about these matters, we implicitly position ourselves as somehow immune from such inadequacies. Using such arguments thus in itself appears to guarantee our rationality and maturity, and thereby distinguishes us from those others whom we take it upon ourselves to protect.

'Active' audiences

Historically, academic research on children's relationship with television and other media has tended to reproduce many of these assumptions. Particularly when it comes to 'violence', the central aim has been to seek evidence of direct behavioural effects. While media violence could conceivably be seen to produce many different kinds of effect – to generate fear, for example, or to encourage particular beliefs about the nature of crime and authority – the central preoccupation has been with its ability to produce aggressive behaviour, particularly among children. The methodological and theoretical limitations of this research are discussed elsewhere in this book (especially in Chapters 7 and 8); but it is important to note that, in many academic disciplines, research on children and television has largely moved beyond these behaviourist assumptions.

While some advocates of the 'hypodermic' or 'magic bullet' theory are still to be found, effects research itself has increasingly emphasised the role of 'intervening variables' which mediate between television and its audience. Far from seeing the audience as an undifferentiated mass, more recent studies have tended to concentrate on individual differences which lead viewers to respond in different ways to the same messages. Thus, for example, research on the effects of television advertising has increasingly challenged the view that children are simply passive victims of the seductive wiles of the 'hidden persuaders'.[3] Likewise, research on the influence of sex role stereotyping has questioned the idea that sexist portrayals necessarily result in sexist attitudes, and that 'heavy viewers' are therefore more likely to adopt traditional roles.[4] Meanwhile, the notion that television viewing inevitably displaces more 'constructive' activities such as reading books, or that it leads to a decline in print literacy, has been systematically undermined.[5] In each of these areas, the potential influence of television has increasingly been studied in relation to other social forces and influences in children's lives.

Over the past two decades, this tradition has been joined by a range of newer perspectives which have defined children as 'active viewers'. The notion of 'activity' here is partly a rhetorical one, and it is often used in rather imprecise ways. Yet what unites this work is a view of children, not as passive recipients of television messages, but as active interpreters of meaning. The meaning of television, from this perspective, is not delivered to the audience, but constructed by it.

For example, within the mainstream psychological tradition, there has been a significant – although in some respects rather belated – incorporation of cognitive or 'constructivist' approaches. Rather than simply responding to stimuli, viewers are seen here as consciously processing, interpreting and evaluating information. In making sense of what they watch, viewers use 'schemas' or 'scripts', sets of plans and expectations which they have built up from their previous experience both of television and of the world in general.[6] Making judgements about the relationship between television and reality, for example, is seen to depend both on children's general cognitive development and on their experience of the medium itself: children use formal or generic 'cues' to build up a growing body of knowledge about the processes of television production, which enables them to discriminate between messages they are prepared to trust and those they are not.

Likewise, uses and gratifications research has emphasised the diverse and active ways in which children and young people use the media for different social and psychological purposes.[7] From this perspective, the socialising role of the media is seen to depend upon the users' relationship with other influences, and upon the diverse and variable meanings which they attach to these influences. Thus, for example, television viewing or popular music will have a different significance depending upon the child's orientation towards the school, the family and the peer group. The influence of variables such as age, gender and social class means that different children can effectively occupy different 'media worlds' – an argument which clearly undermines any easy generalisations about 'children' as a homogeneous social group.

Finally, researchers within Cultural Studies have also drawn attention to the complexity of children's readings of the media, and of the social relationships within which they are situated. In common with constructivists, such researchers regard children as 'active' producers of meaning, rather than passive consumers, although they are also concerned with the ideological and formal constraints which are exerted by the text. One important emphasis here is on the social processes through which meaning is constructed, and the ways in which children define and negotiate their social identities through talk about the media.[8] Children's judgements about genre and representation, and their reconstructions of television narrative, for example, are studied as inherently social processes; and the development of knowledge about the media ('media literacy') and of a 'critical' perspective is seen in terms of their social motivations and purposes. These studies have been complemented by more strictly ethnographic work, which has drawn attention to the diverse social contexts of media use, and the power-relationships which are inherent within them.[9]

While there are undoubtedly several pertinent criticisms to be made of each of these approaches, it is important to acknowledge their complexity and diversity. Uses and gratifications research, for example, is often dismissed as merely individualistic – a criticism which simply does not apply to a great deal of work in the field. Likewise, Cultural Studies research on television audiences has increasingly come to be caricatured as a form of mindless populism, and as a denial of politics – a highly inaccurate view which itself seems to reinforce a very limited and parochial definition of 'politics'.

Nevertheless, it is important to be aware of some necessary qualifications here. The notion that children are 'active', 'sophisticated' or even 'critical' readers is, as I have indicated, partly a rhetorical one – a counter-balance to the more dominant view of them as passive and impressionable. Yet, in some ways, the use of such terms could be seen to perpetuate an inverted form of romanticism, in which children are seen not as innocent but as inherently street-wise. At the very least, this rhetoric merely serves to perpetuate the highly polarised nature of the debate, in which the media are seen *either* as enormously powerful *or* as effectively powerless.

Thus, while it is important to emphasise the *diversity* of children's readings and uses of the media, we must also recognise that that diversity is far less than infinite. Likewise, children's 'sophistication' as viewers has definite limits; and it depends to no small extent on the critical perspectives that are made available to them from other sources, such as parents and teachers. And to argue that children are 'active' viewers is not thereby to suggest that they are not influenced by the media, or indeed that 'activity' is necessarily incompatible with negative effects.[10]

Amid these broader developments, however, research on the effects of media violence has remained something of an anomaly. Despite the more complex views of meaning which have been developed by the various research perspectives mentioned above, much of the work on violence has remained stubbornly tied to behaviourist assumptions. To be sure, there has been some recognition of the social and cognitive dimensions of viewers' responses, but these have largely been conceptualised as 'intervening variables' which mediate between the stimulus and the behavioural response.[11]

At the same time, researchers from other traditions have tended to contribute to this situation, either by strategically ignoring the issue of violence, or by suggesting that the debate is based on theoretical premises which are fundamentally incorrect. 'Violence', they argue, does not exist in the sense that the term refers to a given, socially accepted reality; and the notion of 'cause and effect' is an inadequate basis for understanding the complexity and diversity of audiences' relations with the media. To seek for evidence of 'the effects of media violence' is to persist in asking simplistic questions about complicated social issues.

Academic research and public debate

While these assertions may ultimately be true, they remain essentially negative. And in the heated debates that surround events like the murder of James Bulger they are quickly incorporated into an either/or logic. Are we really saying that the media have *no* effects? Can we prove it? And since we can't, then surely it is better to err on the side of caution. The logic, it would seem, is inescapable – and to challenge it is simply academic obfuscation. In such contexts, the insistence on diversity and complexity which is apparent in the approaches I have outlined above can come to seem not only wishy-washy but also potentially arrogant – as if those who fail to recognise the full extent of this complexity are simply suffering from a lack of rationality or intellectual acuity. Yet again, it would seem that it is only *other* people who are prone to such illogical 'panics'.

This situation is complicated further by the fact that many who seek to challenge assertions about the effects of media violence also wish to hold on to arguments about the power of the media in other areas. Certainly on the left there are widely held beliefs about the influence of the media – in the case of children, in relation to advertising and 'stereotyping' for example – that are based on similar theoretical assumptions (for instance about 'role models') to those espoused by the so-called 'moral majority'. And of course, in some cases, this alliance between the left and the moral right has been quite explicit – most obviously in the case of debates around pornography.[12] In the case of violence, there are many who would dispute the charge that violent television leads to acts of physical aggression, while simultaneously arguing that it encourages an ideology of militarism or traditional forms of masculinity. And there are few on the left who would not advocate some form of state censorship when it comes to issues such as the incitement to racial hatred.

Such tensions and contradictions cannot easily be resolved; but they can quickly lead to a form of paralysis. When compared with the urgency and passion of the pro-censorship lobby, the epistemological meditations of left/ liberal academics are bound to seem frustratingly vague, if not downright perverse. We can all agree to challenge the likes of Elizabeth Newson on the grounds of her lack of evidence and her simplistic theoretical assumptions; but it seems to be much harder to articulate a positive alternative, particularly one which will have any kind of purchase on popular debate. To defend media violence on the grounds of 'freedom of expression' or to base one's argument on claims about 'artistic quality' is almost guaranteed to produce incredulity, particularly in the context of a film like *Child's Play III*. And to challenge censorship on the grounds that it is inevitably 'political' – and that the censorship of violent pornography is somehow to be equated with the censorship of news reporting from Northern Ireland – is to take far too much for granted. Of course, this is not to say that there are not important and valid arguments to be made in such terms; although it is to suggest that they are extremely difficult to sustain in the context of public debate. So what might be the grounds for an alternative approach?

The discourse of 'effects'

One potential starting point here is to look more closely at the ways in which popular discourses about media 'effects' are actually employed. In my own research into children's and parents' views on such issues, I have frequently encountered such arguments.[13] Both groups will regularly define television as a 'bad influence' – albeit, of course, on those other than themselves. Yet it is important to acknowledge the social functions of such arguments, rather than simply taking them at face value.

For parents, assertions about the negative effects of television appear to confer a considerable degree of social status on those who make them. To lament the harmful effects of television violence and to proclaim the need for strict control represent very effective ways of staking out a position as a 'concerned parent'. Such responses are, of course, more likely to be produced in situations where people are addressed and defined as 'parents', not least in response to the earnest investigations of middle-class academic researchers. As numerous studies have shown, there is a 'social desirability bias' written into such encounters, which leads parents to take up such apparently 'principled' positions and to over-estimate the degree of control which they exert over their children.[14]

What is interesting, however, is that these kinds of generalised assertion about media effects often prove difficult to sustain in the face of the evidence, particularly about their own children. Idealised accounts of parental control frequently begin to crack when one is asked to describe the realities and compromises of family life. Parents will often acknowledge that their children imitate what they watch on television, although they will also imply that such behaviour is clearly recognised as a form of 'play', and that it is unlikely to be carried through into real life. Of course, *other people's* children might be led to commit acts of 'copy-cat' violence; but the primary blame for this is seen to lie not with the media, but with what is seen as inadequate parenting.

When talking to children, a similar kind of displacement often occurs. Of course, 10-year-olds will say, television violence can cause violence in real life. But we aren't influenced by what we watch: it's only little kids who copy what they see. We might have done this when we were much younger, but we certainly don't do it now. And yet, when you talk to these little kids, the story is the same: 'other people', it would seem, are always elsewhere. There is a kind of infinite regression here, as children in each age group claim to have already attained the age of reason some years previously. Such anecdotes about media effects are often part of a broader 'narrative of the self', in which children construct a positive identity through disavowing the immaturities of their younger selves.

Similarly, both children and parents will regularly cite cases such as the murder of James Bulger or the Hungerford Massacre[15] as evidence of the negative influence of media violence – despite the lack of evidence which characterises such stories. Yet, at the same time, such arguments are often surrounded with a considerable degree of ambivalence, qualification and inconsistency. In the case of the Bulger killing, for example, most of the people we interviewed challenged the notion that the film *Child's Play III* alone had been to blame; and many of the children in particular mocked such arguments, asserting that they were symptomatic of the hypocrisy and hysteria of the popular press.[16] Unlike most of the press, they insisted on the need to explain such actions in the light of a broader range of social and psychological influences.

Ultimately, however, the concerns of parents and of children were rather different from those of politicians and other social commentators, and indeed from those of most researchers in this field. The central concern among the parents in my research, at least in relation to their *own* children, was not that they would become aggressive as a result of what they had seen, but that they would be emotionally disturbed or upset. Likewise, older children agreed that younger ones should not be exposed to such material, on the grounds that they might find it too hard to handle. In this respect, a 'video nasty' was defined not as a film which would make children do nasty things, but as one which might give them nasty dreams.

As these observations suggest, discourses about media effects carry a considerable social charge: they provide a powerful means of defining oneself in relation to others, not least in terms of maturity and emotional 'health'. Yet, at the same time, we should beware of assuming that people simply swallow such arguments whole – and hence that campaigns to increase the censorship of media violence necessarily represent the views of the population at large, however much appeal they may have for their elected representatives. In this respect, the complaint that 'there is too much violence on television' – a complaint which is, in fact, much less frequent than is often assumed – should not necessarily be taken to reflect a belief in the widespread existence of 'copy-cat' violence.

Defining 'effects'

As I have implied, therefore, there is a need to be much more precise about the *kinds* of effect which are at stake here. Violence on television, for example, may have *behavioural* effects – leading to aggression, or encouraging people to take steps to protect themselves. It may have *emotional* effects – producing shock, disgust or excitement. And it may have *ideological* or attitudinal effects – encouraging viewers to believe that they are more likely to be victimised by particular kinds of people, or in particular kinds of situation, and hence that specific forms of legislation or social policy are necessary to prevent this. These different levels of 'effect' might be related – emotional responses might lead to certain kinds of behaviour, for example – but the connections between them are likely to be complex and diverse. And the question of whether any of these effects might ultimately be seen as harmful or beneficial is equally complex, depending upon the criteria which one uses in making the judgement.

In my recent research, I have concentrated specifically on the question of the emotional 'effects' of television on children.[17] In this area, at least, it is clear that television frequently has very powerful effects – and, indeed, that children often choose to watch it precisely in order to experience such effects. Television can provoke 'negative' responses such as worry, fear and sadness, just as it can generate 'positive' responses such as amusement, excitement and pleasure – and, indeed, it often generates 'positive' and 'negative' responses at one and the same time.

Nevertheless, the question of whether these responses are to be seen as harmful or as beneficial is far from straightforward. Emotional responses which are perceived as 'negative' may have 'positive' consequences: for example, in terms of children's learning. Children (and adults) may be extremely distressed by images of disasters or social conflicts shown on the news, but many people would argue that such experiences are a necessary part of becoming an informed citizen – and, indeed, this was an argument that many of the children made on their own behalf. A fear of crime, for example, of the kind that is sometimes thought to be induced by television reporting, can lead to an illogical desire to retreat from the outside world;

but it may also be a necessary prerequisite for crime prevention. Likewise, children's fiction has always played on 'negative' responses such as fear and sadness, on the grounds that experiencing such emotions in a fictional context can enable children to conquer the fears they experience in real life. In this respect, therefore, the *consequences* of such emotional responses cannot easily be categorised as either 'positive' or 'negative'.

At the same time, children's perceptions of what is upsetting (or, indeed, violent) are extremely diverse. Many children are certainly frightened by horror movies, and by some explicit representations of crime, particularly where they involve threats to the person. But they can also be very upset and even frightened by what they watch on the news or in documentary programmes. And while they generally learn to cope with fictional material – either by developing their knowledge of the genre, or simply by deciding to avoid it – they often find it much harder to distance themselves from nonfictional material. While Freddy Krueger may be frightening at the time of viewing, children can learn to control such fears by reassuring themselves that he is merely fictional; yet such reassurances are simply not available when one is confronted with images of suffering and violence in Bosnia or Rwanda. As they gain experience of watching *fictional* violence, children may indeed become 'desensitised' to images of *that kind* of violence, or at least develop strategies for coping with it; yet the notion that they are thereby 'desensitised' to *real-life* violence is impossible to sustain.[18] Ultimately, there may be very little that children can *do* in response to non-fictional material in order to come to terms with their responses, precisely because they are so powerless to intervene in issues that concern them.

Within these different forms, children are also learning to make fine distinctions between what they perceive to be realistic and not realistic. 'Violence' should not, in this respect, be treated as a single category that can be seen to have singular effects. A great deal depends upon the nature and context of the violence; and upon children's existing expectations and knowledge of the genre and the medium. *Child's Play III*, for example, was described by many of the children in this research as a comedy (in my view quite accurately); yet other horror movies, such as *Pet Sematary*, and even *The Omen*, appeared to be seen as more plausible, and hence more likely to disturb.

Significantly, however, the text that was often described as the most frightening was one that deliberately set out to play with these distinctions: it was not a 'video nasty' but a television film called *Ghostwatch*, transmitted in the BBC's Screen One slot at Hallowe'en in 1992. This programme apparently featured a real-life ghost hunt being conducted at a house on the outskirts of London; and by using all the conventions of an outside broadcast report, including well-known presenters playing themselves, it appears to have succeeded in fooling many viewers (in spite of various pointers to the fact that it was, indeed, a fiction). Yet, while many children found the programme disturbing, a number of the older ones expressed considerable interest in seeing it again.

Rather than simply condemning such material, it makes sense to begin by asking why people – and children in particular – actively choose to watch it. Horror films do frighten most children, in some cases quite severely – but they also give many of them considerable pleasure. Yet the failure to recognise the ambivalence of this experience, the complex relationship between 'distress and delight', is characteristic of much of the research and debate on these issues.

Indeed, many horror films would seem to be implicitly addressed to children, or at least to 'the child in us all'. They are about the ways in which the physical power of adults threatens children; or they are about childlike figures, or repressed dimensions of childhood, taking revenge on the adult world. This may well be why the figure of Chucky from *Child's Play III* proved to be so offensive to many adults: he represents a direct and highly self-conscious affront to cherished notions of childhood innocence. One might even argue that horror provides a relatively safe opportunity for learning to cope with such anxieties, or for indulging in such fantasies. Far from causing lasting psychological harm, the ultimate effects of horror might even be therapeutic.

Rethinking regulation

Particularly since the advent of the domestic video recorder in the early 1980s, the ability of the state to control the traffic in moving images has been dramatically reduced; and with the availability of new technologies such as satellite television and digital multi-media the imposition of centralised regulation is becoming an ever more difficult struggle. On the basis of my own research, there is certainly evidence that substantial numbers of under-age children have seen the kind of material which it is officially illegal for them to watch – and which some would like to ban outright. While they are exceptional, I have interviewed children as young as 6 who have seen films from the *Nightmare on Elm Street* series; and I would guess that a majority of children in their early teens have seen at least one film from this or the *Child's Play* series.

In this situation, much of the responsibility for regulating children's viewing has inevitably shifted to parents, and indeed to children themselves. As I have noted, the debate about media effects has become increasingly tied up with the debate about parenting – a debate which, in the wake of the child abuse cases of recent years, has taken on an increasingly urgent tone.

Nevertheless, the debate about parents' and children's relationship with television has been dominated for much too long by negative arguments. It often seems as though the most responsible thing one can do as a parent is simply to throw out the TV set. Perhaps the most offensive aspect of these debates has been the way in which the blame has been allocated to working-class parents. It is these inadequate parents, living their depraved and aimless lives on council estates up and down the country, who are alleged to have absolved themselves from all responsibility for their children.

Yet, whatever public positions they might espouse, most parents do attempt to control the kind of material their children watch, at least until their middle teens. I certainly do so myself, and throughout several years of research in this field, with children and parents from a whole range of social backgrounds, I have yet to meet or be told about parents who do not. Yet, as I have noted, parents' central concern in relation to so-called 'violent' material is not that they fear their children will become criminals or child-killers. On the contrary, they are seeking to protect their children from material they might find frightening or upsetting. And, at the same time, children are also learning to protect *themselves* from such experiences in a variety of ways.

The problem for parents (and, indeed, for broadcasters) is that it is very hard to predict what children will find upsetting. Many of the children I have interviewed have described very surprising experiences from their early childhood, such as being frightened by *Mary Poppins* or by Fairy Liquid advertisements. Nor is this simply a matter of development: I have inter-viewed 6-year-olds who blithely profess that they were not frightened by *Nightmare on Elm Street* and 15-year-olds who say precisely the opposite. Individuals are often most disturbed by material that is close to their own experience, although this is bound to be very diverse. For parents, this makes it hard to know when or how to intervene. Simply banning material gives it the attraction of forbidden fruit, and means that children will try that much harder to see it elsewhere. Instinctive responses – turning the programme off when it gets too much, or sending the kids out of the room – may deprive them of the reassurance that is provided at the end of the narrative.

Nevertheless, children themselves generally accept that parents are correct to attempt to protect them from such material, at least in principle. In prac-tice, of course, there is a great deal of negotiation over what is seen as 'appropriate' for children to watch, and many children appear to be extremely successful at evading their parents' attempts at regulation. Yet, in claiming the right to make their own decisions about what should be seen, both groups agree that the responsibility for such regulation should be with the family, and not in the hands of others.

A modest proposal

My argument, then, is that we need to begin by exploring what children make of the films and television programmes that *they themselves* identify as upsetting or, indeed, as 'violent' – which, it should be emphasised, are not necessarily those that adults would identify for them. In a debate that is dominated by adults purporting to speak on children's behalf, children's voices have been almost entirely unheard. Yet we also have to engage with the genuine concerns of many parents – concerns which, as I have argued, may be rather different from those of politicians, for whom the media have always served as a convenient scapegoat for rising crime or moral decline.

This is clearly one way of beginning to shift the agenda, although I would acknowledge that it hardly begins to engage directly with the question of censorship. As I have suggested, technological changes are increasingly rendering state-controlled censorship difficult to enforce. And yet wholesale libertarianism is, in my view, an inadequate option, particularly in relation to children. A completely unrestricted trade in media images could never be a realistic possibility – as recent moves to police the Internet clearly demonstrate. Societies will always have to 'censor', to control the images that are made available to young people. The question is not *whether* but *how* and *where* this takes place.

I want to argue that what is often termed the 'liberal' distinction between the public and the private – exemplified most clearly in the Williams Report on obscenity and film censorship (Home Office, 1979) – is one that, for all its problems, should be sustained and actively supported. We need to find ways of backing up parents' and children's attempts to regulate their *own* viewing, rather than seeking merely to increase the state's control over the private citizen – an approach which, at least in this case, is likely to prove ineffective anyway.

At the same time, we should be much more precise about what we mean by children. My research would suggest that the legal notion that childhood stops at 18 (which is also enshrined in the categories of film classification) simply does not square with most parents' perceptions, let alone children's. Most parents seem to agree that, by the time they reach 15 (and in many cases before), children should be free to make their own decisions about what they watch. While parents do take note of the classifications – which thus would appear to serve a useful advisory role – they also frequently dispute them. The notion that stricter censorship legislation would somehow reflect public wishes is, I would argue, highly questionable.

If we are to construct a meaningful alternative to simply increasing censorship, we will need to begin in this way: with children and with parents. We will need to respect their ability to make their own decisions about what is appropriate, and try to support them in doing so. We will need a positive *educational* strategy, rather than a negative one that is based on censorship.

This will mean, first, a more informative and accountable approach to centralised media regulation of all kinds. There should be more objective information for parents (and, indeed, for all viewers) about the content of films, videos and television programmes, particularly where this relates to areas of general concern. Of course, providing such information could well be counter-productive, by identifying forbidden fruit. But we cannot expect parents or children to make informed decisions unless we are prepared to advise them more effectively than we do at present.

Likewise, a great deal more could be done to make the film and video classification system more accountable. The reasons for decisions should be published or made freely available for interested parties (for example, through video shops), and it should be possible for decisions to be challenged by the public and independently reviewed. Steps could be taken to ensure that parents are involved in the decision-making process, or at least consulted – for example, through establishing a representative panel of parents, and by conducting research with children themselves. There is no doubt that decisions such as the granting of a 12 certificate to *Mrs Doubtfire* (a film heavily promoted to a younger audience) brings the system into disrepute among many parents. While there may be good reasons for such decisions, no purpose is served by keeping them secret from the very people on whose behalf they are made.

Second, media education, both for parents and for children, should be regarded as a major priority. It was ironic – and, indeed, really galling – that the Government's plans to increase censorship in the wake of the Bulger case coincided with its attempt to remove media education from the National Curriculum. Yet, if it is to be constructive, media education should be seen not as a prophylactic designed to protect people from things that are deemed to be 'bad' for them; nor, indeed, as something that is solely concerned with 'violence'. On the contrary, it should be regarded as an essential guarantee of an informed and critical audience for all forms of media output.

Third, we need to ensure that the films and television programmes that are produced explicitly for children are both diverse and of the highest quality – while at the same time acknowledging that there are many forms of 'quality'. All too often, the characteristics of films and television programmes for children are defined negatively, in terms of the *absence* of sex or violence or 'negative role models'; as a result, they are often anodyne and conservative. While the Government persistently employs a rhetoric about protecting childhood, and bemoans the negative aspects of children's relationship with the media, it has been conspicuously unwilling to invest in positive alternatives.

Conclusion

These proposals are intended as a modest, practical starting point. Paradoxically, however, I suspect that they avoid what is really at stake. As I have implied, the debate about children and media violence is really a debate about other things, many of which have very little to do with the media. It is a debate that invokes deep-seated moral and political convictions, and it is rooted in people's unsettling experiences of social change and their genuine fears for the future. The issue of 'violence' serves as a cipher for some very diverse, but none the less fundamental, anxieties – about the decline of the family and of organised religion, about the changing nature of literacy and contemporary culture, or, indeed, about the shortcomings of capitalism. How we might engage with these bigger issues is, of course, beyond my scope here. However, in the short term, there may be some benefit in attempting to address the violence issue on its own terms, rather than seeking merely to avoid it.

NOTES

1 Newson (1994). I have discussed the debates surrounding the Bulger case at length in Buckingham (1996).
2 This is well documented, for example by Gans (1974), Ross (1989) and many others. It is also explored by Julian Petley in Chapter 10 of this book.
3 This work is reviewed by Young (1990).
4 For an excellent review of effects research in this area, see Durkin (1985).
5 See Neuman (1991).
6 For reviews of this work, see Bryant and Anderson (1983) and Dorr (1986).
7 See, for example, the studies in Brown (1976) and the extensive Swedish study by Rosengren and Windahl (1989).
8 See, for example, Hodge and Tripp (1986) and Buckingham (1993a).
9 For example, Palmer (1986) and the studies collected in Buckingham (1993b).
10 For a further discussion of these points, see Buckingham (1993a) and Liebes and Katz (1990).
11 For a recent example, see Geen (1994).
12 See Segal and McIntosh (1992).
13 The account which follows is based on Buckingham (1993a), Chapter 5, and Buckingham (1996), particularly Chapters 3 and 8. I am grateful to the Broadcasting Standards Council for funding the latter research, and to Mark Allerton for his assistance.
14 For example, Holman and Braithwaite (1982); Buckingham (1993a).
15 In 1987, Michael Ryan murdered sixteen people in the English town of Hungerford, having allegedly been inspired by the film *Rambo* – which it later transpired he had never seen. For an account of the debates surrounding the case, see Webster (1989).
16 See Buckingham (1996), Chapter 2.
17 The material here is based on Buckingham (1996).
18 Of all the popular hypotheses about the effects of television violence, this is the one that is least effectively supported by the available evidence: see Buckingham and Allerton (1996).

REFERENCES

Brown, R. (1976), *Children and Television*, London: Collier Macmillan.
Bryant, J. and Anderson, D. R. (eds) (1983), *Children's Understanding of Television*, New York: Academic Press.
Buckingham, D. (1993a), *Children Talking Television: The Making of Television Literacy*, London: Falmer.
Buckingham, D. (ed.) (1993b), *Reading Audiences: Young People and the Media*, Manchester: Manchester University Press.

Buckingham, D. (1996), *Moving Images: Understanding Children's Emotional Responses to Television*, Manchester: Manchester University Press.

Buckingham, D. and Allerton, M. (1996), *Fear, Fright and Distress: A Review of Research into Children's 'Negative' Emotional Responses to Television*, London: Broadcasting Standards Council.

Dorr, A. (1986), *Television and Children: A Special Medium for a Special Audience*, Beverly Hills, Calif.: Sage.

Durkin, K. (1985), *Television, Sex Roles and Children*, Milton Keynes: Open University Press.

Gans, H. (1974), *Popular Culture and High Culture*, New York: Basic.

Geen, R. G. (1994), 'Television and aggression: recent developments in research and theory', in D. Zillmann *et al.* (eds), *Media, Children and the Family,* Hillsdale, NJ: Erlbaum.

Hodge, B. and Tripp, D. (1986), *Children and Television: A Semiotic Approach*, Cambridge: Polity.

Holman, J. and Braithwaite, V. A. (1982), 'Parental lifestyles and children's television viewing', *Australian Journal of Psychology*, 34:3, pp. 375–82.

Home Office (1979), *Report of the Committee on Obscenity and Film Censorship*, London: HMSO.

Liebes, T. and Katz, E. (1990), *The Export of Meaning*, Oxford: Oxford University Press.

Neuman, S. B. (1991), *Literacy in the Television Age*, Norwood, NJ: Ablex.

Newson, E. (1994), 'Video violence and the protection of children', *The Psychologist*, June, pp. 272–4.

Palmer, P. (1986), *The Lively Audience*, Sydney: Allen & Unwin.

Report of the Committee on Obscenity and Film Censorship (1979), London: HMSO, Cmnd 7772.

Rosengren, K. E. and Windahl, S. (1989), *Media Matter: TV Use in Childhood and Adolescence*, Norwood, NJ: Ablex.

Ross, A. (1989), *No Respect: Intellectuals and Popular Culture*, New York: Routledge.

Segal, L. and McIntosh, M. (1992), *Sex Exposed: Sexuality and the Pornography Debate*, London: Virago.

Taylor, I. (1988), 'Violence and video: for a social democratic perspective', in P. Drummond and R. Paterson, eds, *Television and Its Audience*, London: British Film Institute.

Webster, D. (1989), '"Whodunnit? America did": *Rambo* and post-Hungerford rhetoric', *Cultural Studies*, 3:2, pp. 173–93.

Young, B. (1990), *Children and Television Advertising*, Oxford: Oxford University Press.

4

LIVING FOR LIBIDO; OR, 'CHILD'S PLAY IV'

The imagery of childhood and the call for censorship

Patricia Holland

In late 1993, when two 11-year-old boys were convicted of murdering 2-year-old James Bulger, battering him to death beside a railway line near their home on Merseyside, the popular press blamed (erroneously) their capacity for such incomprehensible violence on their supposed viewing habits. It could well be more than a coincidence that the video which was the focus of this virulent outcry was called *Child's Play III*. That title drew attention to the dangerous ambivalence of play, but it also did something more. Child's play may be threatening enough, but this was not just child's play pure and simple. It was repeated, insistent child's play, child's play for the third time. It was, of course, the 'compulsion to repeat' that first led Freud away from his belief in the dominance of the life-asserting force of the libido and towards his darker accounts of the human psyche – in particular the death drive (Freud, 1984). The title, and the repeated reproduction of the fearsome cover of the video in the press at the time, mobilised a fear of both children and childhood. It insisted that *play* can indeed be a terrible and murderous activity, not subject to adult social limits.

Jessie Bites

Within the interweaving discourses of contemporary culture, certain images have gained a particular power. They have the ability to resonate back and forth, repeated in different media, accumulating meanings and values as they go, and coming to stand as a shorthand for shared social judgements. These are the *images* that are mobilised within the potent *narratives* of our contemporary media (Holland, 1992). I am here concerned less with real children and actual events than with the construction and reconstruction of such images and narratives as they relate to real children and actual events. Over the last twenty years or so, images of children have figured with increasing frequency in narratives – both fictional and factual – which express the violence of the contemporary world. Certain images of violent children, and of children as victims of violence, have been reflected back and forth between the small screen and the tabloid press. On the occasion of the James Bulger murder and the fear around *Child's Play III*, a series of new dramatic texts was created which also included the imagined children in the audience. In this secondary drama these new players were the potential and possible viewers of corrupting material, and one of the themes was the fear that they would be drawn into a world in which fantasy and horror were indistinguishable from childish reality.

On the cover of the video of *Child's Play III* is one of those images which has resonated through the media narratives. A terrifying face, superhuman and unreal, yet freckled and somehow childish, glares out at the viewer. This is the face of Chucky, the demonic doll at the centre of the story. In the last months of 1993 the picture was insistently repeated on the front pages of the *Mirror*, the *Sun* and other newspapers, now staring out at a wider public, their millions of readers. In the *Sun* (26 November 1993) the image was shown consumed by flames and the headline was: 'For the Sake of ALL Our Kids . . . BURN YOUR VIDEO NASTY.' But this is by no means the only image whose association with childhood and its uncontrollability has placed it at the centre of public anxiety. I would like to compare a sequence from the first (1988) *Child's Play* film with an image from the controversial series of photographs by the American photographer Sally Mann, published under the title *Immediate Family* (Mann, 1992).

The sequence I have in mind from *Child's Play* is that in which Chucky first reveals himself to the single mother who has risked her job and her safety to buy him for her 6-year-old son, Andy. Chucky is dressed in the same outfit as Andy and is almost his height. Terrible things have happened in the first part of the film, and Andy has been blamed. Now, Andy's mother holds the inert doll at arm's length and shakes it, demanding that it speak to her, just as Andy had claimed it had spoken to him. It is her threat to throw the doll on to the fire if it doesn't respond that elicits a stream of abuse in a guttural adult voice like that of the possessed young girl in *The Exorcist* (1973), that archetypal narrative of diabolical childhood. Suddenly we are watching a struggle between a woman and a figure now ambivalently seen as a recalcitrant, resisting child. It is a struggle which ends only when Chucky sinks his teeth painfully into her arm and escapes. The bruising and the tooth marks remain as a terrifying reminder of the 'real' nature of the innocent doll and of Chucky's viciousness.

For me, this sequence recalls the photograph which impressed me most vividly when I first saw Sally Mann's sultry images of her children at play in their home in the foothills of the Blue Ridge Mountains of south-western

Virginia. The black-and-white pictures, showing Jessie, Virginia and Emmett between the ages of about 3 and 10, are heavy with a sensuality normally repressed in the imagery of childhood. Inside the house, on the veranda, or in the immediate rural surroundings, the children occupy their space without inhibition or restraint. They offer themselves to their mother's camera, sometimes naked, sometimes partially dressed or experimenting with clothes and make-up. They may be grubby, bruised by a fall or caught wetting the bed, but they almost never smile at the camera. The picture I have in mind is called *Jessie Bites*. Jessie, aged about 8, lies on a cushion. Her body is partially painted with stripes and dots like the wild young boys in *Lord of the Flies* (1963). A wisp of a feather boa, a remnant from the dressing-up box, rests across her chest. Her expression is intense and remote. Her arm is linked around that of an adult or much older child – the arm and part of a shirt and trousers are all we see of this second person. But on the upper part of the visible arm is a circle of deeply impressed tooth marks.

A mild horror video, certificated as suitable for viewers of 15 and over, and a culturally valued work which has been exhibited on the walls of several prestigious galleries; these two images from very different cultural practices deal in a disturbing territory which is all too easily repressed when narratives are designed only to reassure.

The confusion of tongues

The contemporary focus on children as a centre of adult fears frequently expresses what the psychoanalyst Sandor Ferenczi described as a 'confusion of tongues'. In his celebrated 1932 paper on sexual activity between adults and children, Ferenczi described the confusion between discourse that is appropriate for an adult and that for a child, the 'playfulness' of the child and the passionate 'wishes of a sexually mature person'. To protect themselves, abused children may become prematurely adult and both identify with and attempt to protect their aggressor (Ferenczi, 1932, p. 289). Hence Regan in *The Exorcist* and Chucky in *Child's Play* both speak with adult voices.

I would suggest a parallel confusion between the concepts of child*ren* and of child*hood*. Cinematic and video narratives of demonic childhood – from *The Exorcist*, *The Omen* (1976), *Carrie* (1976) through to the *Child's Play* films in the late 1980s – have become interwoven with those narratives in the tabloid press which envisage a child audience caught up in their demonising influence. My contention is that these films are stories about the nature of child*hood*, a state which survives in the submerged memory of every adult, and have very little to do with actual child*ren*. When they become part of a secondary newspaper-based narrative, the confusion between an exploration of childhood and a commentary on the lives and behaviour of real-life children becomes difficult to disentangle. The two interacting sets of narratives both express a deep disappointment and cynicism at the disappearance of the figure of the romantic child. Nearly two hundred years after its inception, the once inspirational vision of the child as an expression of simplicity and purity has become a shallow stereotype. Peter Coveney associates its disappearance with Freud's 1905 essay on infantile sexuality. Yet its shadow remains, even when sneered at and exposed for the damaging fantasy it has undoubtedly been (Coveney, 1967).

The public discourse around childhood has dramatically shifted. The image of innocence lingers only in the most decadent forms – on Christmas cards and in the truncated language of the moral right. Even greetings cards now offer babies dressed in sunglasses and smoking pipes, or little boys and girls in a pre-pubertal kiss, as often as saucer-eyed moppets. Innocence has become an open invitation to corruption. It is not only Sally Mann's Jessie who is no longer inclined to simper.

A call for censorship which centres merely on the *effects* of corrupting materials on children claims hard-headed factuality. However, it can be seen to be deeply implicated in this web of images and narratives, both as spin-off and exacerbating cause of this shift in consciousness. Just as the purity of the romantic child smoothed over the contradictions of the mid-nineteenth century, the darkness of today's world has found expression in the evanescent figure of the corrupted child. I want to argue that it is anxiety about child*hood* – in other words about the uncertainty of adult status – that is evoked by this new popular discourse, as much as an anxiety on behalf of child*ren* themselves. Tabloid outrage could be seen as less about fears for children than about fears of child*hood* projected on to real children. The repetition of the narrative of fear is itself pleasurable. The call for a violent reaction ('BURN YOUR VIDEO NASTY') is in tune with this narrative, whereas carefully thought out measures for child protection remain much less sexy as front-page material. The belief that children will imitate what they see continues to take precedence over the far more likely consequence that they will be traumatised by it, and thus a call for repressive censorship overwhelms arguments for protective – and enabling – regulation (Buckingham, 1996).

Male fantasies and childishness

As traumatised children take on a precocious adulthood, so the desire to recapture a libidinous childishness has become newly attractive to adults. Alice Miller's injunction to 'nurture the hurt child within' has won her many followers who feel that their own childishness has been denied to them (Miller, 1987).

The action movie genre which flourished in the 1980s can be read as an invocation of such regressive desires. Jean-Claude Van Damme, Arnold Schwarzenegger and Sylvester Stallone live out male fantasies close to those described as pre-Oedipal by Klaus Theweleit (Theweleit, 1987). Their films are expressions of a childish impatience in which impulsiveness is valued above restraint. In *Rambo III* (1988), to take a striking example, Stallone is chubby-bodied and naked like a baby, disregarding the frosts of Afghanistan. His anger, like that of an infant, appears to carry its own destructive force, while he remains unscathed. This is surely the stuff of infantile fantasy. In *Terminator II: Judgement Day* (1991) the 'father' figure, the muscular all-powerful enemy turned protector, can be seen as both a projection of the child's omnipotent fantasy and an expression of the (young) adult male's refusal to mature: Arnold Schwarzenegger as a modern Peter Pan.

Stallone and Schwarzenegger thus both embody the irresponsibility, the infantile narcissism and the terrifying qualities of play. It is at play – that quintessentially childish activity – that children, and particularly boys, are depicted as turning into little monsters.

Rambo has his toys. In his case they are his armoury of guns and his bullet belt. In *Child's Play* and its two sequels the figure which characterises play is the far more domestic image of a doll. An inert, ambivalent thing, without life of its own, it is charged with significance. Like D. W. Winnicott's 'transitional object' or Julia Kristeva's 'abject', it is neither one thing nor the other, neither subject nor object, potentially monstrous (Winnicott, 1965; Kristeva, 1982). Unlike most dolls, Chucky is not waiting to have life breathed into him by an ever-playful child. With an appearance which can be transformed from the bizarre to the downright terrifying, this doll has a life of its own which threatens to take over its owner. Bringing the urban hell of the outside world into the home, Chucky becomes the expression of his play-master's denials: encapsulating sadism and a drive for destruction and amorality in a horrific contradiction of everything childhood has come to stand for. This cannot be the return of the repressed for, in childhood, repression is not yet effected. This is precisely why 'play' is its quintessential expression. Play takes us back to the margins of childhood, to the border with infancy, to a time of confusion and uncertain identity. D. W. Winnicott in his influential radio talks on *Woman's Hour*, which were themselves part of the optimistic post-war child-centred view of the world, explained to his audience of mothers: 'Playing takes place in the potential space between the baby and the mother figure.' It is only when anxiety is too great that the structure of play breaks down to become 'the pure exploitation of sensual gratification' (Winnicott, 1964, pp. 146, 144).

The anxious narratives of the late twentieth century – both the narratives on the screen and the narratives *about* the screen – also focus on the confusion signified by the concept of play, but this time as a 'potential space' between action for 'real' and action as fantasy. Much comment sets out to keep play neatly in a safe, childish compartment. 'Children are meant to play', said Stan Golden, president of Saban Entertainment, which produces the much-criticised children's television programme *Mighty Morphin' Power Rangers*, in which ordinary kids metamorphose into fantasy vigilantes, 'and they are always going to be playing with something' (*Independent*, 24

October 1994). Many texts, including videos and newspapers, deal with this potential confusion. The horror comes when 'play' merges into 'reality'. In this discourse it is also the margin between the experience of being a child and that of being an adult which is at stake. Jon Thompson and Robert Venables acted out those confusions in their most horrific form when they murdered James Bulger.

Exploring the romantic image of early-twentieth-century childhood, Jacqueline Rose points to the 'all too perfect presence of the child'. This figure, she claims, was evoked to 'hold off panic' brought on by the infinite instability of language and identity (Rose, 1984, p. 10). Now, at the other end of the twentieth century, the image of the child speaks chiefly of panic. Innocence is recognised as the most deceptive of appearances. We know that, paradoxically, the attack will come from where we least expect it and that the most dreadful violence underlies the gentlest of exteriors.

Images for the home: images break the home

Observing the changing imagery of childhood, we can detect an increasing tension between a representation of children as central to the home and family, securing its stability, and another image of childhood as *itself* the sign of disruption of the familial social order. My local video shop, Video Forum, used to advertise itself as 'cinema for the home'. The crudely drawn image on its catalogue evoked that withdrawal from a public to a private place. Stately neo-classical pillars reminiscent of a 'picture palace' here enclosed an extended family gathered around a television set in the living room. The grandparents are on the sofa, the young man is inserting the video into the VCR, while the toddler sits on the floor on a cushion. His back is to the set and he is playing with his toes. It is a cohesive image, with children at its centre.

The children of the 1990s may not be part of the workforce, but their economic importance is increasing as the all-consuming market encroaches on this hitherto protected territory. The television-centred, child-centred home is where the economic work of consumption is done, and a popular evocation of the family audience, like this one, insists that this type of work is shown as expressive pleasure. The television set, home entertainment and stories for children *should* secure children's pleasurable presence in that safe environment. They *should* keep them at home and off the streets. But the *content* of that pleasure – the video that this young man is sliding into the machine for his family to watch – may well reproduce those very fears which will blow the cosy family circle apart. Disruption comes from within, from the centre of the home itself. There's no point in bolting the doors because it's Chucky/Andy who is the murderer. The *Child's Play* films make the link with video culture explicit. Andy wanted the doll so badly because of high-pressure advertising aimed directly at kids from his television set.

The child as the centre of the family remains the most potent, and commercially convenient, of images. 'My greatest satisfaction is to sit in an audience surrounded by happy children and their smiling parents', says the producer of Walt Disney's *World on Ice* (*Independent*, 13 October 1994). But this family-based child is closely controlled by the parents and other adults in the family and may be described as the legitimate target of their anger. In the year of the Bulger murder, some of the noisiest newspaper campaigns revolved around the 'right' of parents to hit their children. (On this subject see Petley in Chapter 10 of this book.) In the context of child abuse and violent parents, Andy's mother's threat to throw the resisting Chucky on the fire takes on an unpleasant new meaning.

Our culture continues to take pleasure in the image of the child as a humiliated individual, subordinated to adult power. One of the most popular posters at the National Museum of Photography, Film and Television at Bradford – which hangs in the ladies' toilet, as if suitable only for women's motherly instincts – is a photograph by Wolfgang Suschitzky, entitled *The Orange*. It shows a baby around 1 year old, full-face to the camera. But her face is screwed up in a mixture of pain and surprise. An orange, clearly bitter to the taste, is clasped in her hand at the bottom of the frame. An adult trick has produced a picture which we have learnt to see as amusing, and which sells posters. In this indirect fashion, hatred for childhood, for the child one once was, for the child within oneself, threads its way through contemporary imagery.

In the news pages of the popular press, a horror story about untamed boyhood has been building up over the last twenty years. This is where the bad boys and little monsters have their space, children who have moved beyond the control of their parents. Since well before the murder of James Bulger, a repertoire of images has portrayed boys who are incomprehensible and uncontrollable, little demons running wild in the streets. An image of chaos was used to characterise the riots of the 1980s. Children on the streets were 'undisciplined, prejudiced and arrogant hooligans'. They were wreckers, young thugs, animals, beasts, 'stunted demons' and a 'threat to our sanity' (Holland, 1992, p. 118). When the James Bulger murder occurred, a vocabulary full of references to the demonic and the monstrous was already in place. In reporting the murder the popular press, to a byline, declared that they were dealing with an elemental force. The boys, it seemed, were not just possessed, like Regan in *The Exorcist*, but, like Chucky, themselves embodied evil.

Realism and fantastic fears

In her account of the life of the activist Margaret McMillan, Carolyn Steedman links children's withdrawal from the workforce and from economic activity with their transformation into an object of study (Steedman,

1990). As the century has progressed, a more empathetic study of children has generated its own set of discourses and images, where the very realism of the enterprise, the attempt to capture the lived texture of children's lives – with all the pitfalls that entails – has run parallel to, but sometimes together with, the expression of adult fears. Horrors that are all too real, such as baby-battering, the effects of extreme deprivation, child sexual abuse and playground bullying, have become centres of real concern, as well as enjoyably shocking reading or viewing. Most importantly, there have been an increasing number of spaces for children to make their own voices heard, opening up an embarrassing gap in adult discussions.

In Britain it has been television, produced in a regulated, public-service environment, that has allowed stereotypical definitions to be challenged. From *Grange Hill* (1978–) to Channel 4's *Look Who's Talking* season (1994), a view of childhood from something close to a child's perspective has become part of our regular television fare.

However, despite such advances, the situation remains in which outrage expressed through a frightening image of child*hood* may have the consequence of leaving real child*ren* unprotected. The 'common-sense' solution to the problem of violent movies on television has consistently been that 'the *parent* can always switch off' (or, now, 'use a V chip'), implying a childhood under exclusive parental control. One of the reactionary effects of a resistance to the regulation of television, video and cinema is such a privatisation of childhood. A wider vision would allow children to grow beyond the narrow and over-heated family environment into a diverse public sphere. Regulation is one of the ways in which society as a whole can take responsibility for its children. The 'family viewing policy' reproduced weekly in the *Radio Times* begins, 'Broadcasters expect parents to share responsibility for what children watch', but continues to outline broadcasting policies in relation to the times at which suitable programmes will be broadcast, in order 'to help [parents] decide'. Without such regulatory structures, ordinary, everyday children will have even less opportunity to speak for themselves.

Child's Play will remain horrific as long as children remain silent.

REFERENCES

Buckingham, D. (1996), *Moving Images: Understanding Children's Emotional Responses to Television*, Manchester: Manchester University Press.
Coveney, P. (1967), *The Image of Childhood*, Harmondsworth: Peregrine.
Ferenczi, S. (1932), 'Confusion of tongues between adults and the child', in J. Masson (1984), *The Assault on Truth: Freud and Child Sex Abuse*, London: Faber.
Freud, S. (1984), 'Beyond the pleasure principle', in *On Metapsychology: The Theory of Psychoanalysis*, Harmondsworth: Penguin.
Holland, P. (1992), *What Is a Child? Popular Images of Childhood*, London: Virago.
Holland, P. (1996), 'I've just seen a hole in the reality barrier! Children, childishness and the media in the ruins of the twentieth century', in Jane Pilcher and Stephen

Wagg, eds, *Thatcher's Children? Politics, Childhood and Society in the 1980s and 90s*, Falmer: Falmer Press.

Kristeva, J. (1982), *Powers of Horror*, New York: Columbia University Press.

Mann, S. (1992), *Immediate Family*, London: Phaidon.

Miller, A. (1987), *For Their Own Good*, London: Virago.

Rose, J. (1984), *The Case of Peter Pan, or the Impossibility of Children's Fiction*, London: Macmillan.

Steedman, C. (1990), *Childhood, Culture and Class in Britain: Margaret McMillan 1860–1931*, London: Virago.

Theweleit, K. (1987), *Male Fantasies*, Cambridge: Polity Press.

Winnicott, D. W. (1964), *The Child, the Family and the Outside World*, Harmondsworth: Pelican.

Winnicott, D. W. (1965), *The Family and Individual Development*, London: Tavistock.

5

JUST WHAT THE DOCTORS ORDERED?

Media regulation, education and the 'problem' of media violence

Sara Bragg

Most commonly, public concern about the 'problem' of media violence leads to demands for increased regulation and control of the media themselves. However, some individuals and groups are now promoting educational interventions with audiences as an alternative solution. Comparing the outcome of Greg Philo's research on fans of the film *Pulp Fiction* in the 1990s (discussed in the introduction to this volume) with William Belson's on youth audiences in the 1970s, suggests this may represent a new phase in media debates. Both writers express concern about media influence, but where Belson's report concluded by demanding an immediate reduction in levels of violence in particular programmes, Philo's proposal is 'anti-violence education' (Belson, 1978; Philo, 1997). An article in the *Times Educational Supplement* in 1997 notes that he has discussed this with the Scottish Office and the National Society for the Protection of Children, and has been contacted by the government's junior education minister about his work (Ghouri, 1997).

Media education would seem to be both a less authoritarian and a more practical response to the challenge of new technologies, which make centralised control of media within national boundaries increasingly difficult. Since we know that children spend more time watching television than they do in school, and that they clearly do have access to proscribed material, it makes sense to argue that we should 'do something' to help them understand what they encounter. Furthermore, official interest in such proposals offers the tantalising prospect of enhanced status for media education, in gratifying contrast to habitual press and politician ridicule of it as a non-subject, teaching neither a firm body of knowledge nor useful vocational skills. In the first part of this chapter, I want to consider two existing models of education about media violence. My interest is in exploring the logic and rhetoric of the arguments they employ; and what they suggest about the nature of the media and young people's relationship to them. In analysing the teaching they propose, I do not assess whether or not it is likely to be 'effective' – an approach that would focus narrowly on testable outcomes. Drawing on Elizabeth Ellsworth's work on 'mode of address' in pedagogy, I am concerned rather with how it addresses students and positions them in relation to knowledge, power and authority. That is, who it thinks students are, who it wants them to be, and what 'ways of reading the world' it constructs for them (Ellsworth, 1997).

The first project originated in the Netherlands and was described in an article entitled 'Teaching Children to Evaluate Television Violence Critically: the Impact of a Dutch Schools Television Project' (Vooijs and van der Voort, 1993a; see also Vooijs and van der Voort, 1993b). A modified form is available in Britain as part of a larger pack called *Teaching Television in the Primary School* (Phillips, n.d.). In brief, the Dutch version consisted of a series of six 20-minute television programmes aimed at 10- to 12-year-olds for use in schools, accompanied by student worksheets and teachers' notes. I will refer to it as the *Critical Viewing* or the 'Dutch' project. The second is an American project, *Beyond Blame: Challenging Violence in the Media*, produced by the Center for Media Literacy[1] formerly the Center for Media and Values (CML, 1995). It consists of five programmes aimed at different ages and contexts (the first is for a 'Town Hall' public meeting), each containing teacher's notes, handouts and videos for a set of eight lessons. Two issues of a magazine produced by the CML, *Media and Values*, explain the theoretical underpinnings of the project.

Both projects seem to have gained significant institutional support. The former was funded by the Dutch Schools TV Corporation and shown in 3,500 or a third of all primary schools in the Netherlands, and in Britain, Devon County Council Education funded its distribution free to local schools. James Ferman, as Director of the British Board of Film Classification, hailed it as a 'wonderful introduction to issues about violence and what it means' (Bragg and Grahame, 1997), and it has also been cited in a recent report on 'Violence and the Viewer' (Joint Working Party on Violence on Television, 1998). Meanwhile, the CML claims to have sold some 1,500 copies of *Beyond Blame* at $250 dollars each, suggesting total sales of $375,000. Moreover, as I will show, its arguments may be shared by policy makers in the US concerned with issues of media and youth violence.

Media education as violence prevention: a rhetoric of purpose

Both projects establish the legitimacy of their claims through a discourse of academic expertise and scientific credibility. The Dutch project evolved from Professor Van der Voort's earlier work on children and media violence (Van der Voort, 1986), and both authors are psychologists based at the Centre for

Child and Media Studies at Leiden University. But the CML has its roots in the Catholic Church rather than higher education institutions, although it advertises its *Media and Values* magazines as 'packed with the most current research summaries, statistics and perspectives on the subject of media and violence'. The CML underscores the authority of contributors by giving their academic qualifications and job titles – 'public health advocate', 'professor', 'PhD, child development specialist', 'MD', and so on. It presents quantitative 'evidence' about levels of violence in the media and children's consumption of it. For instance: 'the average child is reported to log roughly 36,000 hours of television by the time he or she is 18, including some 15,000 murders. In prime-time evening shows, our children are served up about 16 acts of entertaining violence (two of them lethal) every night; on the weekend the level of violent acts almost doubles (30.3)'. Such statistics lend an aura of certainty to the project, without acknowledging that they are generated by a methodology that has been subject to challenge and critique, not least because it includes violence in children's cartoons.[2]

Both claim that media violence poses a real social danger, drawing on psychological research into media effects in a manner which suggests that 'the scientific debate is over' (CML). Vooijs and Van der Voort open their article with a list of the 'undesirable consequences of watching television violence'. *Media and Values* declares that there is 'No Doubt About It – Media Violence Affects Behavior'. Both conflate contradictory findings and research perspectives as if they are complementary (Barker discusses this common tendency, in this volume). For instance, *Beyond Blame* insists that the media make audiences more aggressive (an argument which suggests that audiences become more active, and that they 'identify' with the aggressor in violent texts). Yet it simultaneously asserts that they cause audiences to become 'desensitised' (more callous and passive) and to 'fear becoming a victim' (which suggests that we identify with the aggressed). It attributes 'at least' half of the 23,000 murders committed each year in the US to television's influence, on the basis that homicide rates increased with the arrival of TV. This is an absurd argument (the murder statistics correlate equally well with the invention of Velcro, as others have pointed out (Buckingham, 1996: 30)), but no matter; it's a 'groundbreaking' study produced by an 'expert' with a PhD.

In the case of the *Beyond Blame* pack in particular, this discourse anchors more familiar moralistic descriptions of the media. It claims that there is a 'proliferation of realistic-looking mayhem, assault and death' in the media today; that we are 'incessantly bombarded with the images, sounds and emotions of shootings, bombings and rapes'; that 'not a day goes by that we don't get a dose of aggression from the media. And it's getting worse'. One professor of biblical interpretation describes violence as a 'Babylonian' religion, 'the ultimate concern, an elixir, an addictive high, a substitute for relationships'. Much of the concern focuses on 'our' children who are said to be 'awash in depictions of violence as the ultimate solution in human conflicts'. In these well-worn metaphors, media violence is seen as an 'epidemic', a 'disease' and thus a threat to public health, and the media as waging war on innocent victims, turning us into addicts, forcing us to consume with no choice or control (for other examples, see elsewhere in this volume). However, this moral crusade is now presented as a scientific imperative.

Classifying media violence as a medical issue implies in turn that media literacy is an aspect of health education, providing a preventative knowledge, rather than a specific subject discipline. Indeed, an earlier education project was explicitly described as 'immunising' children against effects (Doolittle, 1975). The CML's annual conference in 1998 was called 'Media Literacy: A Paradigm for Public Health'. Similarly, in the *TES* article cited above, Philo compares children's knowledge of 'drug dangers', derived from school, with their ignorance about violence. Just as teaching about drugs can prevent substance misuse, or sex education reduce teenage pregnancy and HIV infection rates, the argument goes, so media education may combat violence and intolerance in society.[3]

Further, a new discourse of environmental as well as individual health has been attached to these older ones. The CML argues that media education is important for a 'healthy *planet*'. According to one writer, recent US congressional investigations defined television violence as part of a larger 'quality of life issue' – a debate about 'What kind of *culture* will give our children the *environment* they need to grow up *healthy and whole?*' (Considine, 1995, my emphasis).[4] Media analyst George Gerbner (a contributor to *Beyond Blame*) launched a campaign on media issues in 1996, the 'Cultural Environment Movement' (CEM). He explicitly compares industries that pollute the environment with media conglomerates that 'discharge their messages into the mainstream of common consciousness'. In Britain, a letter sent in 1994 on behalf of the BBFC to the Schools Curriculum Assessment Authority, during debates about the place of media in the National Curriculum, gives an emblematic account of 'defensive' media education. Describing the 'sinister development' of new technologies which will 'overwhelm' BBFC controls with a 'sheer flood' of material, it claims that media education is 'essential to the survival of our children' by providing the 'knowledge and understanding' that will enable them to defend themselves against 'the blandishments of such material'. And it concludes: 'we regard this letter, and I hope you will, as an *environmental health* warning' (BBFC, 1995, my emphasis).

This discourse of environmentalism marks a shift from arguments about causality (in which the media are the 'stimulus' producing observable 'responses'), to those about 'influence'. The CML website declares that asking whether watching violence causes someone to become violent is the 'wrong question to ask'. Its alternative is: 'What is the long term impact on our national psyche when millions of children, in their formative years, grow up decade after decade bombarded with very powerful visual and verbal messages demonstrating violence as the preferred way to solve problems and normalizing fear and violence as "the way things are"?' This is disingenuous since, as the quotations above demonstrate, the CML does claim that the media directly cause a range of social ills. On its part, the vaguer concept of the 'long-term impact' of the media may be part of a 'belt and braces' strategy where effects research is vulnerable to challenge. However, it does connect with the concerns of a broader spectrum of critics, particularly those on the left who reject simplistic models of effects, but believe in the media's power in agenda-setting, framing public debate, shaping notions of what is valuable and desirable. The 'cultivation analysis' project that Gerbner has pursued over thirty years provides one example here (Gerbner, 1972; 1980; 1995; Signorielli and Morgan, 1990). It endeavours to understand the long-term ideological role of television by correlating dominant values, assumptions and conceptions embodied in media output with the attitudes and beliefs of audiences. 'Heavy' viewers, he argues, articulate views of the world closer to those provided by television than 'light' viewers. Moreover, he offers a more politicised analysis of trends towards homogenisation, concentration and globalisation in media industries, contending that they may limit the range of representations made available. (For challenges to his analysis see Wober, 1978, 1990; Wober and Gumter, 1982, 1988). Likewise, Philo explicitly denies that children will necessarily become 'copycat killers' as a result of watching *Pulp Fiction*, but argues that 'clearly these films do affect their thoughts and ideas' – for instance, in defining killers as 'cool'.

'The environment' may therefore seem a more apt metaphor for exploring these wide-ranging questions about the impact of the media. However, it also brings its own contradictions and dangers. Media campaigners draw from the strength of the green movement to present their own case as having the same claims to validity, urgency and public acceptance, describing it with evangelical fervour as a 'cause'. In practice, it leads to alliances between the left, the moral right, and government bodies: CEM supporters include groups concerned with issues of press freedom, independent and alternative media, the representation of women and minorities, and churches, child protection, drug control and health promotion agencies. This has tended to result in an overwhelming focus on 'media violence' as the one issue that can unite such a disparate range of interests. And crucially, the insistence on media power takes little account of audiences. They become products of their environment, effluent rather than agents making choices in using and understanding the media.

How realistic was that? – Media education to change attitudes

The *Critical Viewing* project is concerned primarily with the influence of television on attitudes and beliefs rather than on behaviour, and focuses on 'realist genres'. This is consistent with Van de Voort's earlier research, which showed that children were well aware of the fictional nature of cartoons and fantasy genres, but saw police and crime series as 'more or less true to life'. (In this respect, it is more nuanced than *Beyond Blame*, which consistently targets the 'violence' of children's cartoons.) The aim of the teaching is to make children aware of the 'factual differences between film and real life' (Vooijs and van der Voort, 1993a: 140). If crime programmes can be made to seem less real, their violent content or values – such as, the notion that violence is an acceptable way of solving problems, or approval of the use of unjustified force by 'good guys' – will have less of an impact.

In the teaching, extracts from crime dramas such as *Miami Vice*, *Hill Street Blues*, *Frank Buck* and *Magnum* are screened. These show improbably glamorous lifestyles, heroism, marksmanship, or police delight in shooting a suspect. Children are then presented with video footage of 'actual' law enforcement officials. For instance, in the Devon version, kindly West Country policemen chuckle over how rarely they themselves use firearms. In a section from an American documentary, a police officer describes the traumatic effect on his life and marriage when he shot and killed a suspect. Dutch officers explain how they are 'put through the mangle' after a shooting, emphasising the 'punishing' process of investigation to which they are subjected by superiors, the press and politicians, especially if their victim came from an ethnic minority and they are suspected of racial prejudice. Finally, another drama clip is shown and children are asked to watch out for the differences between reality and fiction (e.g. 'how would real police officers react?') that they are assumed not to notice in their everyday viewing.

This model suggests that television offers a 'distorted' view, which can be corrected by comparing it to what happens in real life. One consequence is that the teaching focuses on the content and not the construction of texts; interviews and documentaries are treated as 'the truth' rather than as different versions of the meaning of crime and violence. It is not clear how this approach might deal with more recent programmes such as *Chopper Coppers*, *Police, Camera, Action!* and *Cops* which blur the line between fact and fiction by using actual footage from police work, albeit edited in highly selective ways. Second, the question of what is real or unreal, true or false, factual or fictional, is seen as self-evident and simple. In the Devon pack, worksheets are provided that ask 'Did you think that the action (in a clip) was very realistic?' with a box for 'yes' and one for 'no'. The context might make it clear what the 'right' answer is, although I'm still pondering the tactful response to a dilemma posed by the Dutch project: 'In detective programs, most female detectives look lovely. Are real female detectives beautiful too?' Answer: yes / perhaps / no.

Yet the question of 'modality' (the reality attributed to a message) is a complex one, because there is no fixed relation between fantasy and reality. Hodge and Tripp's (1986) work, for instance, shows that it is a continuing, even contradictory, process of discrimination and judgement, made in relation to audience understanding of both textual conventions and of the world. Indicting the media instead for giving impressionable children 'false notions about social reality' (Vooijs and van der Voort, 1993a: 139), highlights the political dimension of the project. '"Reality" in this view is what children *ought* to think, not how things are, because they will act on the basis of what they believe things to be' (Hodge and Tripp, 1986: 101). The teaching is a struggle to control children's perceptions of the world – as is evident from its attempt to persuade them that the police are 'in fact' benevolent, sensitive, cautious and (arguably) non-racist.

Children are defined here primarily through what they lack; that is, adult knowledge, experience or skills of discrimination. This is a consequence of the authors' reliance on a normative model of development in which children are seen to progress through stages to a more adequate adult understanding. Indeed, the success of the teaching was explicitly assessed in part by how far children's responses to questions about 'perceived television realism' or knowledge of police procedure moved closer to those of a 'norm' group of adult students. Moreover, it is a premise of the work that attitudes can be changed by 'new information', provided it is supplied by a 'credible source'. By assuming that children will perceive 'experts' such as policemen and detectives in this way, the authors position them as subordinates who willingly accept the trustworthiness of authority figures.

The project is not only paternalistic but, in viewing the media primarily as sources of information about the world, it is also overly rationalistic. It has little interest in exploring how texts might resonate for their audiences at quite other levels – in terms of their own feelings, pleasures, and even violent fantasies, for instance. (The fact that the project uses dated programmes is also relevant here, since they are more easily mocked than the contemporary television fare in which children may have more investment.) Therefore, whilst evaluations of the project found that students (dutifully?) stated that they found the lessons 'instructive and useful', it is revealing that some criticised the input from experts and that most stated that watching the drama clips was the most 'attractive' part. These comments may provide evidence of children's resistance to the 'adult' perspectives they were offered, since they might have known these were not really the desired responses in this context. Or, we might just note that recognising a text as 'unrealistic' does not necessarily shake our emotional involvement with it. To take such a road would radically undo this entire approach.

'As with the rat . . .' – media education as behaviour modification

The *Beyond Blame* pack shares some elements of the *Critical Viewing* approach, although the latter presents evidence of the serious nature of real-life violence, and the former asks students simply to imagine it. So, one session is entitled 'What's missing from Media Violence?' Here, video extracts illustrate 'violent acts shown without their logical consequences'. One of these (40 seconds long) is from the film *Witness* (1985); Harrison Ford punches a man who says 'boo' to him, leaving him with a bloody nose. After viewing, children have to answer questions like: 'Who will be sad? Who will clean away the mess? Who will have to go to the hospital? How long will they have to wait to be seen by a doctor?' In the next lesson, 'Violence Doesn't Solve Problems, It Causes Them', a longer (90 second) extract from the same scene is screened.[5] This time, it shows the events running up to the fight: the man daubs an ice cream over the face of another character, who does not respond. It is said to illustrate the 'cycle of violence' in which minor events lead to greater violence, and students are encouraged to 'break the cycle' by providing a non-violent resolution.

A teacher who dealt with *Hamlet* by requiring students to 'resolve the problems shown without recourse to violence', or to respond to the blood-bath of the final scene by discussing 'who will clean away the mess?' might rightly be considered to have completely missed the symbolic meaning of the violence. *Beyond Blame*'s answer to such criticism lies, unsurprisingly, in the distinction between 'high' and 'low' culture, 'art' and 'entertainment'. It tells us that in 'great drama' violence occurs 'only to portray the rise and fall of a character who eventually recognises and regrets her or his terrible acts'. In 'action-adventure entertainment', by contrast, violence is 'gratuitous', 'an end unto itself', 'formulaic' and 'sanitised', used just to 'keep the action moving, to create emotional shock or to showcase special effects'.

These specious distinctions refuse to allow that media texts might them-selves have anything to say about the issue of violence. Its use of *Witness* ignores the fact that the film is itself a meditation on the limits and advan-tages of pacifism. Harrison Ford plays John Book, a big city cop forced to stay in the Amish community in order to protect an eight-year-old boy who has witnessed a murder. The narrative explores the tensions between the lifestyle of the non-violent Amish and the more aggressive Book, finding something of value in each. It is worth noting that the man Book attacks is a coward, who only bullies the Amish because he thinks they will not fight back, and that Book has just learnt that his police partner has been murdered by the corrupt cops who are trying to track him down. The scene described therefore invites us to debate both the motivations behind brutal acts, and how far non-violence is an appropriate response to those who are prepared to use force themselves. Yet at the climax of the film, the police chief (who is both the villain and a 'family man') is not killed, but shamed into surrender by Book's words and the presence of the Amish neighbours who have run to offer support. However, such subtleties are irrelevant here. This is not education about the media, but about violence, with texts used only to engender criticism or illustrate predetermined hypotheses.

Whereas the *Critical Viewing* project wants to make children view television violence in a new way – a cognitive goal – *Beyond Blame* aims to make them watch less of it – a behavioural goal. (The equivalent in English might be teaching books in order to stop children reading.) To achieve this, teachers 'share' the findings and theory of effects research. So, in one session, students multiply the number of hours of TV they watch by the number of violent acts they are said to contain, to produce a figure for the total number of violent acts they view per week. In another, 'Why is everyone watching?', children are told that producers attract audiences by using 'jolts' (moments of excitement), in order to keep them watching 'until the commercials come on!' They then view clips, such as a promotional trailer for a film called *Terror In The Night* and 'count the jolts'. A contributor to the *Media and Values* magazine outlines the theory of 'jolts', as one explanation of why we watch media violence. Referring to a classic laboratory experiment, he writes that 'Programmers learned long ago that *as with the rat*, regular jolts of empty stimulation are the easiest and cheapest means of keeping viewers glued to the screen'. 'Jolts' give us a 'generalized rush of adrenalin' and their 'addictive power' hypnotises us into carrying on watching (Johnston, 1993, my emphasis). Other research has challenged this view of audiences as so bedazzled by the formal features of the medium that they are unable to concentrate on its meaning.[6] But in the classroom, it functions to offer children a view of themselves as innocents who have been haplessly conditioned into consuming violence and lack a 'real' understanding of how they have been 'fooled or mesmerized' by the media. A behaviourist understanding of audiences results in behaviourist teaching strategies: facts provide the corrective to erroneous feelings, as a route to attitude change and thus to virtuous conduct.

Although the pack uses a rhetoric of 'empowerment' through 'inquiry-based' education, in which teachers are merely 'facilitators' and 'co-learners' about media violence, it constructs traditional relations of power and authority in its address. For instance, it instructs teachers on how to control and silence dissenting voices, in the following terms:

If the students describe TV violence as being fun or entertaining, explain that *people who study the effects of media violence* have found that violence has negative effects even if the audience 1) Thinks it's fun and entertaining and / or 2) Knows that media portrayals are not real (my emphasis)

Students then receive handouts outlining the 'four effects' of viewing media violence. They are not invited to debate their own views on them, or informed how the findings have been reached. Instead, they are asked to contribute anecdotes that illustrate their validity – to 'remember a time when they themselves or someone they knew was affected by TV or media violence'. Examples are supplied to get them started, such as 'My older sister, who watches a lot of gory movies, doesn't trust anyone who is walking by on the sidewalk'. (This utterly fallacious reasoning somewhat belies the claim that media literacy teaches 'critical thinking'. A similarly constructed statement, such as 'my brother, who eats cornflakes for breakfast, doesn't like to leave the house', does not 'prove' that cereal consumption causes agoraphobia.) Again, students are situated as 'empty vessels', subservient to the authority of scientific researchers and other experts.

Likewise, it proclaims its commitment to a new literacy, which will enable children to 'create as well as read' media texts, and to 'participate actively in the public discussions that shape policies about media, and media violence, in our world'. Whilst we might welcome in principle any attempt to 'give children a voice', in practice the project merely views them as handy conscripts into its own campaign. Thus, students are exhorted to take direct action (e.g. lobbying broadcasters through postcard campaigns), to produce posters to express their concerns about media violence, or to create their own non-violent TV shows or heroes.

Those in Britain who have argued long and hard for media teacher-training courses might also be somewhat alarmed by the CML's view of teachers. 'With *just a couple of hours of preparation*', its website declares, '*any teacher* or group leader new to this subject can begin to teach media literacy with basic resources developed by our Center' (my emphasis). The lack of centralised support or funding for media education in the US opens a gap in the market for the CML to fill, advertising itself as a 'first-stop shopping service' to which purchasers should 'stay tuned!' to 'choose with confidence' the 'must-have' items from its catalogue. 'Your Guarantee of Quality is knowing your resource is "Selected, Evaluated and Distributed by the CML",' the 'source you can trust', it intones, in the language of a nineteenth-century fairground hawker flogging talismanic remedies.

Media education: moral panics and moral technology

The pedagogies here might be seen as what Terry Eagleton has termed a form of 'moral technology', that seeks to instil 'quite specific kinds of value, discipline, behaviour and response' in students (Eagleton, 1985/6: 96–7). There is perhaps nothing inherently sinister in this; some critics have argued that teachers are inevitably involved in the 'ethico-political' formation of students (Hunter, 1994). However, the projects are profoundly unreflexive. Their teaching demands precisely the passive consumption they accuse the media of promoting, and is oblivious to students' likely familiarity with received public messages about media violence and influence. As David Buckingham's research has found, in interviews even young children readily trumpet their contempt for 'silly' and unrealistic texts, or express concerns about their bad influence (on other people), without any teaching at all. Deploying such arguments functions to underscore one's own identity as socially responsible, rational and sophisticated; it might work in the context of the classroom, but is unlikely to transfer to the playground where talk about the media is used for quite different purposes (Buckingham, 1993). Further, the authors' judgements on the 'meaning' of popular texts promote a particular cultural agenda, as Jeffrey Sconce has discussed (Sconce, 1993). They prioritise an aesthetic of realism, probability, complexity, the portrayal of motivation and moral consequences, over the formulaic, spectacular, excessive (that is, of elite culture over mainstream Hollywood products) and thus reinforce rather than overcome differences of taste and 'cultural capital' between teachers and students.

We should certainly question how far these projects are a response to a genuine problem and meet children's needs, or whether, as with other moral panics, they serve as vehicles for general social anxieties about trends in contemporary life or are tactical for specific interest groups. (For more on moral panics see Jenkins, 1992; Goode and Ben-Yehuda, 1994; Thompson, 1998, and other contributors to this volume.) CML contributors often write from 'a parent's perspective'; its publications offer parental 'Better Viewing Guides', suggesting how and what children should watch on television and more desirable activities they should be involved in ('sports, hobbies, reading'). In *Media and Values*, effects researcher Edward Donnerstein attacks slasher films on the grounds that 'a young male or female's first introduction to anything that might deal with human sexuality and the nude body could take place in a violent context'. This paternalistic concern is echoed by Philo when he writes in his *Pulp Fiction* research about one girl 'with a cherubic face and golden curls' who wrote that she remembered 'things from the Bible and lots of swearing, motherfucker, shit, fuck, things from the bible'. The projects may reflect adults' desires to control young people's sexuality, behaviour and access to information, maintaining the power of the privatised family against the influence of the public media. We might also see here a 'politics of substitution', in which a specific problem is focused on because another cannot be addressed directly (Jenkins, 1992: 10). Technological change enabling marketing to 'niche' audiences, and a more liberal moral climate, make it difficult for groups with a conservative social agenda to denounce graphic violence as long as it is seen as a private issue for adults. Basing claims about on its effects on children circumvents this problem, as they can more easily be presented as victims.

We also find, in the debates outlined here, a number of influential claims-makers, each with a set of interests. For an agency such as the BBFC, turning its attention to educational initiatives may be a means of redefining its role in the face of potential redundancy. Educators, campaigning groups or individuals such as Philo may have an independent stake in bringing the issue to the fore, since it will help advance their status, power, and material resources (Goode and Ben-Yehuda, 1994: 139). And, of course, it is easier for government agencies and policy-makers to denounce the culture of media violence than to tackle more complex issues underlying youth violence, such as poverty and unemployment. 'Critical viewing' cannot be a panacea for these many tensions here, and we should be wary of any claims that it is.

Learning from the media: a case study

As should be clear, the two projects above invite students to see the mainstream media as trivial or dangerous and their own investments in them as valueless, rather than as a potential source of learning and pleasure. Whilst *Beyond Blame* 'gives a voice' to children to create media texts, it does so only on condition that they use it for socially approved purposes. However, other educators in Britain have proposed more open-ended models, which begin from a more positive valuation of the media. They invite students' own unofficial, informal knowledge and interests into the curriculum by asking them to construct representations within genres with which they are familiar. Subsequently, they seek to build understanding by asking students to reflect on their own work, on the grounds that such analysis may be more thought-provoking to them than being drilled in teacher-pleasing responses to existing texts (Buckingham, 1986; 1990; 1993; Buckingham and Sefton-Green, 1994; Buckingham *et al.*, 1995).

I do not have the space to explore these arguments fully. However, I want to consider here a piece of practical video work, which might appear initially to be a 'worst case scenario' of what might be produced within this paradigm. It arose from an A-Level module on the horror genre. As part of their assessment students were asked to write a plot for a new horror film, on the basis of which they then produced a video cover and an opening sequence consisting of still images taken with a digital camera and dubbed onto videotape with a soundtrack. One student offered the following outline of a film called *White Gloves*:

> It's set in a hospital . . . and, what it's going to be is, he's like Spanish and he's against, like, the English, he doesn't like the English, he's got some sort of chip against them, and he's working in the old wards, and, the old people like annoy him and that, so he begins to get frustrated and it's so easy just to kill em off anyway, just, you know, because they're old and there's no question why they're dying, because they're old anyway, so he starts beginning to kill em off and he gets this, like, great sense of buzz out of just killing these

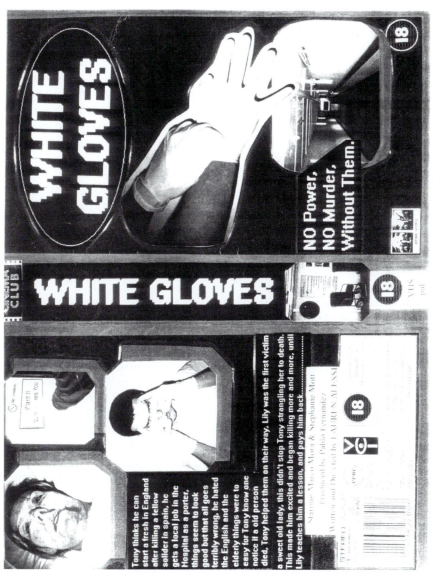

Figure 5.1 Video cover: Lauren carefully follows the conventions of video cover lay-
out. She uses the setting of the hospital to create images that are ironic
('Ward 11 Welcomes You') and sinister (the deserted corridor and the
empty wheelchair). She has attended to details by applying make up (white
powder and red 'blood') to the face of the 'victim'. Practical production
offers an empowering role to students as 'teller of the tale', which Lauren
marks by writing her own name, with her surname changed, in capitals on
the credits.

women – and men, and then it sort of moves along, because the buzz sort of goes after a while, because it's getting boring, you know, and he begins, like, the young nurses n that, following them home, raping them, slaughtering em, you know, beating em up in the forest nearby and then an undercover detective gets set on the case to investigate and and he – as a porter – and he, no one suspects this like kind Spanish man to be doing this, but then a lot of investigation goes on and they do end up finding him, but he goes back to Spain, and then so, that's the ending – but I don't know, I think I've gotta make a better ending cause like –

Sara: So he gets away with it?

Student: Well I *think* he does, yeah, but you know, he kills, he moves on to the nurses and it gets more gory and it begins to get a bit more sexual and every time he does his murder he puts like the white gloves on, them latex gloves on, so I've got loads of pictures of the latex gloves and everything . . . he does it very cleverly and no fingerprints . . . so that he wouldn't get caught or anything.

The opening sequence of the video which this student subsequently produced shows the killer arriving after dark at the hospital where he works, moving down empty corridors towards his victim who is strangled and left bleeding in her bed.

Anti-violence educators might say that this piece proves that immersion in media violence leads to an unthinking acceptance of sexist, ageist, and racist values. According to those definitions which take only the rejection of violence as evidence of 'being critical', it has failed to evaluate the media critically. It regards ethnicity as a sufficient motivation for murder (the Spanish killer has 'some sort of chip' against the English), and old people as superfluous and dispensable (on the video cover, they are described as 'the elderly things'). In reproducing the dominant conventions of serial killer films, in which men victimise women through rape and slaughter, it teaches male audiences to revel in their own power and female audiences their subordinate place in the patriarchal order (Gerbner might describe it as a 'lesson in gender roles, fear and power').[7] However, since its producer, Lauren, was neither delinquent nor passive, but a mature 16-year-old, well able to hold her own and participate in a class generally dominated by boys, I want to pursue instead the question of what we can learn from her.

My first points concern the role of genre, which has implications for how we understand both the aesthetics of horror and audience involvement with it. As recent work has argued, genres are not just types of films, but are constituted by the knowledge of the 'rules, norms and laws' appropriate to different media materials, that is shared by both audiences and film-makers (Neale, 1990: 46). The more familiar audiences are with these conventions, the better they understand what to expect from texts. They are able to make sense of events and characters on screen, to anticipate what will happen next and why – and even to decide whether it is worth carrying on watching. Moreover, different genres carry different cultural weight, as noted above. 'Realist' texts, which refer outwards to what is held to be 'true' about society, tend to be more highly valued than fantasy genres whose rules obey a more internal logic ('in horror, having sex means you will die') or refer to other belief systems such as witchcraft (Neale, 1990: 46–8).

Horror is particularly interesting in this respect, because it is so formulaic, even ritualistic. Its repetition of familiar characters, events, locations and even shot types has made it a highly self-conscious and frequently parodic form. Relatively few critics have analysed horror with the sustained attention given to higher status genres. Those that do commonly emphasise the importance of the 'insider knowledge' of conventions acquired by seasoned audiences, which enables them to read and play with the different levels of meaning in the text rather than responding only to its 'violent' content. Pleasure is provided through a combination of the films' transparency and predictability, and the innovations and surprises they deliver – especially through special effects or scenes of 'intense visual excitement' (Brophy, 1986; Sconce, 1993; Pinedo, 1997; Kermode in this volume). Audience involvement thus takes on the aura of a participatory game, rather than empathy with individual characters. Moreover, recent psychoanalytically-oriented critics have explored the cross-gendered fluidity of audience identifications, with victims as well as monsters. They have thus challenged the common-sense view of sadistic male audiences cheering on male killers, and underlined instead the masochistic elements in horror spectatorship (Williams, 1991; Clover, 1992; Lehman, 1993).

Such analyses lead me to suggest that Lauren understands the conventions and aesthetics of horror rather well. What counts in her film is precisely the performance of familiar set pieces (death scenes), rather than narrative or character development. She is aware that she is addressing an audience, and carefully directs our interpretation. For instance, her scenario plays with a typical theme in horror, the distinction between appearance and reality (Barker, 1984) – 'no one suspects this kind Spanish man to be doing this'. The audience, however, is given knowledge denied to the fictional characters. Killer and victim are introduced in two credit shots at the beginning of the video that reveal the nature of their characters. 'Tony' is clearly villainous, since he is shown in close up, using a low camera angle; 'Lily', posed rather helplessly in a medium, high angle shot, is set up as a future victim. When these images are repeated, shortly before the murder, our response to them has already been established. For much of the sequence, Tony is shot from behind, so that his identity and expression are partially hidden, creating a sense of threat and foreboding. For viewers familiar with the genre, the lack of point-of-view shots attributed to Lily would also be significant in marking her victim status (Clover, 1992). Other images too are complex and sophisticated,

Figure 5.2 This image of the killer's battle with himself before the murder problematises Lauren's conscious understanding of male violence as natural and
normal, as do the 'white gloves' of the title.

using long shots of empty corridors, and the signs in the hospital ('Ward 11
Welcomes You'), to sinister and ironic effect. Thus, our participation in the
film is guided through a series of cues; suspense is created through the contrast between our knowledge and Lily's ignorance, but we should not be
shocked by her death, nor are we meant to 'identify' with either character.

Production work has necessitated a certain critical distance here. Lauren's
control of the form alone indicates that she is not in thrall to the conventions
(still less 'bombarded' by them), but able to use them for her own purposes
of communication. Additionally, video work offers particular pleasures that
students find 'empowering'. They can position themselves as 'creators',
rather than reproducers of teachers' ideas, as essay-writing requires. The
process of filming itself often disrupts school routines and established relationships between students and their 'actors' – whether friends, teachers, or
in Lauren's case, her mother and boyfriend. Lauren may be relishing, not the
content of the film, but the role of director, of 'teller of the tale', the novelty
of which she marks on her video cover by changing her surname from 'Mott'
to 'Alessi'.

However, demonstrating Lauren's skill and understanding may evade a more fundamental question, of whether such images of male power and female victims promote women's oppression. Anti-sexist and anti-racist pedagogies frequently focus on replacing 'stereotypes' with 'positive images', often by a logic of simple role reversal – if women are generally shown as weak, dependent and domestic, then students should see or produce stories in which they are instead strong, independent and career-minded. Large claims have been made for the liberating potential of such strategies in allowing a new sense of agency and identity for girls and ethnic minority students (Davies, 1993). (For criticisms see Walkerdine, 1990; Cohen, 1991.)

Influenced by these ideas, I asked Lauren why she had not 'challenged conventions' in her work. She read this as a request to replace a violent male monster with a female one – to show, in her words, how 'a woman could, like, control a man'. The profound challenge this would have presented became clear to me in one interview, in which Lauren described her collection of books on serial killers and she and two female friends expressed considerable interest in horror and true crime genres. I therefore asked what they thought about 'female serial killers in real life',[8] at which all three recoiled. Lauren exclaimed: 'They make me sick, they do make me sick, I don't know why, they make me more sick than the blokes doing it. Probably because I'm a woman anyway . . . it just makes me feel really ill and I think that Rosemary West, oh, just wanna get her face and smash it, I mean that's how it makes me feel'. All three agreed that women murderers are somehow 'worse' and 'weirder' than male ones; 'with men you can understand it', but 'with women it's not normal'.

Lauren and her friends are thus caught in a dilemma. On the one hand, images of mutilation, death and (male) violence clearly held a potent fascination for them. (Other research too has shown that horror is popular with women audiences; Cherland, 1994; Buckingham, 1996). However, their view of gender assumes that there is a 'natural' element of aggressiveness in male sexuality that makes men's (sexual) violence against women normal or at least comprehensible. The violent woman, on this understanding, is more evil and abhorrent than the violent man, because she betrays her ascribed gender role of nurturance and motherhood. (For the record, this is not a quirk of ignorance on the part of teenage girls, but a view shared by most non-feminist 'experts' and commentators on the trials of the Yorkshire Ripper or Rosemary West. For discussion of these tendencies see Hollway, 1981; Cameron and Frazer, 1987; Cameron, 1996; 1996/7). Further, as Lynda Hart points out, both aggression and desire are qualities that our society codes as masculine, hence fictionalised portrayals of violent women are always shadowed by the image of the lesbian (Hart, 1994). Admitting the possibility of female violence is fraught with risks for young women who, like Lauren and her friends, identify as heterosexual – although it can more easily be imagined to avenge a wrong, as Lauren fantasises 'smashing' Rosemary

West's face.[9] Even being interested in horror is defined as a masculine pursuit, as Lauren herself noted when she remarked quietly in one lesson 'I like horror, I must be abnormal'. The question might more realistically be, not why Lauren does not 'challenge the conventions', but whether the process of the practical work has enabled her to work through any of the contradictions of the gender discourses available to her.

For instance, we might argue that the male killer acts as a convenient and valuable cypher that allows Lauren to explore those feelings and desires – for power and control, for instance – that are socially prohibited to her as a woman. This might account for the fact that, as so often in horror, her killer is the most interesting character, both visually and narratively. Alternatively, it could be said that she has simply disowned her own unacceptable emotions by projecting them outwards onto the monster, hence explaining the positioning of the audience as observer of the killer, which encourages a moral distance from his actions. He, like Dracula, is foreign, coming from elsewhere to disrupt the safe space of an English suburban hospital; Lily's name underlines her 'whiteness' in contrast to Tony's ethnic otherness. His probable punishment and despatch in the final sequence might then reinforce existing value judgements of what is 'normal' and leave us and her feeling virtuously detached from the on-screen mayhem.

However, Lauren's name-change, from 'Mott' to the more exotic, less British-sounding 'Alessi', may suggest she is assimilating herself to the Spanish killer rather than firmly externalising him. We might also recall her initial lack of narrative closure – Tony may 'get away with it', or at least, his punishment is not what most interests her. Moreover, her visual construction of the killer emphasises his psychic struggle and subsequent remorse. Before the murder, he is shown praying by an altar; afterwards, standing in front of a mortuary with his hands up to his face, and in the final shot, on his hands and knees in a posture of despair. These images problematise her own conception of male violence as normal or requiring no special explanation. The theme of the 'white gloves' is also significant. They give the film its title, and an image of two hands pulling on the gloves, accompanied by the by-line 'NO Power, NO Murder, Without Them', dominates the cover. The gloves hold the naturalness of male violence at a distance. Power, in this account, is not a property securely possessed by virtue of (male) gender. Rather, it is a practice, which requires something else – an additional layer – before it can be achieved. Potentially, therefore, this power is available to women too, as I would argue that the process of production has offered a particular form of empowerment to Lauren. When she describes the killer's 'cleverness' in leaving no trace of his crimes, and the 'buzz' he experiences, she is also expressing her own pride in creating the story and constructing the images. In the play of identity and identifications across many surfaces, Lauren has been able to denaturalise the meanings of male violence and power; but she has done so on her own terms, using horror as a 'tool to think with', and without giving up on her pleasures, knowledge and investments.

Lauren began an A-Level course in Psychology before taking up Media Studies, but gave it up in disappointment. She had thought it might enable her to understand 'the mind of a serial killer', but soon found it did nothing of the sort; it was Media Studies that enabled her to pursue her own interests from outside the classroom. I am tempted to read this as a general comment on the inadequacies of the psychology-based projects of *Critical Viewing* and *Beyond Blame* which, by insisting that students 'reject' violence, create 'positive images', use only a prescribed 'critical' discourse, and so on, similarly stop learning short in its tracks.

Conclusion

We should be wary of any calls for media education based primarily on concerns about media violence and 'influence', or which see it as an alternative method of censorship. Media education will not deliver self-regulation, if by that is meant that it will stop children thinking Quentin Tarantino films are 'cool', watching adult material, or forming passionate attachments to disapproved genres. Still less will it stop violence on the streets or 'save the planet'. To think that it could do any of these things is to accede to the faulty logic of the projects discussed in the first part of this chapter. Media education is not a solution to the problem of violence, not just because the media do not 'cause' it in the first place, but because education should not be a behaviour modification therapy, a means by which adults prescribe how children are to see the world, or a moral crusade that makes teachers responsible for social ills that lie beyond their control. It has a more banal and infinitely more complicated task: a matter of trying to enable students to understand their own tastes and pleasures, to locate them in relation to other possibilities, and to participate in the media culture around them. If education is to achieve this constructively, it should not depart from predetermined moral positions on the worth or meaning of media texts, but acknowledge the learning and understanding they offer. To create 'conditions which favour dialogue' (Richards, 1998: 17), it might start by paying attention to what students have to say, but it should not expect them to come to the conclusions that teachers might wish to hear.

Since I have focused on one specific example in order to explore what might happen if we did this, I will finish with a more general one, encapsulated by a story I have heard many times from students. The details change, but the basic elements remain the same: A student working on a Media Studies project decides to photograph a murder scene. She gathers her materials – tomato ketchup, a knife, a red light bulb – and asks a friend round to play the victim in the bathtub. When she takes the photos to the developers, however, they become suspicious and call the police, who arrest her and keep her 'all day in the cell'. She's only released when the friend turns up to prove he's still alive . . . The truth value and provenance of the story are unclear,[10] but it seems to have taken on something of the status of an 'urban legend' amongst media students, perhaps because it articulates so well the kinds of conflicts that go on around young people's investments in the media. On the one side, we have the student. She is not the complete innocent in need of protection that we so often find in writings about media violence, since she is fascinated by the gruesome and ghoulish, but nor is she guilty of the crime of which she is accused. Primarily, she is skilful and expert, absorbed (and successful) in her task of constructing convincing special effects. On the other side, we have the fundamental stupidity of authority figures, who misinterpret both representations and audiences, taking fantasy for reality, playful intent for vicious acts. 'Paying attention' to what young people say, then, might just involve trusting them a little more, and recognising that they may be better able than adults to read and respond to the media images they know. And pedagogy might be well advised to work with, rather than try to rule out, the pleasures the media can offer.

I would like to thank Lauren Mott for agreeing to let me write about her and her work, and for her encouraging comments on an earlier version of this article.

NOTES

1 'Media literacy' is the term more commonly used in the US than 'media education'.

2 The figures derive from content analysis, a familiar methodology in the social sciences, in which researchers take a limited sample of television programmes and count the number of violent incidents in them, which match their own supposedly objective, pre-determined definition of violence. For example, George Gerbner defines violence as 'the overt expression of physical force (with or without a weapon) against self or other, compelling action against one's will on pain of being hurt or killed, or actually hurting or killing' (cited in Gunter and McAleer, 1997: 94). This method has been criticised on a number of grounds. It assumes that 'meaning' is something contained within the text, which can then be quantified. It ignores ambiguity, the contexts in which 'violent acts' occur and are watched, and audiences' own definitions of violence. Cartoons thus emerge as the most violent programmes on television – even though other research has shown that audiences consider them as 'fantasy' and thus do not count them as violent (Dorr, 1983; Gunter, 1985). (For a general critique of content analysis see Winston, 1990.) It is important to note that the Dutch project does not adopt this approach and departs from children's own understandings to a greater extent, as I explain below.

3 This logic serves to put the case for funding media education on a different footing. See for example, Eron, who claims that although the causes of aggression are multiple, if television violence explains 9–10% of it, then education might be able to reduce it by the same percentage. Moreover, he argues that if teaching can indeed successfully reduce aggression, 'that would be evidence of a causal effect as persuasive as that demonstrated in a carefully controlled laboratory experiment'

(Eron, 1986). Accepting media education's special claim to public money, then, involves accepting the causative argument. On the failings of education in relation to HIV prevention, see Britzman, 1998 or Patton, 1990.

4 Considine is referring to a 1993 conference, *Safeguarding Our Youth*, convened by the Department of Justice, the Department of Education and the Department of Health and Human Services.

5 This extract is one of the longest contained in the pack. Another session, for instance, presents clips from a range of genres (mostly children's films and cartoons, such as *Home Alone* or *The X-Men*) said to exemplify 'Types of Violence' found in the media (crashes and explosions; violence with and without a weapon; verbal violence). They are so short that it is almost impossible to explore the narrative contexts in which 'violent acts' occur and which (from a Media Studies perspective) help shape their meaning: hence what seems to be an argument about how to rescue someone in danger, for instance, is classified as 'verbal violence'.

6 See, for instance, Huston and Wright. They argue against criticisms of programmes such as *Sesame Street* which hold that its formal features – such as fast pace and editing, which might be seen as equivalent to the notion of 'jolts per minute' – lead to reduced attention spans, poor comprehension, little time for reflection and general intellectual passivity. One of their arguments is particularly relevant here; that children are in fact active, selective viewers whose attention is guided by what they find interesting or comprehensible, not by formal features alone. Rapid pace does not hold attention, but may be used by children to help them decide whether particular content is worth watching, e.g., whether it is geared at a child or adult audience (Huston and Wright, 1994). Anderson offers a similar argument (in Bryant and Anderson, 1983).

7 Such is Gerbner's description of Red Riding Hood (CEM website, 'Letter from the Founder').

8 My question was of course misleading. Some feminist critics have argued that female serial killers do not in fact exist, with the possible exception of Rosemary West (Cameron, 1996; 1996/7).

9 Lauren in fact changed her scenario in response to teacher feedback that the first two shots, in which she 'introduces' her victim and killer, seemed to imply that 'Lily' would play a greater role in the film, as early victims are not usually given extended credits. It was, I now feel, based on a misreading of the function of the shots. However, Lauren rewrote the ending to escape this criticism, bringing back Lily from the dead to haunt the killer and make him 'regret everything'. In an interview she was quite well able to assert the pleasures that this would bring for women audiences: 'she has the power – I know she's dead and that, but she has got the power when she comes back by haunting him and making him really like ill and crazy, so they'd probably be the good bits because, seeing him suffer for what he's done?' So she has access to a more 'feminist' discourse about horror; however, it again involves notions of female violence as vengeance rather than an inherent potential.

10 The student who told me this version said she had read it in *More!*, a teenage girls' magazine – which already indicates that it has travelled around the country. In other accounts, students position themselves as the subject of 'weird' or 'suspicious' looks when they go to collect their photographs. It combines elements from popular mythology and news events, such as the story of the movie *Snuff*, rumoured (erroneously) to portray an actual death, and the accusation against the newsreader Julia Somerville, whose photographs of her child in the bath were seen as paedophilia by developers and investigated by the police.

REFERENCES

Barker, M. (1984), *A Haunt of Fears: the strange history of the British horror comics campaign*, London: Pluto Press.

Belson, W. (1978), *Television Violence and the Adolescent Boy*, Farnborough: Saxon House.

Bragg, S. and J. Grahame (1997), 'An Interview with James Ferman of the BBFC', *The English and Media Magazine* **36**: 33–36.

British Board of Film Classification (1995), Annual Report for 1994/5, London: British Board of Film Classification.

Britzman, D. P. (1998), *Lost Subjects, Contested Objects: Toward a Psychoanalytic Inquiry of Learning*, New York: SUNY.

Brophy, P. (1986), 'Horrality – the textuality of contemporary horror films', *Screen*, **27**: 1, Jan.–Feb., pp. 2–13.

Bryant, J. and D. Anderson, eds (1983), *Children's Understanding of Television*, New York: Academic Press.

Buckingham, D. (1986), 'Against Demystification', *Screen*, **27**: 5, September–October.

Buckingham, D. (1990), *Watching Media Learning: Making Sense of Media Education*, London: Falmer Press.

Buckingham, D. (1993), *Changing Literacies: Media Education and Modern Culture*, London: Institute of Education / Tufnell Press.

Buckingham, D. (1993), *Children Talking Television: the making of television literacy*, London: Falmer Press.

Buckingham, D. (1996), *Moving Images: Understanding Children's Emotional Response to TV*, Manchester and New York: Manchester University Press.

Buckingham, D., J. Grahame, and Michael Morgan (1995), *Making Media: Practical Production in Media Education*, London: The English and Media Centre.

Buckingham, D. and J. Sefton-Green (1994), *Cultural Studies Goes to School*, London: Taylor and Francis.

Cameron, D. (1996), 'Wanted: the female serial killer.' *Trouble and Strife*, **33**: Summer, pp. 21–8.

Cameron, D. (1996/7), 'Motives and meanings.' *Trouble and Strife*, **34**: Winter, pp. 44–52.

Cameron, D. and E. Frazer (1987), *The Lust to Kill: A Feminist Investigation of Sexual Murder*, Cambridge: Polity Press.

Center for Media Literacy (1995), *Beyond Blame: Challenging Violence in the Media (teaching pack with 5 guides and videos)*, Los Angeles USA: Center for Media Literacy.

Cherland, M. R. (1994), *Private Practices: Girls Reading Fiction and Constructing Identity*, London: Taylor and Francis.

Clover, C. (1992), *Men, Women and Chainsaws: Gender in the Modern Horror Film*, London: BFI.

Cohen, P. (1991), *Monstrous Images, Perverse Reasons: Cultural Studies in Anti-racist Education (Working Paper no. 11)*, London: Centre for Multi-cultural Education, Institute of Education, University of London.

Considine, D. (1995), 'Are we there yet? An update on the media literacy movement', *Educational Technology*, **35**: 4, pp. 32–43.

Davies, B. (1993), *Shards of Glass: Children reading and writing beyond gendered identities*, Sydney: Allen and Unwin.

Doolittle, J. C. (1975), *Immunizing Children Against Possible Anti-social Effects of Viewing Television: a curricular intervention*, University of Wisconsin-Madison (unpublished PhD).

Dorr, A. (1983), 'No shortcuts to judging reality', in J. Bryant and D. Anderson, eds, *Children's Understanding of Television*, New York: Academic Press.

Eagleton, T. (1985/6), 'The subject of literature', *Cultural Critique*, **2**, pp. 95–104.

Ellsworth, E. (1997), *Teaching Positions: difference, pedagogy and the power of address*, New York: Teachers College Press.

Eron, L. D. (1986), 'Interventions to mitigate the psychological effects of media violence on aggressive behavior', *Journal of Social Issues*, **42**: 3, pp. 155–69.

Gerbner, G. (1972), 'Violence in TV drama: trends and symbolic functions', in G. Comstock and E. Rubinstein, eds, *Television and Sound Behaviour: Reports and Papers*, Vols 1–5, Washington DC: US Government Printing Office.

Gerbner, G. (1995), 'Television violence and the art of asking the wrong questions', in *Beyond Blame: Challenging Violence in the Media (teaching pack with 5 guides and videos)*, Center for Media Literacy. Los Angeles USA, Center for Media Literacy, pp. 12–16.

Gerbner, G. and L. Gross (1980), in E. L. Palmer and A. Dorr, eds, 'The violent face of television and its lessons'. *Children and the Faces of Television: Teaching, Violence, Selling*, NY and London: Academic Press.

Gerbner, G., L. Gross, and Nancy Signorielli (1980), 'The "mainstreaming" of America: Violence profile no. 11.' *Journal of Communication* **30**(3): 10–29.

Ghouri, N. (1997), 'Films Linked to Violent Crime.' *Times Educational Supplement*, 6 December, p. 1.

Goode, E. and N. Ben-Yehuda (1994), *Moral Panics: The Social Construction of Deviance*, Oxford UK and Cambridge USA: Blackwell.

Gunter, B. (1985), *Dimensions of Television Violence*, London: Gower.

Gunter, B. and J. McAleer (1997), *Children and Television*, London and New York: Routledge.

Hart, L. (1994), *Fatal Women: lesbian sexuality and the mark of aggression*, Princeton University Press.

Hodge, B. and D. Tripp (1986), *Children and Television*, Cambridge: Polity Press and Blackwell.

Hollway, W. (1981), '"I just wanted to kill a woman" Why? The Ripper and Male Sexuality.' *Feminist Review*, **9**: October, pp. 33–40.

Hunter, I. (1994), *Rethinking the School: Subjectivity, Bureaucracy, Criticism*, St Leonard's, NSW: Allen and Unwin.

Huston, A. and J. C. Wright (1994), 'Educating children with TV: the forms of the medium', in D. Zillmann, J. Bryant and A. Huston, eds, *Media, Children, and the Family: social scientific, psychodynamic, and clinical perspectives*, Hillsdale, New Jersey; Hove, UK: Lawrence Erlbaum Associates.

Jenkins, P. (1992), *Intimate Enemies: Moral Panics in Contemporary Britain*, New York: Aldine de Gruyter.

Johnston, C. M. (1993), 'Strung Out On Aggression.' *Media and Values*, 62, pp. 6–7.

Joint Working Party on Violence on Television (1998), *Violence and the Viewer*,

London: British Broadcasting Corporation, Broadcasting Standards Commission, Independent Television Commission.

Lehman, P. (1993), '"Don't blame this on a girl": female rape-revenge films', in S. Cohan and I. R. Hark, eds, *Screening The Male*, London and New York: Routledge.

Neale, S. (1990), 'Questions of Genre', *Screen*, **31**: 1, Spring, pp. 45–66.

Patton, C. (1990), *Inventing AIDS*, New York: Routledge.

Phillips, M. (n.d.), *Teaching Television in the Primary School*, Devon County Council Education.

Philo, G. (1997), *Children and Film / Video / TV Violence*, Glasgow: Glasgow Media Group.

Pinedo, I. (1997), *Recreational Terror: Women and the Pleasures of Horror Film Viewing*, New York: State University of New York Press.

Richards, C. (1998), *Teen Spirits: Music and Identity in Media Education*, London and Bristol, Pennsylvania: UCL Press.

Sconce, J. (1993), 'Spectacles of death: identification, reflexivity, and contemporary horror', in J. Collins, H. Radner and A. P. Collins, eds, *Film Theory Goes to the Movies*, New York and London: Routledge.

Signorielli, N. and M. Morgan, (eds) (1990), *Cultivation Analysis: new directions in media effects research*, Newbury Park, London, Delhi: Sage.

Thompson, K. (1998), *Moral Panics*, London and New York: Routledge.

Van der Voort, T. (1986), *Television Violence: A Child's Eye View*, Amsterdam, Holland: Elsevier Science Publishers.

Vooijs, M. W. and T. H. A. van der Voort (1993a), 'Learning about television violence: the impact of a critical viewing curriculum on children's attitudinal judgements of crime series.' *Journal of Research and Development in Education*, **26**: 3, pp. 133–42.

Vooijs, M. W. and T. H. A. van der Voort (1993b), 'Teaching children to evaluate television violence critically: the impact of a Dutch schools television project.' *Journal of Educational Television*, **19**: 3, pp. 139–52.

Walkerdine, V. (1990), *Schoolgirl Fictions*, London and New York: Verso.

Williams, L. (1991), 'Film bodies: gender, genre, and excess.' *Film Quarterly*, **44**: 4, pp. 2–13.

Winston, B. (1990), 'On Counting the Wrong Things', in M. Alvarado and J. O. Thompson, eds, *The Media Reader*, London, BFI: pp. 50–64.

Wober, J. M. (1978), 'Televised violence and paranoid perception: the view from Great Britain.' *Public Opinion Quarterly*, **42**: 3, pp. 315–21.

Wober, J. M. (1990), 'Does television cultivate the British? Late 80s evidence', in N. Signorielli and M. Morgan, eds, *Cultivation Analysis: New Directions in Media Effects Research*, Newbury Park, California: Sage.

Wober, J. M. and B. Gunter (1982), 'Television and personal threat: fact or artifact?: a British view.' *British Journal of Social Psychology*, **21**, pp. 43–51.

Wober, J. M. and B. Gunter (1988). *Television and Social Control*, Aldershot: Avebury.

6

ONCE MORE WITH FEELING

Talking about the media violence debate in Australia

Sue Turnbull

I'm waiting – waiting for that phone call from a radio station inviting me to participate in an on-air discussion about media violence. This time it will be about the news item in yesterday's *Sunday Herald Sun* newspaper (24 October 1999) entitled 'Video Stabbing Boys Guilty' which briefly reports on the trial and sentencing of Daniel Gill (14) and Robert Fuller (15) in Yorkshire, England. Apparently, although we have heard little about the case here in Australia, the two attacked their 'friend' with a knife 'only hours after watching the horror film' *Scream* at the 'home of a convicted drug dealer'. Because that would seem to be about all that the *Sunday Herald Sun* has on the case, the author of the article pads it out by recycling an earlier story in the same newspaper ('Girl Trapped in Evil Video', *Sunday Herald Sun*, 26 September 1999). This second story is about a 10-year-old Australian girl who, after watching *Scream* at a friend's birthday party, had to spend almost two weeks on a psychiatric ward, so disturbed was she by the experience. This newspaper article thus typifies a classic move in the media violence debate: the juxtaposition of unrelated incidents connected only by a tenuous link to a particular media product.

And I'm wondering, as I wait for the inevitable call, how will I tackle it this time? Will I be up against a well meaning but mis-directed spokesperson from some society for the protection of the family? Or a psychologist with the evidence of 'thousands of clinical trials' at hand? Or an insidiously reasonable interviewer who will sweetly and deviously offer a 'common sense' interpretation, implying that my academic approach is out of touch with the community and its values? All I can be sure of is that the whole exercise will probably render me angry and frustrated with a desire to kick something inanimate, prompting the inevitable conclusion that there's nothing quite like the media violence debate for inciting violence in media studies academics.

Meanwhile back at the *Sunday Herald Sun* article there's so little to go on, so many questions to ask. I don't know much about the British case, but what the article does tell me is enough get me thinking. What were the 'behavioural difficulties' of the two accused referred to by the judge? How come they were watching videos at a drug dealer's home? What kind of a social context does this imply for these two boys? And as for the Australian case: who was this girl, and why should she have responded in such an extreme fashion to a film which thousands of teenagers and under-age students have watched and loved, including our 10-year-old son? Shall I tell them that I currently have a postgraduate student writing a fine paper on slasher film spectatorship and the interactive teen audience (Downing, 1999) in which she explores the possibility that the watching of a horror movie may in itself constitute a type of embodied and participatory performance: a possibility which film maker Wes Craven knows only too well, and knows his audience knows too? Shall I tell them that this knowledge is enacted even more obviously in the ironically self-reflexive *Scream 2*, which is not only a horror film about watching a horror film, but is also a horror film about making film sequels?

But if I talk about irony and postmodernism I know that I will run the risk of sounding too academic in my response. They'll like the bit about 'our son' though: I always include him somewhere in these discussions in order to demonstrate that I'm not speaking just as an academic but also as a mother. It's a cheap move (of which I'm secretly ashamed) but it occasionally works, although it can backfire as it did when, much to my son's delight and my husband's distaste, a television crew arrived to watch the former watching television. Do the ends justify the means in this debate? Or will my arguments be discredited not only as overly academic and therefore irrelevant to daily life, but also because I'm 'obviously' an atypical mother and clearly take an irresponsible attitude to my own son's moral and psychological welfare? It can get dirty out there in media pundit land.

And so I'm waiting, rehearsing my moves and rhetorical strategies and wondering why I bother, although the answer is not hard to find. I bother because I care, not only about the ways in which this debate is repeatedly rehearsed in the media and by the media, resulting in serious violence to important ideas, but also because I care about the same things that everyone engaged in the debate claims to care about, namely: how, and on what terms, we relate to each other as human beings. It's just that I don't search for an answer to the problem of violence in the same place as those who look to the media as both the source and the solution. After sixteen years of participation in this debate, and caring passionately about the issues involved, I am more than ever convinced that the single most significant factor predicting violence is the social context of the individual or individuals concerned – not the media at all. But how can one get this across?

Of course, it all depends to whom I am talking and in what context. As a media academic with a particular history and investment in this debate, I regularly find myself addressing all sorts of groups on this topic, each group requiring a different approach, a different strategy and a different discourse, although the issues remain essentially the same. And then there are those social occasions at which you hardly dare to tell anybody what you do (teach Media Studies) because you can sense an opinion coming on, usually based on something someone has recently read or seen about the media violence debate (like the *Sunday Herald Sun* article, for example). And so you either back out gracefully, or get stuck into a discussion which runs the risk of becoming severely over-heated, because if there is one thing which everybody seems to 'know' – except, of course, those of us who have spent our lives studying media and communications history and theory – the media make people violent. And how do people know this? Because the media (which has a vested interest in emphasising its own power) tells them so? Because it's easier to believe that the media are to blame rather than people like themselves? Because it's obvious?

Talking to teachers

I am often asked to talk to teachers about the media violence debate because 'media issues' constitutes one section not only of the Victoria State's upper secondary media curriculum, but also of its English curriculum. The teachers to whom I speak may therefore be secondary media teachers, with some background in Media Studies, or English teachers (as I myself once was) who have no such background. I'm therefore expected to give them that background along with some useful strategies to use in the classroom, and all in under two hours. It doesn't take long to undo any assumptions based on a simplistic model of cause and effect which may already be firmly entrenched, or to put across any substantial theoretical issues. My strategy in this instance, therefore, is to begin where I myself entered this debate in 1984: as a secondary school English teacher just arrived in Australia on an overseas scholarship and undertaking her first piece of independent media research as a masters of education.

Because I had been a secondary school teacher, and imagined that I would be again, I was particularly interested in the relationship between young people and the media, and especially in what they consumed and why. I'd read Paul Willis' seminal study, *Learning to Labour* (1977), which examines the processes whereby secondary school boys get working class jobs, but I kept wondering just how the media might have figured in the landscape which he described. What particularly inspired me about Willis' work was his attempt to understand how, within the social context of the school, the boys' specific codes of masculinity might articulate with particular attitudes towards teachers and academic work to produce particular forms of social action and moral choice. I was also extremely impressed by the fact that, as a teacher working for a year in a particular school, Willis was able to theorise the complex social environment of which he was a part

However, while Willis certainly shed considerable light on what was essentially a masculine attitude to school and schooling, I was particularly interested in exploring my own female experience and social context. In other words, I wanted to find out how and why secondary school girls might be opting out of and resisting school in the ways which I myself had perceived in ten years of teaching in the UK and the US. Opposition and resistance seemed to be the buzzwords back then in educational research. And so when one of my media lecturers mentioned that, while trawling through a box of correspondence at a TV station, he had come across a letter from a headmaster to the producers of the television soap, *Prisoner*, arguing that this controversial series about women in prison had had a detrimental effect on the girls (but not the boys) in his school, I was primed and ready for a spot of Willising.

Prisoner is, of course, something of an Australian television phenomenon. Originally produced in 1979 for the Grundy organisation by Reg Watson of *Crossroads* fame, *Prisoner*, or *Cell Block H* as my American high school students knew it, is probably showing somewhere in the world right at this very moment. It has been one of Australia's most successful TV exports and has prompted a number of academic studies and articles (Stern, 1982; Curthoys and Docker, 1989; Docker and Curthoys, 1994). At the height of its popularity in Australia during the early 1980s, it was the top rated show for young people in the 13 to 17 age group, or at least for those allowed to watch it, since it included strong language, overt lesbianism and a great deal of aggression, both verbal and physical.

And it was the aggression, both verbal and physical, which had particularly worried the headmaster who had written to the TV network; lesbianism wasn't even mentioned. Instead, the letter referred specifically to the ways in which girls in the school were copying the language used in the show and were also forming 'gangs'. Two incidents in particular were recounted in which violence had been threatened (note – only threatened); in the first, one group of girls had threatened another and, in the second, a girl had been injured by a member of the public who had chosen to intervene in a confrontation which otherwise would probably have resolved itself without violence. Although the events described were already two years old when I contacted the media teacher at the school and asked if I could come to talk to him about the events described in the letter, he told me that some of the students involved were actually still in attendance, and that I was more than welcome to talk to them myself. Glossing over the elaborate negotiations with the aforementioned headmaster and the local education authority (which were a necessary prelude to undertaking any research), I set off for the school as a would-be educational ethnographer, not sure what I would find or even do there.[1]

What I did find was a very informative media teacher who told me how, as a result of the headmaster's letter, a producer from the show and one of the actresses (Betty Bobbitt – in costume) had come to the school to talk to twenty 'specially selected' students about the difference between real violence and fictional violence, getting on together, drug use and, oddly enough, euthanasia, since the character played by Bobbitt had originally been imprisoned for helping her friend commit suicide. Even more fortuitously, because a new video camera had arrived in the media department that very week, the whole event had been taped by the media students and made into a documentary entitled *Whose Prisoner?* in which they also interviewed their peers about the show. After viewing this video I then arranged to return to the school and to talk with eleven of the original 'selected' pupils.

It's hard to recall my initial impressions, but I can remember feeling enormous sympathy for those girls who said their school was like a prison and that their teachers were just like 'screws': I'd been both a school student and a teacher and thought I knew what they meant. But I was also acutely aware (thanks to Willis) of all sorts of class issues and (thanks to feminism) of all sorts of gender issues seething away beneath the surface. In the essay I wrote at the time, I talked about gender roles in society, the expectation that 'nice' girls wouldn't swear, form gangs and fight, and how *Prisoner* showed women doing exactly that. I also speculated on how attractive such alternative images might be to young women rejecting those aspects of polite middle class femininity represented by their school and teachers. But it was when the girls started to talk about their futures that the poignancy of the parallels really hit home. Three of them wanted to be policewomen, a not unsurprising number given their obvious interest in crime and punishment. Three wanted to be hairdressers. One wanted to win the lottery and run a farm. Two wanted to study computing but had been excluded from class because their grades were too low. And two had no idea of a future at all, except they knew that they didn't want to get married. All of them were doing very poorly at school in an area of high unemployment. The reality of their futures was, to put it mildly, somewhat bleak: the local shoe factory or the dole loomed.

What I took away from these encounters with the school, the teachers, the students and the neighbourhood was a sense of futility and frustration, especially on the part of the girls to whom I spoke who, even if they had ambitions, already knew that they were unlikely to achieve them. Just as surely as Paul Willis' working-class boys were locked into working-class jobs, these girls were locked into a future of economic hardship, one likely to be further compounded by their almost inevitable choice of motherhood with its subsequent loss of income.

My conclusions were that *Prisoner* as a television series functioned for the girls as an elaborate metaphor for the experience of being female, working class and disempowered: an experience which might well be expressed in aggression towards authority, towards others or themselves. The girls were therefore 'using' the television show *Prisoner* as a reference point for the acting out of their own aggressive rejection of a system which they perceived as both hostile and repressive. The girls were just as hemmed in by economic, cultural and gender constraints as the prisoners were by their bars.

And it's at this point, when talking to teachers, that I usually make my next set of moves. Firstly to point out that the girls' opposition to school and their resistance to polite forms of middle-class femininity was by no means unique or even particularly uncommon. Teachers, if they have any breadth of experience at all, already know this to be true. It's then just a quick side-step to the proposition that *Prisoner* might not have been the 'cause' of the girls aggressive acting out, as suggested by the headmaster. Instead, the girls' mimicry of aspects of the show might have more to do with the ways in which it offered a metaphorical expression of a much bigger and more intractable set of problems in relation to their experience of school, class and gender.

From this point I can go in any number of directions, including showing how this story might illustrate a 'uses and gratifications' approach to media consumption. Alternatively, I might head off into a discussion of the active reader and of reader response theory which would stress how people make sense of the media they consume on the basis of their specific social context and interpretative schema. I might even get into questions of ideology and the ways in which *Prisoner* challenges conventional expectations about how women should look, act and appear in both the media and the wider society, and how disturbing this might be for some – particularly headmasters. And I will also offer a set of handouts, a summary of the topics covered and a list of background books for the teachers to follow up, knowing that, over-worked as they usually are, they'll be hard pressed to find the time to read them.

The telling of my *Prisoner* story is therefore an opening gambit intended to connect teachers' thinking about teaching with different ways of thinking about the role of the media in society. The main point of the anecdote is to direct attention away from the embedded violence of the media product, and back to the potential for violence within the social context in which it is consumed. When I'm addressing student groups, I'm likely to start some-where else.

Talking to students

Undergraduate media students are the easiest to talk to about the media violence debate. This is because my fellow lecturers at La Trobe University and I don't even raise the issue until we've done considerable groundwork in the history of communication theory, of the mass culture debates and of the ways in which media audiences have been constructed in both academic and popular discourses. By the time our students arrive at the media violence debate, they know enough to understand that the relationship between violence in the media and violence in the wider society is not obvious at all.

Talking to secondary school students is a different matter. This I am also asked to do on a regular basis, usually in a very limited time frame and without the opportunity to give them the kind of background to the debate with which we provide our university students. There's also the attention problem: how to make these issues vivid, immediate and engaging, since many of either think they know it all already ('it's obvious, isn't it?') or they're simply not that interested (they weren't going to do that option anyway). And so I tell my Port Arthur story: a story intended to demonstrate that the ways in which the media reports violent crime may be not only misguided but also deliberately misleading and mischievous when they start to speculate on media violence as a causal factor (Turnbull, 1997).

The tragedy of Port Arthur, when 28-year-old Martin Bryant took an automatic rifle to the historic tourist site of Tasmania's first penal settlement and killed 35 people, happened on 28 April 1996. Within days, media speculation about Bryant's motives began to include references to his taste for violent videos, including *Child's Play II*. This latter 'fact', obtained during a cheque book interview with Bryant's alleged girlfriend, immediately sparked an explosion of media speculation which involved a tenuous link to the James Bulger case in England. The fact that the video allegedly involved in the Bulger case was *Child's Play III* didn't bother the Australian press, just as the fact that there was no real evidence that the two 10-year-old boys accused of murdering 2-year-old James Bulger had ever seen that film, let alone been influenced by it, didn't bother their British counterparts (Smith, 1995: 242; Young, 1996: 133–37). The involvement of the supposedly offending video could only be asserted, not proved. Nevertheless, within two weeks of the Port Arthur tragedy, the 'facts' of Bryant's apparently perverse media habits and their connection to other 'similar' cases were being rehearsed in both the tabloid and the broadsheet press. Thus, for example, Melbourne's usually careful *Age* newspaper ran a piece in its television guide entitled 'Do Movies Make Murderers? (*Age Green Guide*, 10 May 1996), linking Wade Frankum, the 'Strathfield Plaza gunman', to the film *Taxi Driver*, and Jon Venables (one of the boys convicted of killing James Bulger) to *Child's Play III* and Bryant to both.[2]

My presentation involves showing these headlines and articles on overheads as I explain how suspicious I was about the kinds of connections that were being made, given that I already had some knowledge of the Bulger case and the ways in which the extremely tenuous link to *Child's Play III* had been exploited in that instance. However, it is at this point that I myself become directly involved in the unfolding of events since, as a result of one of those radio interviews about the media violence debate initiated by the media coverage of Bryant's supposed video habits, I was contacted by a group of lawyers, judges and family conciliators in Hobart, Tasmania, who invited me to speak to them about the coverage of the case on mainland Australia.

And so, six months after the tragedy at Port Arthur and just before Bryant's trial was due to begin, I found myself staying in the very same hotel in downtown Hobart where Bryant had gone for a drink on the eve of his fateful exploit. As the last speaker at the end of a long afternoon, I thus found myself addressing a room full of people, many of whom had been directly affected by the murders, either in their professional or personal lives. Why were these people so interested in the media coverage of the case, given that they themselves had been so immediately concerned? It was quite understandable really. Two days after Bryant's arrest, both the *Hobart Mercury* and a national newspaper, *The Australian*, had published an illegally obtained photograph of Bryant in which the eyes had been digitally altered to make him look more maniacal. The Director of Public Prosecutions in Tasmania had therefore ordered a media blackout because of the risk of prejudice to the outcome of the trial.

So there I was, before the trial began, with my portfolio of headlines and newspaper articles, and my account of the ways in which Bryant was constructed by the press as an innocent child (even though he was 28) corrupted by an evil mass media. The judge who chaired my session kindly reassured me that he didn't think my presentation contravened the media blackout. I chose to believe him.

At the conclusion of my presentation I was approached not only by a TV network, who gave my comments 30 seconds of national coverage, but also (more significantly for my story) by Dr Ian Sale, the forensic psychiatrist who had been the first person to interview Bryant and who had accompanied the police when they searched Bryant's house, which had been left to him by his wealthy benefactor on her death. What Sale told me confirmed my suspicions. There were not 2,000 videos in Bryant's collection, but 1,200, most of which had belonged to his benefactor. Said Sale, with the black humour of those in the caring professions when confronted by the terrible banality of violent crime: 'When we found three copies of *The Sound of Music* and a Kamal tape, we knew we were dealing with a seriously disturbed man.'

What the students to whom I tell this story already know is that Kamal is a middle-aged Sri Lankan singer whose recordings are very popular with elderly women in Australia. And when I tell them that the most disturbing aspect of Bryant's media practices, according to Sale, was the fact that he cited Disney's *The Lion King* as his favourite film, they do seem to get the point.

Of course Bryant was disturbed, as the psychiatric report by Professor Mullen presented at his trial clearly demonstrated (Mullen, 1996). The psychological tests and educational profiles which had been conducted on him when he was a child had already revealed that he was well below average intelligence and emotionally immature. Bryant had always been a problem, displaying all the familiar signs of disturbance such as enjoying torturing small animals and being unable to make and sustain friendships. He was even more socially isolated as an adult, particularly after the suicide of his father, which he blamed on the consequences of an ill-fated property deal with the owners of the Broad Arrow cafe, which is where he first opened fire. Bryant was a volatile cocktail of seething resentments, but what made him even more dangerous was the fact that he was very wealthy as the result of an inheritance from his elderly benefactor, who had promised his deceased father that she would look after him. Bryant had used the money to make long plane journeys which he enjoyed, he said, because he could talk to the people sitting next to him – people who, as Professor Mullen pointed out in his report, 'presumably being strapped to their seats had no choice but to appear friendly (Mullen, 1996)'. But he also used the money to buy a semi-automatic weapon over the counter in Hobart and to wreak his revenge on a community which he considered had rejected him. One of the only good things to come about as a result of the Port Arthur incident was an imme-diate decision on the part of the Prime Minister, John Howard, to effect a tightening of the gun laws in Australia (Stockwell, 1997: 56).

I tell this story dramatically. I am shameless in my use of rhetoric and narrative. But this is also quite deliberate since I want my story to compete for credibility and persuasiveness with those told by the media. I want to encourage students to question what and how they 'know' about the rela-tionship between the media and violence, especially when that knowledge is obtained from the media itself. This they grasp fairly swiftly, since they are usually already ironic and distanced viewers of most media content. What I want them to question is not only the way in which the media will tell a story, but also how it will seek to persuade by using the voice of apparent author-ity, quoting science and experts and seemingly irrefutable facts. To do this I will help them to pull apart a newspaper article (I have a fileful) which cites the statistic that by the time a child is 14 he or she will have witnessed sixty million acts of aggression, or the expert opinion of a child psychologist who states that over a hundred billion clinical trials have proved a direct link between exposure to violence on television and aggressive play. And I will talk about the problems with content analysis and the relevance of scientific methods to measuring complex human behaviour. I may not use terms like empiricism and positivism but these in fact are what I am dealing with. What I will also do is to ask the students to consider the significance of the social context in which violence occurs and how this might be related to questions of moral choice and action.

And so I ask them to relate the issue of media violence back to themselves. What counts as violence in the media? What difference does the context or the genre make? How does violence in the media make them feel? Can it ever be enjoyable? (You bet – I am a huge fan of Hong Kong martial arts films and World Federation Wrestling.) Are some kinds of violence more disturbing than others? What makes them angry and why, and what do they do about it? What I'm trying to do here is to make the students understand that not all violence in the media is the same, and that people make distinctions all the time about what they are watching. Furthermore, that such distinctions are made, not only on the basis of the context of the violence portrayed, but also on the basis of the social and cultural context of the viewer. What worries me most about the media violence debate, and what I want students to interrogate, is the way in which questions of moral responsibility (on the part of both the offender and the offended against) can be neatly avoided by the assertion: the media is to blame. And issues of moral responsibility inevitably lead me towards another set of encounters – those with government.

Talking to government

In many respects, the recent history of government intervention in the media violence debate in Australia repeats the pattern familiar in countries such as Britain and the United States. That is, after a violent incident or series of incidents has galvanised public concern, the government of the day reacts by instituting an inquiry into the relationship between violence in the media and violence in society at large. Thus after two such incidents in Melbourne in 1987 involving two different but similarly disturbed lone gunmen, the so-called Hoddle Street and Queen Street massacres, the Labour government initiated a number of public inquiries, including one conducted by the regulatory body responsible for the broadcast media at the time, the Australian Broadcasting Tribunal (ABT).[3]

As Stuart Cunningham has argued, the terms of reference for the ABT inquiry, *TV Violence in Australia*, clearly embodied a set of assumptions about the portrayal of violence in the media and its consequent undesirable social effects; it was expected that what would emerge would be a set of recommendations for stricter policing and regulation (Cunningham, 1992: 153). The inquiry thus proceeded along what looked like fairly predictable lines. Over 1,100 submissions from members of the public and interested groups were received, briefing sessions with relevant academic and industry researchers were conducted and nation-wide public conferences were held (I attended and spoke at one of these). Although some original research was conducted, this was focused primarily on public perceptions of violence in both the media and the wider society. When finally released in 1990, the conclusions and recommendations of the inquiry were regarded by many of the more conservative forces in the community and government as a cop-out. They were, however, greeted by media academics like myself with some glee because of their insistence on the social and economic roots of violence. The

Tribunal showed itself to be well aware that many factors contribute to violence in society, and argued that watching violence on television is only one of the many which may facilitate aggression away from the television screen, major ones being poverty, stress, unemployment, low self-esteem, family breakdown, challenges to traditional values, and prejudice (ABT, vol.1, 1990). Having pointed to the social and economic roots of violence in society, the Tribunal firmly stated that, in its opinion, the answer to the problem of violence in the media lay not in censorship but in public media education, debate about rules and practices within and across the networks, and an industry-wide self-regulatory code (Cunningham, 1992: 154). If only this enlightened attitude had prevailed.

One of the problems with talking to government about media violence issues is that power is constantly shifting, and that there is a great deal at stake for the government in being seen to be responsive to public concerns. While the ABT inquiry suggested a way forward which was welcome to many, by 1992, following a new Broadcasting Services Act, the Tribunal was replaced by the Australian Broadcasting Authority (ABA) (Spurgeon, 1994: 55). While the ostensible purpose of the new Authority was to oversee the opening up of access to broadcasting licenses and the deregulation of the media industry in Australia in the interests of greater 'diversity', other branches of government were pulling in another direction altogether.

It is an ironic contradiction of capitalism that demands for freedom from economic regulation frequently exist alongside desires for moral constraints, and that these may well work against each other: nowhere was this more evident than in the debate over the introduction of pay television in Australia. At the same time that the Labour government was pushing for deregulation, the upper house of parliament, the Senate, established a Select Committee on Community Standards which effectively stymied (at least for a while) some of the government's deregulatory impulses. The punch-up over whether or not R-rated material should be shown on pay television is described in detail by Spurgeon (1994).[4]

My knowledge of the series of events surrounding R-rated material on pay TV was augmented by a conference encounter with two of the researchers involved in the controversy; they provided me with their own vivid take on the proceedings, and this has inevitably coloured the account which follows.

The brief provided for the researchers, to be addressed under the auspices of the new ABA and overseen by the Senate Select Committee, was to conduct extensive Australia-wide qualitative and quantitative research into community standards of taste and decency in relation to classifications for pay TV and into the permissible levels of sex and violence in this particular medium (Spurgeon, 1994: 57). Having done this, and having found that the community seemed to want R-rated material to be available on pay TV, the researchers presented their findings to the Senate Select Committee, only to be told that they were all wrong: their questionnaires were faulty (they had posed the question about the R-rating too 'positively'), their samples were unrepresentative and, in short, they should go back and do the whole thing again, which they accordingly did. When they presented their findings a second time (which endorsed and even augmented their original ones) they were told that the whole study was fatally flawed; the committee then moved to recommend that R-rated material be banned altogether from pay TV.

Despite this recommendation, however, the Labour government chose to allow the pay TV providers to show R-rated material, as long as they ensured that adequate blocking mechanisms were in place. This decision thus demonstrated the triumph of the economic over the moral and presented me with something of a moral dilemma since I was not sure whether to be delighted or dismayed. In other recent instances, such as the proposed scrapping of a public health system, or the privatisation of the national telecommunications provider, I have been less than happy about arguments based on economic imperatives. The problem with the pay TV debacle was that the right outcome was achieved, but for all the wrong reasons. Despite these contradictions and my own ambivalence about them, what the intervention of the Senate Select Committee served to demonstrate is that there are still those in government who are simply unwilling to entertain a more relaxed attitude to media violence, even when this is apparently endorsed by the public – and especially when it is advocated by academics.

This reluctance became even more apparent as a consequence of yet another disheartening series of incidents in 1995, when the Committee began to make pronouncements about appointments to the board of the Office for Film and Literature Classification, which had established the guidelines on R-rated material in the first place.

Various members of the Committee made it clear on several occasions that, in their opinion, 'film critics and lecturers' should be excluded from membership of the board because their opinions were out of touch with those of the community in general (Huntley, 1995: 7). Apart from the obvious slight to academics and critics, what is even more disheartening about this intervention is that the Senate Select Committee has continued to speak and act as if they, and they alone, are in touch with the community on issues of media censorship and regulation. Furthermore it is clear that this 'community' excludes not only academics and film reviewers but also the gay community and anyone else who isn't considered 'normal'.

And so we come to the crux of the problem with talking to government about media violence: what do they want to hear? Clearly some members of the government are happy to listen to some academics but not to others, and government in general seems very selective in its use of academic opinion and research in the media violence debate. What is wanted are academics who will let them off the hook and cheerfully tell them that of course the media is to blame. What is not wanted are academics who suggest that if government continues to abrogate its responsibility for the moral and social welfare of society (as represented by its investment in education and hospitals, child protection and support services, psychiatric beds and prisons) then violence in society will not only continue but worsen dramatically (Turnbull, 1999).

Talking to myself

Shall I shut up? During the course of the week in which I wrote this chapter while waiting for the telephone to ring, I listened to the radio. My favourite station is a public service network called Radio National, where the emphasis is primarily on talk. Listening to a programme in their *Background Briefing* series on 26 October 1999, I heard the compelling account of a brutal murder committed by an 'intellectually disabled' young man who was deemed fit to plead and sentenced to life imprisonment, although it was doubtful that he had indeed committed the crime or even understood what was going on at his trial. In a coda to the show it was noted that 30 per cent of prisoners in Australian jails have some form of intellectual disability.

On another Radio National programme, *Late Night Live* on 1 November 1999, I heard British journalist Beatrix Campbell revisiting the Bulger case and describing the rehabilitation of one of the two convicted boys, Bobby Thompson.[5] In her account of how this rehabilitation had been achieved, and how it might be reversed if Thompson were transferred to the brutalising conditions of an adult prison, details of Thompson's shocking treatment at the hands of his father and brothers were recalled. I sat in the car even after I had arrived at my destination, listening with anguish to Campbell's description of Thompson's quite appalling childhood, realising that what it revealed, yet again, was the significance of social context and experience in the production of violence in society.

So I won't shut up. It's stories like these which need to be told until the message about media violence gets through. To worry about the alleged effects of violence in the media on violence in society is to worry about the wrong set of issues entirely.

I would like to think that things are changing in Australia, that the debate has gone round so many times that the ground has begun to shift, that people in the community of which I am indeed a part despite what the Senate Select Committee might think are beginning to question the 'obvious' relationship between media representations of violence and violence in the community. I also console myself with the knowledge that every year a new set of media students who have learned to think about the media violence debate in more complex and challenging ways graduates from high schools and universities. Some of them find work in the media, some of them teach. Most of them will, I hope, become well informed and enlightened members of the community who will make themselves heard in this debate, so that they can no longer be spoken for by those who assume to do so, including academics like me.

By the way, the telephone didn't ring. I neither heard nor read any further discussion of the *Scream* stories anywhere. What does this mean? Have they heard it all before? Is it a case of *déjà-entendu*? Is the debate moving on or has it simply got stuck? Perhaps now is the time to try something different: a discussion about the social and moral responsibility of individuals, communities and government for the well-being and safety of us all, a discussion in which the media itself might play a really constructive role. Maybe I'll ring them.

NOTES

1   Note the 'would-be'. I know that the research methods I employed in this case could hardly be called ethnographic. Three years later I undertook another project which might come closer to that description, spending a whole year in a school and studying the media usage of twenty-two young women in the context of their school, family and social experience. This constituted the research component of my PhD dissertation entitled *The Media and Moral Identity: Accounting for Media Practices in the Lives of Young Women*, La Trobe University, 1992.

2   While the Bulger case is familiar to many, that of Frankum is probably less well known. In 1991 taxi driver Frankum killed seven people in a suburban shopping mall in Sydney before turning the gun on himself. His actions were linked by the media not only to his known consumption of X-rated videos and pornography but also to Brett Easton Ellis' already notorious novel *American Psycho* which was reportedly found on his bedside table after the event.

3   The Australian Broadcasting Tribunal (which replaced the Australian Broadcasting Control Board in 1978 and was itself replaced by the Australian Broadcasting Authority in 1992) was the government-funded body responsible for the handling of all commercial TV and radio licenses in Australia. It was also responsible for conducting research into aspects of broadcasting content and policy, a responsibility also assumed to some degree by the Australian Broadcasting Authority.

4   R-rated material is defined in the guidelines of the Office of Film and Literature Classification (OFLC) as material which is legally restricted to adults and as being unsuitable for those under 18 years of age because it contains issues or depictions which require an adult perspective (OFLC 1999). The OFLC is the body which replaced the original Film Censorship Board in the 1980s in Australia and which has responsibility for classifying not only films and videos but also electronic games and printed material. Whilst responsible to government, the Board is supposedly free from government intervention. The issues or depictions requiring an adult perspective include 'violence' which, according to the guidelines for the R classification, should not be excessive, frequent, gratuitous or exploitative; 'sex', which may be simulated but should not be the 'real thing'; and ' coarse language', which is completely unrestricted at this level. R-rated material therefore sits somewhere towards the 'dangerous' end of a spectrum of classification which has at one extreme G for general and at the other RC or Refused Classification. Between RC and R sits X which 'contains sexually explicit material' and which is available on video in only two states: the Northern Territory and the Australian Capital Territory which, coincidentally, is the home of the federal parliament in Canberra.

5   The web site address of Radio National is: http://www.abc.net.au/rn. Transcripts

and tapes of some programmes are available from this site although, at the time of writing, information about the two programmes referred to had not yet appeared.

REFERENCES

Australian Broadcasting Tribunal (1990), *TV Violence in Australia*, 4 vols, Canberra: Australian Government Publishing Service.

Bourke, T. (1990), *Prisoner: Cell Block H, Behind the Scenes*, London: Angus and Robertson.

Cunningham, S. (1992), *Framing Culture: Criticism and Policy in Australia*, Sydney: Allen and Unwin.

Cunningham, S. and Jacka, L. (1996), *Australian Television and International Media-scapes*, Cambridge: Cambridge University Press.

Curthoys, A. and Docker, J. (1989), 'In praise of *Prisoner*' in J. Tulloch and G. Turner (eds) *Australian Television: Programs, Pleasures and Politics*, Sydney: Allen and Unwin.

Docker, J. and Curthoys, A. (1994), 'Melodrama in action: *Prisoner* or *Cell Block H*, in J. Docker, *Postmodernism and Popular Culture*, Cambridge: Cambridge University Press.

Downing, L. (1999), 'The screaming zone: slasher film spectatorship and the inter-active teen audience', *Metro* (in press).

Huntley, R. (1995), 'Queer cuts: censorship and community', *Media International Australia*, 78, pp. 5–12.

Mullen, (downloaded October 1996), 'Psychiatric Report: Martin Bryant', http://www.theage.com.au.

Office for Film and Literature Classification (1999), *Guidelines for the Classification of Films and Videos (Amendment no. 2)*, www.oflc.gov.au (downloaded December 7, 1999).

Smith, D. (1995) *The Sleep of Reason: The James Bulger Case*, London: Arrow Books.

Spurgeon, C. (1994) 'Black white & blue: program classifications for pay TV', *Media Information Australia*, 72, pp. 55–61.

Stern, L. (1982), 'The Australian cereal: home grown television', in S, Dermody *et al.*, eds, *Nellie Melba, Ginger Meggs and Friends*, Malmesbury, Victoria: Kibble Books.

Stockwell, S. (1997), 'Panic at the Port', *Media International Australia*, 85, pp. 56–61.

Turnbull, S. (1995), 'Dying beautifully: crime aesthetics and the media', *Australian Journal of Communication*, 22: 1, pp. 1–13.

Turnbull, S. (1997), 'On looking in the wrong places: Port Arthur and the media violence debate', *Australian Quarterly*, 69: 1, pp. 41–59.

Turnbull, S. (1999), 'Lolita: neither seen nor heard', *Metro*, 119, pp. 22–7.

Willis, P. (1977), *Learning to Labour*, Farnborough: Saxon House.

Young, A. (1996), *Imagining Crime: Textual Outlaws and Criminal Conversations*, London: Sage.

7

I WAS A TEENAGE HORROR FAN

Or, 'How I learned to stop worrying and love Linda Blair'

Mark Kermode (Age 36)

My first introduction to the world of horror and sci-fi came in the early 1970s through watching a regular spot on ITV called 'The Monday X Film'. At around about 11.00, when everyone else was in bed, I would sneak down into the family living room and sit entranced by a selection of creaky (but crucially *always* colour) horror flicks, usually from the Hammer or Amicus stable. No matter that I had to have the volume turned down so far that it was impossible to hear anything that was being said: what was captivating was the electrifying atmosphere, the sense of watching something that was forbidden, secretive, taboo. It was, indeed, my first real experience of discovering something that was uniquely *mine*, something that existed outside the domain of my parents' control and authority.

I also sensed from the very beginning that there was something incomprehensibly significant about the actions being played out on-screen, something which spoke to me in a language I didn't quite understand. Like a novice watching opera for the first time and recognising something in the gestures but nothing of the language, I felt from the outset that beyond the gothic trappings these movies had something to say to *me* about *my* life. I just didn't have any idea what . . .

Like any enthusiast, I rapidly discovered that there was secondary literature available about my particular obsession. I remember first finding a copy of *Castle of Frankenstein* in a local newsagent, and being both thrilled and terrified, desperate to buy it, but frankly scared of what buying it would *mean*. What would the newsagent think? Would he look at me in a different way from then on? Would he tell my mum? More important, would he actually sell it to me? The bizarre realisation that the newsagent neither noticed nor indeed cared what I was buying soon gave way to a weird sense, first, of anti-climax, then of dawning horror when I finally got to read *Castle of Frankenstein*. What was disappointing was the fact that the magazine didn't talk about any of the movies I had actually seen – although I'd watched only a handful, I just assumed that any horror magazine would deal in detail with the twenty or so movies that I'd stumbled across. Instead, *Castle of Frankenstein* opened the door on a frankly incomprehensible world of films of which I had never heard, people I didn't recognise, from countries I never knew existed.

From furtive but devoted fan, I was suddenly (and terrifyingly) transformed into a know-nothing dilettante who had no right even to profess an interest in horror movies. Here were people who *knew* what they were talking about, grown-up people who had been doing this for *years*, who actually *understood* what these movies were about. (Flicking back through those early issues, I notice that no less a notable than Joe Dante served as assistant editor on *Castle of Frankenstein*.) I still remember vividly the cold, clammy, slightly panicky feeling I got sitting on a wall opposite Christ's College School in Finchley, realising that I was simply never going to get up to speed with the back catalogue of horror which stretched back to the 1930s and beyond. I was *never* going to be able to remember Boris Karloff's real name, pick out Elsa Lanchester in a line-up, or name any of the directors, writers and cameramen who had steered Hammer through the hey-day of the 1960s. I was completely at sea, drowning in the realisation that the scab I had been gently picking had suddenly fallen away to reveal a vast, gaping, chasmic wound.

The second event of real significance in my education as a horror fan came with the British release in 1974 of *The Exorcist*, William Friedkin's ground-breaking shocker which sparked off an international wave of media-fuelled hysteria. My first knowledge of the movie came via a feature on the early-evening BBC magazine programme *Nationwide*. In a three-minute segment, Sue Lawley quickly recapped the film's plot (a young girl becomes demonically possessed), recounted Stateside tales of audience hysteria, questioned the involvement of teenage actress Linda Blair, and wondered whether the film shouldn't be banned in the UK. I was transfixed. Unlike the classic gothic horror fantasies which had played on late-night TV, here was a movie set in the present day, with everyday people, apparently based on real-life experiences, which (if the reports were to be believed) was literally driving viewers insane. The idea of such a movie scared the living daylights out of me and, oddly, drove me straight back to the safer pastures of Karloff, Lugosi and Lee, in whose company I now began to feel profoundly safe. Reading about (and even watching) the classic chillers began to seem almost a respectable pastime, compared to the ground-shaking horror that lurked out there in the form of *The Exorcist*.

I began to pursue a pseudo-scholarly interest in pre-1970s horror, deceiving myself that I had no interest in the shocking turn which the genre had taken in the wake of *The Exorcist*. What I really wanted to know about, I told myself, was how much nice, avuncular Vincent Price or Peter Cushing could remember about the good old days of horror. Yet whenever any of my older friends (I was 11 or 12 by now) claimed to have seen *The Exorcist* I would pump them mercilessly for information about it, demanding that they recount each scene as if they were witnesses to some appalling crime. And all the time I insisted that I *really wasn't interested in it at all.*

What was infuriating was that, for the most part, neither were they. They hadn't sat there (as to my mind they should have done) taking notes, drinking in every scrap of information on-screen, studiously committing to memory every image that passed before their eyes. Maddeningly, they had seen the film, been scared by it, then wandered out of the cinema and back into the mundanity of their everyday lives. It had not had any profound impact upon them whatsoever. And they really weren't that interested in talking about it. They generally wanted to talk about girls and football, both of which seemed to me as alien as the blob-headed monsters in *This Island Earth.*

For the second time, I was made profoundly aware of the absolute divide between horror fans and everybody else in the world; only by now I knew absolutely which side of the divide I was on. Finally, frustrated by the inability of anyone else to tell me what I needed to know in the kind of depth and detail that I needed to know it, I succumbed, and turned back to the new breed of horror and fantasy magazines that were arriving from the States to fill the gap. I first fell into the company of *Cinefantastique* through a newsagent in Muswell Hill which had clearly stocked it by mistake. Inside its pages I found interviews with the writer, director, cast and crew of *The Exorcist*, along with sombre under-stated stills (any graphic material was fiercely defended by the film's distributors), and a series of in-depth readings of the film. Unable to trace any further copies of the magazine locally, I began to venture into central London, where a series of vintage magazine and movie memorabilia stores sat cheek-by-jowl with seedy-looking strip-clubs and porn vendors. Going up to Soho on a Saturday became a regular quest to track down back issues of *Castle of Frankenstein, Famous Monsters, C.F.Q.* and *Quasimodo's Monster Magazine.*

Then, in 1979, the new bible of hard-core horror fandom, *Fangoria*, began to arrive in the UK, bringing with it a garishly modern approach to horror which seemed oddly in tune with the post-punk nihilism blighting British youth culture. It wasn't for nothing that *Fango* earned the affectionate nickname 'Exploding Heads Monthly'. For all its up-market production values, *Fango* was the Sex Pistols of horror fanzines, loud, noisy, visually graphic and absolutely guaranteed to send your parents apoplectic with righteous indignation. It was terrific! At around the same time I started frequenting the Phoenix cinema in East Finchley which every Friday and Saturday night played late-night double bills of the sort of culty horror and fantasy films that I'd by now read so much about.

From around the age of 15 (1978 or so) it was possible to get into X-rated movies with ease, particularly late-nighters, and I began to spend every weekend either at the Phoenix or at the Scala, losing myself in *Night of the Living Dead, Rosemary's Baby, The Possession of Joel Delaney, The Crazies, Eraserhead* and, of course, *The Exorcist*.

Going to see these movies was essentially a lonely pursuit since no one at school shared my enduring enthusiasm for horror. Most of them would go and see a current mainstream horror picture maybe once a year – *Halloween, Friday the Thirteenth, Carrie* and so on – and considered it something to be endured, a test of machismo, an instantaneous thrill (and often a great way to cop off) but nothing more. Only at the late-nighters would I find myself surrounded by other 'loners' who, like me, weren't there to impress anybody but themselves, and who were clearly getting more out of the movies than passing scares, watching them again and again, learning them, studying them.

Although I almost never said anything to any of these people (one thing we seemed to have in common was that we were all lousy conversationalists) an odd bond was formed by seeing the same faces at the same cinemas, watching the same movies, time after time. In fact, there was something profoundly 'conversational' about the act of watching the movies, something that joined us together as a group in our increasingly knowing reactions to what was happening on-screen.

A prime element in this was the fact that the movies themselves seemed acutely aware of their audience. More than any other genre, horror movies play to and feed upon the knowledgeability of their fans. Directors, writers, actors, even special-effects men, all become recognisable to devotees who provide the hard-core fan-base for the genre. Through the pages of *Fangoria* – and later *Gore Zone* – we had met these people in their natural surroundings, seen photographs of them goofing around with severed latex heads, and read their behind-the-scenes accounts of how the movies got made. We understood that when special-effects maestro Tom Savini popped up on-screen as 'third bystander from the left' (as he did with increasing frequency) it was the film-makers' way of winking at the fans in the audience, to which the correct response was a knowing laugh. I remember forming a fleeting bond with a fellow movie-goer at a screening of *The Fly* at the Manchester Oxford Road Odeon in the 1980s when an on-screen doctor preparing to abort Geena Davis' insect foetus turned out to be director David Cronenberg. While everyone else cringed, the two of us chuckled smugly from opposite sides of the auditorium, like ships signalling each other in deep fog. I don't know who the other person was, but I bet they had a stackful of *Fangos* under their bed.

Just as film-makers' faces are familiar to the horror fans, so generic conventions of plot, narrative, character and dialogue become the play-things of writers and directors well versed in the genre, as do recurrent visual motifs and archetypal images. While Quentin Tarantino litters his hugely popular

129

movies with nods and winks to the films which inspired him, so horror has a tendency endlessly to recycle its own history. Like the climactic sequence from Joe D'Amato's *Anthropophagous* in which the ravenous cannibal disembowels himself only to begin chomping upon his own intestines, so horror movies have habitually found sustenance from devouring their own flesh. For the horror fan, the recognition of these recycled elements is a crucial part of the enjoyment and appreciation of the movies.

At its most basic, this is merely a rarefied form of 'getting the joke', of feeling 'in the know', of understanding that a knife is never just a knife. Produce a chainsaw on-screen in a horror movie, and the devoted fan will automatically click into a celluloid history dating back to Tobe Hooper's ground-breaking *Texas Chainsaw Massacre*, and marauding to the present day via the parodic excesses of *Motel Hell, Hollywood Chainsaw Hookers, Bad Taste, The Evil Dead* and, of course, *Texas 2, 3* and *4.* To the genre fan, a chainsaw is not a threatening weapon – it's a magical talisman, conjuring up a heritage of horror.

Gory special effects, constantly the target of attacks by the censors and media pundits alike, work upon disparate audiences in a similarly polarised manner. A key problem in persuading non-horror fans that genre devotees are not a pack of marauding sadists hell-bent on destruction (I wish!) lies in the recurrent inability of untrained viewers to see past the special effects, puncture the gaudy surface of the movies, pull apart their rubbery rib-cages and grasp their dark thematic hearts. Essentially a surrealist genre, contemporary horror demands to be read metaphorically rather than literally. Throughout the 1980s, advanced latex special-effects processes allowed directors like David Cronenberg, Brian Yuzna and Clive Barker to stretch the envelope of on-screen surrealism with a previously impossible ease.

Yet the work of all these directors is meaningless if taken at face value. The bizarre physical mutations of *Videodrome*, the body 'shunting' of *Society*, the skin-flailing tortures of *Hellraiser* – none of these on-screen wonders are intended to be read as depictions of 'real' physical possibilities. Instead, each film uses body-based special effects to address a range of issues (the power of the televisual image, the nature of inter-class conflict, the sadomasochistic allure of desire) which have little or nothing to do with actual bodily contortions. The horror fan understands this, and is thus not only able but positively compelled to 'read' rather than merely 'watch' such movies. The novice, however, sees only the dismembered bodies, hears only the screams and groans, reacts only with revulsion or contempt. Being unable to differentiate between the real and the surreal, they consistently misinterpret horror fans' interaction with texts which mean nothing to them. Just as, to me, all opera is basically fat people shouting at each other, many opera fans clearly believe that all horror is crazy people torturing and killing each other. Neither of us has an effective take on the chosen fetish of the other. The only difference is, I don't go round calling for opera to be banned.

One clear example of the way in which fans' knowledge affects their viewing of a movie is the case of Sam Raimi's *The Evil Dead*. A gruesomely satirical first feature, *The Evil Dead* is in essence a horror farce, a violent comedy which strives to elicit a response of startled hilarity from its audience. The movie was shot in America in the early 1980s using finance raised from local shop-keepers, dentists and hardware store owners by a group of enthusiastic young film-makers, equally well versed in the traditions of horror and slapstick. Praised in the horror press for its feisty verve, *The Evil Dead* scored a major hit with fans, but ran into trouble with British censors. In UK cinemas, the movie was cut by forty seconds by the British Board of Film Classification, who recognised its ghoulish flair, but couldn't countenance its self-parodic excesses. In February 1983 (before the introduction of the Video Recordings Act) Palace Video released this cut version on to the video rental market, unfortunately coinciding with the rise of press-fuelled hysteria about 'video nasties'.

In the panic that followed, *The Evil Dead* was cited by the Director of Public Prosecutions as potentially likely to deprave and corrupt, and a number of video dealers stocking the title were prosecuted (with varying results) under the Obscene Publications Act. In courts up and down the country, juries utterly unfamiliar with the horror genre or the audience which it attracts, were asked to respond either to key scenes from the movie or to written check-lists of the violent acts depicted therein. Unsurprisingly, their reaction tended to be one of shock – to them, the catalogue of on-screen dismemberment which the movie offered was nothing more than unashamed sadism, designed to delight those who would revel in pain.

Crucially, this is not how the movie plays to horror fans. It's not just that the juries who considered this sadistic pleasure to be the primary function of *The Evil Dead* were over-reacting to the on-screen atrocities; it's that they were literally seeing an entirely different movie from that which had delighted *Fango* readers the world over. To the uninitiated viewer, *The Evil Dead* was a gruelling horror picture in which human bodies were mercilessly hacked to pieces. To erudite horror fans, it was *The Three Stooges* with latex and ketchup standing in for custard pies, a knockabout romp in which everything is cranked up to eleven, and in which pain and suffering play no part. As James Ferman rightly observed: 'With *The Evil Dead*, the name of the game is excess.'

The reason for this disparity of opinion between jurors and genre-hounds is not (as is sometimes suggested) that horror fans have become hardened or insensitive to violence through years of exposure to sadistic material. The truth is simply that the experienced horror fan understands the on-screen action in terms of a heritage of genre knowledge which absolutely precludes the possibility of sadistic titillation. Nowhere in *The Evil Dead* does the horror fan see the actual torture, mutilation or violation of the human form (as they *would* do in a movie like John McNaughton's solidly unfunny

Henry: Portrait of a Serial Killer). What they do see is the playful trashing of a tradition of special-effects work, in which the refining of various latex additives has opened up vistas of possibilities for enthusiastic amateur film-makers everywhere. To the horror fan, *The Evil Dead* is about as threatening as a pop group smashing up their guitars on stage – it's stupid, but it's huge fun none the less. And just as it's impossible for any modern pop group to ram a guitar through the front of a vast Marshall stack without invoking the ghost of axe-wielding legend Pete Townshend, so it is impossible for any horror fan to see the chainsaw sequence in *The Evil Dead* without indulging in a knowing laugh. They're not laughing at pain, they're laughing at the movie. Or, more precisely, they're laughing *with* the movie.

This is not to say that all horror movies rely upon humour. Far from it – there is clearly very little to find funny in films as diverse as *The Haunting*, *Night of the Living Dead*, *The Exorcist*, *Dead Ringers*, *The Vanishing*, *Cronos* or *Henry: Portrait of a Serial Killer*. These are movies which work because they are *deadly* serious, and horror fans understand absolutely the difference between these brutal masterpieces and the up-beat buffoonery of *The Evil Dead*. Yet, crucially, those ill-versed in the genre generally have no means of distinguishing between these wildly different strands. To the average bleary-eyed juror, there is simply no difference between the gory goings-on of the farcical *Brain Dead* or the bleaker-than-bleak *Dawn of the Dead*. But, to the horror fan, these movies are as unalike as *Apocalypse Now* and *Whoops! Apocalypse*.

Similarly, experience has taught me that only those who have dutifully ploughed through hour upon hour of indescribable European dreck tend to have any truly valid concept of the difference between a good and bad horror movie. And, as the fans know only too well, even within the infinite sub-divisions of the horror genre there are vast differences between the good and the bad, whether it be cannibal movies (*Cannibal Holocaust* vs *Cannibal Ferox*), serial killer movies (*Manhunter* vs *The New York Ripper*), zombie movies (*Dawn of the Dead* vs *Zombie Flesh Eaters*), latter-day vampire movies (*Near Dark* vs *Innocent Blood*), demonic kids movies (*The Omen* vs *The Good Son*), psycho-automobile movies (*Duel* vs *Christine*), or even Freddy Krueger movies (*Nightmare on Elm St. Parts 1, 3* and *7* vs *Parts 2, 4* and *6*).

Knowing, understanding and arguing about the difference between these movies is an integral part of horror fandom. And the place where these debates rage is across the pages of the current horror magazines, the direct descendants of *Famous Monsters* and *Castle of Frankenstein* which them-selves owe a hereditary debt to EC comics and their ghoulish predecessors. What is most encouraging about the best of these publications is their inter-national dimension, the fact that no self-respecting horror magazine (unlike the majority of mainstream cinema mags) is considered complete without in-depth coverage of the works of European film-makers like Mario Bava,

Dario Argento, Lucio Fulci, Michele Soavi, Guillermo del Toro, even the irredeemably tiresome Jess Franco. It's not for nothing that Britain's own *Shivers* accurately described itself (before its disappointing relaunch) as 'The Global Magazine of Horror'. Nor would any self-respecting horror fan be unprepared to discuss in detail the often minute dissimilarities between English, French, Italian, German and Japanese versions of the same horror movie. In fact, I can think of no other cinematic genre in which internationalism is so genuinely championed, and in which linguistic boundaries are so nimbly over-stepped.

The watch-word of horror fans is 'completist', and it is in this arena that publications such as Tim Lucas' indispensable *Video Watchdog* really come into their own. Only a die-hard horror devotee such as Lucas could have made internationally viable a magazine whose primary purpose was to document the tiny differences between versions of movies available across the world. And, unlike the mainstream film magazines which can blithely pass over the small factual blips and inconsistencies which litter their pages, *Video Watchdog* is subject to the sort of intense scrutiny usually afforded only to legal documents. Horror fans *need* to know this kind of detailed information, and they are very unforgiving of inaccuracy. As director Joe Dante has said, *Video Watchdog* is less a film magazine than a survival manual – it simply cannot get things wrong. Indeed, in a market-place in which there is no legal requirement for a distributor to declare that a film may have been abridged from its original format, *Video Watchdog* is often the only source of product information which in other areas would be strictly monitored by trading standards and weights-and-measures laws. If only such publications existed for all areas of cinema!

A logical extension of the on-going consumer dialogue pioneered by horror fanzines is the horror film festivals which flourished in Britain in the late 1980s, and which have a healthy tradition throughout Europe and the States. In Britain, the ground was broken by the indefatigable 'Shock around the Clock', which brought together spotty adolescents from around the country to pig out on twenty-four hours of international terror. Organised by Alan Jones and Stefan Jaworzyn, the mercurial talents behind the UK horror magazine *Shock Xpress*, 'Shock around the Clock' paved the way for subsequent festivals like 'Black Sunday' (a Northern riposte to the capital-based 'Shock'), 'Splatterfest' and, ultimately, 'Fantasm' at the National Film Theatre, an up-market affair which continues to delight audiences with its varied range of international shockers. (The fact that the air in the 'Fantasm' auditorium is generally breathable and that the projectionists usually put the reels through in the right order also adds a charm often lacking in other such gatherings.)

In Europe, the horror festival brand-leader for many years was Milan's currently dormant 'Dylan Dog' festival, an absolute riot of an event in which thousands of screaming kids greeted each new chiller with a rock star's reception, chanting, cheering, whooping and whistling. And here's a bizarre thing – for some unfathomable reason, the teenage horror devotees who roamed the streets of Italy and crowded out the 'Dylan Dog' enormodrome *weren't* the malnourished, acne-ridden pasty-faces that we know and love in Britain. On the contrary, they were sparkling young things, dashingly elegant in their designer jeans and logo-blasted T-shirts, hair cut *à la mode*, and generally paired off in a manner that suggested sexual achievement. In a frankly inexplicable biological quirk, Italy has somehow managed to breed good-looking movie geeks, a fact I find more profoundly shocking than anything I have ever seen in a horror movie. Elsewhere in Europe, Sitges and Oporto continue to play host to popular annual horror festivals (and public entrance to these tends to be on the increase); while, in America, *Fangoria's* annual conventions get bigger each year. For British fans, cut ever deeper by the UK's censorious scissors, these festivals are becoming increasingly important. Where else can British fans see these movies as they were intended, and not in the BBFC-approved bastardised versions, which have been slashed to pieces by people who have neither any affection for, nor understanding of, the horror genre?

And here is perhaps the greatest irony of horror fandom in the UK. For here an obsession which absolutely demands rigorous attention to detail, which thrives upon intense research and the patient devotion of the true completist, is utterly thwarted from the outset by the clumsy bludgeoning of genre-illiterate censors. If there were ever a genre in which cutting and banning could do nothing but harm to both the movies and their audience, then it is the horror genre. It is perhaps unsurprising that, of all the issues which recur through the pages of British horror mags past and present such as *Samhain, Fear, The Dark Side, Shivers, Eyeball, Ungawa!* and *Shock Xpress*, censorship has generally commanded more column inches than any other subject. Personally, I look forward to the time when European trading laws make a legal mockery of the senseless snippings and belligerent bannings which blight so many horror films in the UK. In the mean time, as I slip my uncut copy of *Texas Chainsaw Massacre 4* into the video machine, I remember the illicit thrill I got as a child sneaking downstairs to ogle 'The Monday X Film' undetected by my parents. It doesn't matter if the movie isn't any good (and, believe me, *Texas 4* is no good at all). It's the fact that you're not supposed to be watching it which makes it fun.

8

'LOOKS LIKE IT HURTS'

Women's responses to shocking entertainment

Annette Hill

'It was very violent, very gory but I really, really enjoyed it – so
there you are.

(21-year-old female student)

In the early days of our relationship, my partner often took me to the
movies. We saw *Reservoir Dogs*, *Bad Lieutenant*, *Man Bites Dog*, and *Henry,
Portrait of a Serial Killer* all in the space of a few months. These films had a
reputation; they were examples of a 'new brutalism' in cinema, and we were
warned by family, friends and concerned film reviewers to steer clear of
them, in case this new breed of violent movies warped our minds, and gave
us murderous intentions.[1] We loved them. The films were challenging, exciting, in-your-face. And we were not alone. Other people enjoyed watching
these movies too.

This chapter is about movie-goers, like me, who enjoy watching shocking
entertainment. The media effects tradition commonly perceives fans of violent movies as either social deviants or vulnerable viewers (Barlow and Hill,
1985; Van Evra, 1990). In Ben Elton's *Popcorn*, a novel about media effects,
the psychopathic murderer is a fan of violent movies: he tells a Hollywood
director 'you make killing cool' (Elton, 1996: 282).[2] Such stigmatisation of
viewers of violent film dominates discussion of audiences and media violence.[3] My research into fans of violent movies problematises the media
effects tradition and its presumption that viewing pleasure is based on
deviancy, and amorality.

In this chapter I summarise this research. My main research aim was to
give fans of violent movies a voice. Scanning through the many books on
media violence I realised the natural audience for violent movies was almost
invisible.[4] What is more, the natural female audience for violent movies
appeared to be in hiding.[5] I told myself: I like to watch violent movies; I am
not a psychopath (trust me on this); there must be more people like me who
want to talk about watching shocking entertainment. I was right. There isn't
space in this chapter to outline the full findings of my discussions with

viewers of violent movies (see Hill, 1997; 1999), but there is space to explore some of the main points people made when explaining why they like to watch films which are notorious for their violent content. Their discussion illustrates the complex reasons why people are attracted to violent movies.

In particular, I want to reflect on my own personal relationship with other fans of violent cinema. How did my experience of watching *Reservoir Dogs*, or *Pulp Fiction* compare with other fans? In one discussion, a 27-year-old female college teacher commented: 'I don't know a woman who wouldn't go and see these movies but I know plenty of women who would, who wouldn't think it was odd, they shouldn't be watching it or they shouldn't be exposed to it.' Her comment struck home. During the research, I wanted to give voice to male and female fans of violent movies, but I was particularly interested in understanding why other women liked to watch violent films. My taste in violent cinema is often interpreted by other people as 'odd', particularly by other women who shake their heads, in confusion and ask me 'why would you want to watch something like that?', 'something like that' meaning violent films are unspeakable, repulsive and often involve violence towards women.[6] The representation of violence in cinema is a topic for another chapter, but my aim here is to explore the attractions of 'new brutalist' films for women. I want to show this attraction is not based on deviancy or amorality, but rather it is an attraction to the aesthetics of film, the range of emotional and physical responses to watching film, and the experience of testing responses to violent cinema.

Some notes on the research process

This research into people who watch violent movies draws on the qualitative research tradition. I conducted self-contained focus groups, as the advantage of focus groups is that they provide an opportunity to collect data from group interaction (see Morgan, 1988). Men and women, aged 18+, who had seen three or more target films, were recruited to take part in the focus group discussions.[7] The majority of participants were British and aged between 18 and 30 years old.[8] The discussions were transcribed and analysed using qualitative data analysis, which allowed me to focus on language use, and look for repetition, and emergent themes in the raw data (see Morgan, 1988). The quotations in this chapter are illustrative of a range of issues that emerged from the data and are typical articulations of the sample as a whole.[9]

The target movies discussed and shown in the focus groups are typical examples of the kinds of movies commonly reported as embodying 'extreme violence'.

Released in Britain during 1990 to 1995, they were categorised by the popular press as extreme, and brutal 'violent' movies. When *Reservoir Dogs* was released in the UK in January 1993, journalists and film critics

Film	Director/Year
Reservoir Dogs	Quentin Tarantino, 1992
Pulp Fiction	Quentin Tarantino, 1994
True Romance	Tony Scott, 1993
Natural Born Killers	Oliver Stone, 1994
Man Bites Dog	Belvaux, Bonzel, Poelvoorde, 1992
Henry, Portrait of a Serial Killer	John McNaughton, 1990 (Prod. 1986)
Bad Lieutenant	Abel Ferrara, 1992
Killing Zoe	Roger Avary, 1994

highlighted Tarantino's 'cinema of viscera'.[10] Shaun Usher, in the *Daily Mail*, wrote a review of *Reservoir Dogs* titled: 'Deadly Dogs Unleash a Whirlwind of Violence.'[11] A week after the UK release date of *Reservoir Dogs* (8 January 1993), *Man Bites Dog* was released, and only a few weeks after that *Bad Lieutenant* gained its theatrical release (19 February 1993).[12] This prompted journalists to speak of a 'new wave' of visceral films which re-fuelled the debate about screen violence. The *Daily Telegraph* asked the question, 'Are These Films Too Violent?',[13] and interrogated James Ferman of the British Board of Film Classification about why he released these 'new brutalist' films. The hype surrounding the release of *Reservoir Dogs* and related films ensured my participants were well aware of the notoriety of these 'violent' films, through reading newspapers and magazines, watching TV entertainment programmes and talking to friends.

What's new about 'new brutalist' films?

Although 'new brutalist' films like *Reservoir Dogs* were primarily talked about in the popular press in relation to extreme scenes of violence, many women in my study chose to highlight aesthetic issues, such as narration and characterisation, as one of the main reasons they liked these films. Hannah, a 21-year-old student, explained: 'With *Pulp Fiction* and *Reservoir Dogs*, I enjoyed the plot and I enjoyed the story and I enjoyed the characters and the violence was just something that happened in it.' Her repetition of the word 'enjoy' in conjunction with narrative and characterisation makes a clear point that the reason she liked this film is not solely because it is 'violent'. Katie, a 30-year-old administration assistant, echoed this response: 'For me, *Reservoir Dogs* is an excellent film and violence is fourth or fifth on the list of what was interesting about it.' Like many women in the study, Hannah and Katie saw the 'violence' in new brutalist films as incidental to their enjoyment of these movies.

What is 'interesting' and 'enjoyable' about these films is that they offer something distinctive to the viewer. One common theme in the discussions was these types of films were perceived as different to other violent movies, in particular Hollywood action movies (Hill, 1999). Angela, a 31-year-old homeopath, explained why she thought 'new brutalist' films were different to action movies:

> I think what's interesting about the sort of Tarantinoesque films is that you can't necessarily [anticipate the violence] but with a major Hollywood film you know it's coming because of things like the music and the scene building and the – you definitely know what is going to happen in a *Terminator 2* situation or a you know a *Die Hard* sort of film but with the new sort of violent cinema I think it's more difficult to anticipate and that makes it – scarier – well more challenging, it makes it much more challenging, much more interesting. It is much more imaginative.

In order to explain what is different about these films, Angela lists common devices in Hollywood film which cue the audience when to expect a violent scene. However, the 'new' films are 'interesting' and 'challenging', and Angela uses these adjectives twice to emphasise how *Reservoir Dogs*, or *Pulp Fiction* offer something beyond the traditional action movie.[14] Her comparison with other films only serves to show what is different about the experience of watching 'new brutalist' films. What exactly is this difference?

When I asked Angela if she had experienced anything like watching 'new brutalist' films before, her friend, Alison, a 31-year-old student, interjected 'It's a new experience every time you see something like that.' For Alison what is 'new' about these films is linked to her uncertainty about the characters' motivation and actions: 'I think the thing that does it for me is the unpredictability of the actors. You don't know what they are going to do whereas in *Die Hard* you know exactly what is going to happen, you know the plot.' For Angela, on the other hand, what is challenging about these films is linked to her strong emotional and physical response:

> I get palpitations quite often, mm, it's quite awful to admit but I often feel a sense of excitement when I watch violence. Actually, if I'm totally truthful, suppressed anger that I've got working its way out. When I go to see a violent film I often feel quite high after I've seen it, you know you come out from a – maybe not so much with the more realistic stuff, you know, like *Pulp Fiction*, or whatever, but, no, I do actually. I think it can breed excitement in a sense. I think it's the adrenalin as well, you know. Yeah you do feel that kind of heightened awareness I think after you've seen violence.

The films are stimulating; they breed, multiply excitement. For Angela, her admission she often exorcises her anger through watching violent films leads to what she calls a 'heightened awareness'. This heightened awareness is what makes the films challenging to watch. The films are challenging not only because of the violence, although this is part of it, but because the combination of characterisation and narrative used in the films can generate excitement, anger, uncertainty, in short, a rollercoaster of emotional and physical responses. Angela's reaction to the ear-amputation scene from *Reservoir Dogs* illustrates this range of response:

> I felt my heart was slightly beating a little bit faster and I felt kind of, you know, that adrenalin kind of feeling when you're frightened or upset by something. I don't think it's in terms of a conscious, you know, like imagination of what's happening but there is that awful feeling of – oh my God something violent, something disgusting is going on, you know. It's not that I was playing it out to make a scene in my head but I was sort of experiencing something, sort of a bit horrifying, I suppose, but not on a very conscious level. It was very good, I liked it.

Jill, a 27-year-old college teacher, described her attraction to *Reservoir Dogs*:

> You just kind of feel that although it is really, really funny, you know, you are also invited to think, why am I laughing at this, you know, this is really painful, look what's happening. And then as if you didn't get a reminder of just how bad it can be to be shot, you know, you get the shot of Tim Roth on the floor, bleeding to death, you know. I think if the film can encourage you to sort of think, instead of watching *Die Hard* where you just accept the violence as a matter of course. I mean if you can sort of be made to think about it in some way? . . . I think you go and see a film like *Reservoir Dogs*, you know, and, I mean, I don't feel de-sensitised to it because it's dealt with in such a different way that it looks like it hurts, you know, it really looks like it hurts and so it still strikes me every time I see it how painful it is, you know.

Like the other fans in the study, Jill classifies these films as different to Hollywood action movies. Her language – 'painful, bad, shot, bleeding, hurts' – emphasises her response to the violence in the film. For her, 'new brutalist' films deal with extremes, in this instance the extremes of humour and pain in *Reservoir Dogs*, and this encourages her to reflect on the issue of violence.

The way these women describe their responses to 'new brutalist' films is certainly something I can relate to. The films are different to action movies. I like action movies, but the spectacle of violence in action films invites a more undemanding response.[15] Sometimes I want this kind of experience, particularly after a stressful day at work, but when I see a film like *Reservoir Dogs* I know the narrative, characterisation and style of the film work to explore violence in a more extreme and challenging manner. So far, fans of violent movies have said that what is challenging about these films is the unpredictability of the characters and stories, the invitation to experience powerful emotional and physical responses, such as anger, excitement, laughter and surprise, and the film's invitation to make you think about the consequences of violence. What also makes these films challenging is the personal response of the viewer to violence depicted on screen. If the violence 'looks like it hurts': why would anyone be attracted to this?

The attractions of film violence

There is something about watching a violent movie like *Pulp Fiction*, or *Man Bites Dog*, which is challenging on a personal level. At least, that is my experience, and one that fans of violent movies repeatedly discussed in their response to these films. As this 34-year-old mother succinctly put it: 'You are always having to push against boundaries.' Another woman, a 31-year-old video tape operator, described her response in a more energetic manner: 'I love the thrill of daring yourself to watch a violent scene – that's a real kick – no, I'm not going to watch and then, yeah, just do it, make yourself watch it.'

For female fans of violent movies, the fact that society does not usually expect women to watch violent films, in particular notorious violent movies, means there was a twofold reason for testing boundaries.[16] For some women, watching violent movies was seen as a masculine domain. Angela, who spoke about her heightened awareness after watching films like *Reservoir Dogs* in the previous section, echoed other women in the study when she reflected on the perceived gender difference in responses to violent film:

> I think there is a difference between the way men and women react to violence and I think a lot of it is a conditioned response, you know. And it is okay for women to scream but it's, you know, a lot of men don't feel comfortable doing that kind of thing . . . Generally I find that I do try to make myself watch things actually. I find that interesting. Why people don't watch it, why is it men make themselves watch, you know, and I find I've got an element of that in my personality as well, that I will force myself to watch things – kind of like a test or something.

Angela's reaction to violence in film is to test her responses. Although society may expect her to be squeamish about representations of violence, she challenges this view of herself as a moviegoer. Angela combines her own psychological response to violent cinema with a consciousness of how others define her as a movie-goer. Her complex response emphasises her social awareness of herself as a woman, and as a filmgoer.

There is a certain achievement in watching a violent scene you know you find disturbing. I remember watching a distressing rape scene in *Man Bites Dog*, in fact half watching through my fingers, and after the experience, I certainly felt satisfaction that I had challenged my fears of rape, a common fear for women. The challenge, for me, was in the choice to watch or not watch a scene I knew I found disturbing. But I also know there is a part of me that doesn't like to watch things I find distressing. In my study, female fans highlighted the relationship between self-censorship and their attraction to violent movies. Samantha, a 26-year-old student, described her reasons for watching violent films:

> Yes I think, oh God, yes, yes I think, I think quite a lot of these ones are [entertaining]. I think *Reservoir Dogs* was and *Pulp Fiction* was and *True Romance* was. *Natural Born Killers* – yes I think they are because I think you can choose at what sort of level you become involved in and I think that's what it boils down to me for me. I can just sit there and I can bear to watch and I can kind of – that I can self-censor if I want to, so, I think I have a choice there, so I do find it entertaining.

Samantha's comment emphasises the importance of choice to the viewing experience. When she searches for a reason why these films are entertaining, she focuses on self-censorship. Samantha's repeated use of 'I think' as she works through her reasons for enjoying the films highlights a process of discovery ('I think, I think quite a lot of these ones are', 'I think you can choose'). Her animated response leads to a declaration of independence: she can watch or not watch. Her explanation also highlights a process of self-discovery: this is her response ('so, I think I have a choice there', 'I think that's what it boils down for me'). Through discussing her response to 'new brutalist' films, Samantha reflects on her own emotional and psychological reasons for enjoying violent cinema. Like me, Samantha enjoys the challenge to watch or not watch something she finds disturbing, but the reasons why we are attracted to these films, and why we half-watch, or look away at certain violent scenes, are not necessarily the same. There is self-reflection to watching violent movies which links the 'challenging' aspects of violent cinema with viewers' own personal reasons for watching the films.

For the female fans in my study, watching violence and exploring their emotional responses to these films is not something just for men. Indeed, their individual responses to violent cinema run counter to traditional perceptions of women's cultural tastes, and women as moviegoers. The ability to self-censor adds an important ingredient to the viewing experience. I would argue another ingredient is self-awareness. For female fans, the knowledge that, traditionally, women are not perceived as a natural audience for violent cinema leads to a cognizance about how women do watch scenes of violence.

The women in this study challenge social boundaries concerning taste and gender, and they also challenge their personal responses to violence in film.

There is a case to be made that boundary testing and self-censorship can be related to personal experience. The relationship between personal anger or fear and the attraction of watching violent film is complex, and varies with each individual. For example, Alison, a 27-year-old student, explained:

> I think it is very much a personal experience that influences your own censorship or decision to watch a film, because if I know there is a rape scene in it, it has a very different effect on me whether it is something I want to see or not, regardless of whether it has been reviewed or recommended – and female violence – I didn't really like that – it's very personal, I mean, I just don't like it.

Alison would only watch *Reservoir Dogs* on video to give herself more control of the viewing experience:

> I was prepared to see it on video rather than at the cinema because I knew that obviously I could walk out of the room, or I could feel comfortable averting or switching off, or do something else – pick a magazine up if it did have a bad effect on me, if I wasn't happy watching it.

There were personal reasons why Alison wanted to control her viewing experience: she was attacked in real life:

> If there is a knife involved I just – I get quite angry and it has definitely affected me as a person as well because I sort – it sort of brings out – I have a lot of violence in me actually. For me – I know this is a very important thing to say but for me I kind of will it to happen again so that I can act it out – although I wasn't violently attacked, there was no violence at all apart from a knife. I didn't – in that respect I keep thinking I wish I could have fought back and so if I see things like a rape scene I think – wouldn't it be great if she could just do something violent, do this and do fucking that.

The violence within her, the violence Alison contains as a result of her personal experience of a knife attack, spills out when she describes her fantasy to become the aggressor and protect herself. She chooses to self-censor knife scenes. In the focus group, she looked away when we watched the ear-amputation scene from *Reservoir Dogs* ('I just didn't want to watch it. It really has a horrible effect on me'). But she also chooses to watch other scenes which depict violence towards women in order to relive her attack in such a way that she is no longer the victim. Here, the decision to look or not look is usually part of the attraction, but in this instance the repulsion, of violent films.

There were other women in the study who also described personal reasons why they wanted to watch violent movies. I want to examine one case in some detail to highlight the complex relationship between attraction to violent cinema and self-awareness about the role such films can play in people's own life histories. Sally, a 28-year-old student, had personal reasons why she chose to watch 'new brutalist' films:

> Well, me and my friend both ended five-year relationships at exactly the same time last year. I always said I hate violent films but I just thought what the hell, I'll go and do something now to counteract the relationship. For a four- or five-month stint we only saw violent films, to prove we could do it . . . I think we've both been boundary testing a hell of a lot and therefore sort of going to see sort of things that I'd never even considered that I'd wanted to see in my past life – which has really been interesting actually. I think maybe a lot of women would feel the same . . . It is something I did in defiance of what people thought that – what they thought I should actually be doing. I thought I was a sensitive person. I thought I didn't like violent films. I shied away from them. And then you go through a stage where all your boundaries just dissolve and you don't know where the hell you are and you feel liberated.

There are many aspects in her statement that deserve highlighting. Sally's new desire to watch violent films stemmed from her feelings of disempowerment after a relationship breakdown. She was aware of other people's perception of her in the past and used viewing violent movies as a way to challenge this. Before the breakdown of her relationship, she considered herself a person who would never watch violent cinema. She uses the phrase 'boundary testing' twice in conjunction with a new sense of liberation from her past self. There is a way in which Sally hardens herself from the pain of her failed relationship, and she talks about her self in the past tense ('I thought I was a sensitive person'). However, the fact that she watches violent films does not mean she is desensitised to violence, she has empowered herself. When Sally reflected on what she gained from her new experience, she explained:

> Achievement that I've got myself out and I'm doing things because I did feel better able to define boundaries between myself and the cinema, exhilaration because of the action on the screen and also because I was doing something which wasn't anything that I'd done before. Also, kind of laughing at the whole thing which was extremely – me and my mate – feeling really awful but we're going to

go out and see these horrible films just for our own benefit. With a particularly violent episode such as the ear scene in *Reservoir Dogs* 'I will see this and I will get something out of it and I will test myself', yeah, yeah? Seeing all these films, it's been like quite fun and quite liberating. I still – the one time I did see someone get their head kicked in, literally, I felt like I was going to be sick. I'd previously seen cinema as kind of extension of this activity, which I obviously was not wanting to be involved in, but I was now prepared to see it because it's art and it's fiction and I wanted to test boundaries.

As in the previous extract, the word 'boundaries' occurs several times, indeed it frames her speech. Sally tests personal and cultural boundaries. She explores a different side to her personality; she develops a new taste for a genre she previously found distasteful (indeed, which was labelled as nauseating in the popular press). The substance of Sally's experience relates to self awareness: there is a real energy in her language, she is re-invigorated through watching violent movies. However, testing boundaries does not relate to real experience of violence, and her memory of acute distress at witnessing real violence reinforces her new understanding that responses to fictional violence are not the same as responses to real violence.[17] This understanding comes as a result of exploring her emotions through viewing violent cinema.

In the previous section Jill, a 27-year-old college teacher, discussed her sensitised response to the violence in *Reservoir Dogs*, the way in which the violence 'looked like it hurts'. Jill watched violent movies to safely examine her personal fear of violence:

> I think it's just a safe way, isn't it, to experience the things that you might be really, really frightened about in your own life. I don't want to be beaten up, I'm scared of real violence but I am not as scared when I watch a fictional representation of it because I feel I can safely get out all my fears. That's why I can safely watch the punching, it scares me but I know, you know, I can deal with it in a legitimate way.

Her juxtaposition of emotions like fright and fear in relation to safety, her repetition of the words 'scare' and 'safe', emphasises Jill's desire to guard herself from real violence and *at the same time* explore personal fears through watching fictional violence. This relationship between fear of real violence and interest in fictional violence is another reason why women are attracted to watching violent films. Laura, a 31-year-old care worker, reflected on the relationship between real violence and fictional violence:

> I mean, having seen violence in the past against friends, you just, like, avoid it. I avoid it at any costs.

AH: You avoid real violence but go to see fictional violence?

Yeah, because it's fictional and you do know it's fictional . . . I think that's why a lot of people moved to London as well because it doesn't happen in London so much than if you're living in the sub-urbs where it does happen, it's a regular thing. Violence does happen in pubs in those towns where they've got nothing else to do so if you want to avoid violence you come to London and you go to the cinema, whereas at home, where I was brought up, you know, violence on a Saturday night between two different pubs, that's how it was. Real violence is horrible, but we'll go to the cinema to see it – it's a safe way.

Laura and Jill are aware their attraction to violent movies is, in part, linked to their repulsion to real violence. Not all female fans of violent cinema have personal experience of violence. Not all women want to watch violent movies for therapeutic reasons. Nevertheless, in my research, the majority of women explored their emotional responses to violence in the 'safe' environment of a fiction film.

What is the attraction of violent movies? Earlier, I discussed the signifi-cance of testing boundaries and self-censorship in understanding the attrac-tion of violent movies. Boundary testing also relates to the way female fans talk about their personal responses to violence. For some women, their satis-faction in challenging themselves to watch a violent film can be related to life biography and personal development. For others, their attraction to violent cinema can arise from less personal motives – the opportunity to watch a 'good' film which is marked by its difference from 'standard Hollywood fare.' For most women in my research it was in fact a combination of both. Laura and Jill may have personal reasons why they explore their responses to violence, they may find watching violent movies at times therapeutic, but this doesn't stop them from enjoying the experience. As they explain, new brutalist films may be challenging, but they can also be entertaining:

Reservoir Dogs I found entertaining because it was completely differ-ent to anything I've seen before and quite exciting for all that but at the same time quite disturbing and horrific. So it was the entertain-ment side but it was also the other side which isn't what I'd call entertaining. *Pulp Fiction* I found thoroughly entertaining in every way. I mean, I personally loved the fact that the two main protagon-ists of the violence either died or took a decision to be pacifists for the rest of their lives.

When Patricia Arquette picks up the toilet seat in *True Romance* you just want to be there . . . Something like *Reservoir Dogs* or *Pulp*

Fiction and *True Romance, Natural Born Killers*, they are the ones that for me are quite exhilarating.

Their responses highlight a strong interest in characterisation and narrative, in characters' decision-making processes, and although these films contain scenes of 'violence' the violence is not essential, but only one ingredient in their enjoyment of new brutalist films.

Conclusion

Talking to fans of violent movies is an illuminating experience, especially if you are a fan yourself. The aim of my research was to understand why people, like me, were attracted to 'new brutalist' films, films which were cat-egorised by the popular press as gruesome and notorious for their extreme violence. I summarised in this chapter the complex reasons women liked watching these films. Female fans of violent movies were not attracted to these films solely because of the 'violence'. Films like *Reservoir Dogs* and *Pulp Fiction* offered something 'new', something different from Hollywood action movies: they contained strong narrative and characterisation, unpredictable stories, extreme emotions – they were 'good' films. What is more, these films invited a range of physical and emotional responses from the viewer: fear, anger, excitement, laughter, surprise. Female fans liked to test boundaries whilst watching these films. Some women explored their emotional responses to real violence through watching fictional violence.

What I observed from listening to women talk about their attraction to violent movies was that their responses had to be explained on a number of levels. I learnt there is no simple answer to the question of why people enjoy watching media violence. Female fans responded in localised ways to violent cinema, in ways which could not be generalised to stand in for women as a whole. For many women in my study, their responses to violence often led to a self-awareness of their own psychological reasons for watching violent cinema. They were also aware of how society expected women to be repulsed by, rather than attracted to, violent cinema. Female fans challenged the traditional perception of women as either non-viewers, or squeamish viewers of violent cinema, and in the process tested personal, social and cultural boundaries. For this community of moviegoers, women enjoyed watching violent movies on their own terms.

NOTES

1 Jim Shelley (1993a: 7; 1993b: 12), refers collectively to these films as 'heralding the arrival of "the new brutalism"' in cinema. The very category 'new brutalism' refers to the media effects tradition, as it implies violent entertainment *brutalises* viewers.
2 Elton's novel regurgitates many of the comments made by Michael Medved in his populist tract *Hollywood vs. America* (Medved 1992).

3 Barker (1984), Cumberbatch and Howitt (1989) and Gauntlett (1995) note the way that the stigmatisation of fans of media violence hinders open and objective research into this topic.

4 For research into viewers of media violence, and emotional responses to horror films, see Brigid Cherry (1999), Cantor *et al.* (1984), Cantor and Hoffner (1990), Sparks (1989, 1991), Tamborini *et al.* (1990), Zillman *et al.* (1986), Buckingham (1996) amongst others.

5 See Cherry (1999), Dresser (1989) and Auerbach (1995) for discussion of female fans of horror films, Weaver and Tamborini (1996) on gendered reactions to horror films, and Jenkins (1992) for discussion of television fans.

6 The discrepancy here may be more apparent than real. Some women in my research saw themselves as part of a group of movie-goers who shared similar tastes, and who did not perceive watching violent cinema as 'odd' or unusual for women (in their group). I would categorise this group as women who had a strong interest in cinema, and who saw 'new brutalist' films as part of their wider taste in 'independent' cinema, i.e. non-Hollywood, or non-mainstream cinema. However, for others, going to see 'new brutalist' films was something they saw as 'different' to the type of films they would normally choose to watch. These women also noted other people thought their choice of films unusual, and not traditionally associated with women's tastes in film. This group of women went to the cinema less often, and saw new brutalist films as different to the standard Hollywood fare, and also different to the standard repertoire of films they would normally watch.

7 Recruitment was conducted using the snowball technique. The format for the focus group discussions was standardised, although, where appropriate, allowance was made for specific issues raised by participants in a given group (see Hill, 1997 for further details).

8 The most common age bracket was between 18–30, with 10 participants aged between 18–20, and 16 participants aged between 20–30, making a total of 26 participants aged 30 or under taking part in the discussions. Only 10 participants were over 30, and only one out of that figure was over 40. The majority of participants were British (33), with only 3 participants being of a different ethnic origin (1 Indian, 1 Australian, 1 Chinese). All participants were educated to GCSE level/ A level standard, with 21 participants having finished a technical or vocational course or part of a university course and three participants who had completed a postgraduate course.

9 The names given to participants in this chapter are fictional.

10 Manohla Dargis, 'Pulp Instincts' in *Sight and Sound*, Vol.4, Issue 5, May 1994: 6.

11 Usher, S. 1992. 'Deadly Dogs Unleash a Whirlwind of Violence' in the *Daily Mail*. 22 December 1992: 26. The *Guardian Weekend* magazine describes Tarantino as 'a connoisseur of cruelty' (Lynne Segal, 'Killing Jokes' in the *Guardian Weekend Magazine*, 11 September 1994: 24–8). Quentin Tarantino told Geoff Andrew in *Time Out*: 'I don't think you can go too far with violence if what you are doing is right for the movie. What's too far?' 1994. 'Killing Joke' in *Time Out,* 21–28 September 1994: 24–26.

12 Soon to follow in 1993 was the re-release of *Mean Streets* (Martin Scorsese, 1973), and the UK release of *Hard Boiled* (John Woo, 1992), the Australian film *Romper Stomper* 1992 and the video release of *Henry, Portrait of a Serial Killer*.

13 Guttridge, Peter, 1993. 'Are These Films Too Violent?' in the *Daily Telegraph*. 22 January 1993: 18.

14 Many of the participants may have used *Die Hard* (John McTiernan, 1988) as an example of a traditional action movie because they were prompted to discuss action movies such as the *Die Hard* series or the *Terminator* series in the focus

group, and also because *Die Hard with a Vengeance* (John McTiernan, 1995) was on general release at the time of the focus groups.

15 For research into fans of science fiction action movies see Barker and Brooks (1998).

16 See popular press response to media violence in Barker (1984), Buckingham (1996), and also audience research such as Schlesinger *et al.* (1992).

17 This prior expectation that fictional violence and real violence are not the same thing is an important ingredient in the attraction of 'new brutalist' films. Although the women in my study said they found films like *Reservoir Dogs* and *Pulp Fiction* more realistic than action movies, they made a distinction. Of all the target films, the two films which people said were the most challenging (*Man Bites Dog* and *Henry, Portrait of a Serial Killer*) were the most 'realistic' in their depiction of violence. *Man Bites Dog* and *Henry, Portrait of a Serial Killer* use documentary techniques (hand held cameras, black and white film, a cinema verité style) to depict violence in a particularly disturbing manner, one woman called both films 'relentless and grim'. These films were challenging to watch because they were more akin to the experience of watching a documentary (see Hill, 1997). Only about half of the people in my study watched these two films, whereas everyone had seen *Reservoir Dogs* and *Pulp Fiction*. Although each person responded to the target films in an individual way, drawing upon their own tastes and personal experiences to define their responses to violent movies, there was a pattern to the attraction of some films over others. Thus, *Reservoir Dogs* and *Pulp Fiction* were more popular, less grim and relentless, than *Man Bites Dog* or *Henry, Portrait of a Serial Killer*. It would be good to explore further the relationship between boundary testing and different types of violent movies.

REFERENCES

Auerbach, N. L. (1995), *Our Vampires, Ourselves*, Chicago: University of Chicago Press.

Barker, M. (ed.) (1984), *The Video Nasties: Freedom and Censorship in the Media*, London: Pluto Press.

Barker, M. and Brooks, K. (1998), *Knowing Audiences:* Judge Dredd, *Its Friends, Fans and Foes*, Luton: University of Luton Press.

Barlow, G. and Hill, A. (eds) (1985), *Video Violence and Children*, London: Hodder and Stoughton.

Buckingham, D. (1996), *Moving Images: Understanding Children's Emotional Responses to Television*, Manchester: Manchester University Press.

Cantor, J., Ziemke. C. and Sparks, C. (1984), 'Effects of forewarning on emotional responses to a horror film' in *Journal of Broadcasting*. 28: 1, pp. 21–31.

Cantor, J. and Hoffner, C. (1990), 'Forewarning of a threat and prior knowledge of outcome: effects on children's emotional responses to a film sequence' in *Human Communications Research*, Vol. 16, No.3, pp. 323–54.

Cherry, Brigid (1999), 'Refusing to Refuse to Look: Female Viewers of the Horror Film' in Melvyn Stokes and Richard Maltby, eds, *Identifying Hollywood's Audiences: Cultural Identity and the Movies*, London: BFI Publications, pp. 187–203.

Cumberbatch, G. and Howitt, D. (1989), *A Measure of Uncertainty: the Effects of the Mass Media*, London: John Libbey & Company Ltd.

Dresser, Norine (1989), *American Vampires: Fans, Victims, Practitioners*, New York and London: WW Norton and Company.

Elton, B. (1996) *Popcorn*, London: Simon & Schuster.

Gauntlett, D. (1995), *Moving Experiences: Understanding Television's Influences and Effects*, London: John Libbey.

Hill, Annette (1997), *Shocking Entertainment: Viewer Response to Violent Movies*, Luton: John Libbey Media.

Hill, Annette (1999), 'Risky business: film violence as an interactive phenomenon' in Melvyn Stokes and Richard Maltby, eds, *Hollywood and its Spectators*, London: BFI Publications pp. 175–86.

Jenkins, Henry (1992), *Textual Poachers: Television Fans and Participatory Culture*, London: Routledge.

Medved, M. (1992), *Hollywood vs. America: Popular Culture and the War on Traditional Values*, New York: HarperCollins.

Morgan, D. L. (1988), *Focus Groups as Qualitative Research*, London: Sage Publications.

Schlesinger, P., Dobash, R. E., Dobash, R. P. and Weaver, C. K. (1992), *Women Viewing Violence*, London: BFI.

Shelley, J. (1993a), 'The boys are back in town' in the *Guardian*, 7 January 1993, p. 7.

Shelley, J (1993b), 'Down these mean streets many men have gone' in *The Times*, Saturday Review, 20 February 1993, p. 12.

Sparks, G. G. (1989), 'Understanding emotional reactions to a suspenseful movie: the interaction between forewarning and preferred coping style' in *Communication Monographs*, 56: 4, pp. 325–40.

Sparks, G. G. (1991), 'The relationship between distress and delight in males' and females' reactions to frightening films' in *Human Communication Research*, 17: 4, pp. 625–37.

Tamborini, R., Stiff, J. and Heidel, C. (1990), 'Reacting to graphic horror: a model of empathy and emotional behaviour' in *Communication Research*, 17: 5, pp. 616–40.

Van Evra, J. (1990), *Television and Child Development*, Hillsdale, New Jersey: Lawrence Erlbaum Associates.

Weaver, James, B. and Tamborini, Ron (eds) (1996), *Horror Films: Current Research on Audience Preferences and Reactions*, Mahwah, New Jersey: Lawrence Erlbaum Associates.

Zillman, Dolf *et al.* (1986) 'Effects of an opposite-gender companion's affect to horror on distress, delight and attraction', *Journal of Personal and Social Psychology*, 51.

9

RESERVOIRS OF DOGMA

An archaeology of popular anxieties

Graham Murdock

On the morning of Wednesday, 13 March 1996, Thomas Hamilton, a middle-aged man with no criminal record, walked into the primary school in the small Scottish town of Dunblane, shot sixteen children and a teacher and then killed himself. It was a deeply disturbing incident and, although there was no evidence that he had a particular interest in watching screen violence, it prompted a rash of commentary condemning the morality of popular film and television. Here is Andrew Neil, writing in the *Sunday Times*:

> There are some crimes so horrific that they make us all wonder what kind of country we have become . . . It should be cause for concern that, in the values and mores of modern society, we have created a quagmire from which monsters are bound to emerge . . . far too much of what passes for popular entertainment pollutes our society and creates a new tolerance in which what was thought to be beyond the pale becomes acceptable. Young minds are particularly vulnerable.
>
> (Neil, 1996, p. 5)

An almost identical catalogue of complaint followed two other traumatic events of recent years: Michael Ryan's random shootings in Hungerford and the brutal murder of 2-year-old James Bulger by two boys of 10. Again, although there was no firm evidence of direct 'effects' in either case, screen violence was singled out as a major contributory cause. In recent discussions, a small number of films containing scenes of violence have come to stand for the state of contemporary cinema. Quentin Tarantino's début feature *Reservoir Dogs* has been a particular target. One popular cartoon, which appeared in the wake of the intense debate on the James Bulger case, showed two children sitting in front of a television set displaying the film's title. One is turning to the other saying: 'Let's go and drown some puppies.'

This simple image of direct effects draws its power from a deep reservoir of social fear and dogma which first formed in the mid-nineteenth century as commentators began to link the social costs of modernity with the proliferation of new forms of popular entertainment. Then, as now, the perceived disorders of the present were often counterposed against an idealised image of the past.

> Once upon a time, so the story runs . . . violence and disorder were unknown in Britain . . . But now all that is no more. Now violence and terror lurk in the once-safe streets. The family no longer holds its proper place and parents have abandoned their responsibilities.
>
> (Pearson, 1983, p. 3)

Here is Andrew Neil again:

> There was a time, within my memory, when popular culture sought to lift our spirits and encourage what was good, honourable and just in our society. We aspired to what we saw on our screens, and evil was generally given a bad press.
>
> (Neil, 1996, p. 5)

This is a startling case of selective recall. Though Neil grew up in the 1950s he has conveniently forgotten the moral panics about media 'effects' which greeted the American 'horror comics', the hard-boiled pulp thrillers of Mickey Spillaine and Hank Janson, and the 'Teddy Boy riots' in cinemas showing early rock 'n' roll films. For a newspaperman, he also displays a woeful ignorance of the long history of condemnation that has accompanied popular media throughout the modern age.

By the 1850s the core patterns of modern social life had begun to crystallise, and popular fictions, dramas and journalism were assuming their familiar contemporary forms. The blood-soaked melodramas playing in the 'penny gaffs', the lurid stories carried by the 'penny dreadfuls' and the sensationalised coverage of crime in the populist Sunday newspapers established traditions of representation which are still very much with us. Violence and lawlessness were one of their principal stocks-in-trade. They paraded the dark side of modernity's promise of progress, the monstrous doubles of order and respectability, the animalistic potentials that continually elbowed and jostled sobriety and rationality. Commentators were quick to see them as both a potent symptom of moral decline and a powerful new incitement to anti-social behaviour. Because they supposedly lacked an adequate training in moral and social restraints, young people were widely seen as particularly open to suggestion. As the critic who reviewed a series of recent publications on juvenile crime for the *Edinburgh Review* in 1851 lamented:

> One powerful agent for depraving the boyish classes of our popula-
> tion in our towns and cities is to be found in the cheap concerts,
> shows and theatres, which are so specially opened and arranged for
> the attraction and ensnaring of the young ... when our fear of
> interfering with personal and public liberty allows these shows and
> theatres to be training schools of the coarsest and most open vice
> and filthiness – it is not to be wondered at, that the boy who is led on
> to haunt them becomes rapidly corrupted and demoralised, and
> seeks to be the doer of the infamies which have interested him as a
> spectator.
>
> (*Edinburgh Review*, 1851, p. 409)

This attractively simple notion, that what young people watched was directly linked to what they later did, rapidly moved to the centre of debate. Despite the serious reservations that have been lodged against the research evidence claiming to 'prove' these connections (e.g. Murdock and McCron, 1979; Cumberbatch and Howitt, 1989; Gauntlett, 1995) studies in this tradition are still routinely cited by commentators arguing for more stringent controls on film and video. According to Melanie Phillips of the *Observer*, for example:

> The remarkable fact is that there is a vast amount of evidence, more
> than 1,000 studies carried out in the United States and elsewhere,
> demonstrating a link between screen violence and aggressive
> behaviour in children ... True, there are problems with this kind of
> research ... But there are simply too many studies all pointing the
> same way to be ignored.
>
> (Phillips, 1994, p. 25)

Anyone who questions this conclusion is presented as an arrogant, self-opinionated member of 'the progressive, libertarian intelligentsia', out of touch with the justified concerns of ordinary people.

The attraction of these 'many studies' is not simply that they offer the illusion of strength in numbers, but that they fit perfectly with the common-sense assumption that, since 'it stands to reason' that there must be a link, responsible research is simply confirming what reasonable people already know, and that refusing to accept this is patently unreasonable.

As we shall see, this circular relationship between empiricist science and common-sense thinking was built into academic work on media 'effects' from the outset. The dominant research tradition adopted the definition of the 'problem' already established in popular and political commentary. The result was banal science, which failed to ask awkward questions, to pursue other possible lines of inquiry or to place 'effects' in their social contexts. But because its investigative procedures corresponded to common-sense notions of what 'proper' science was – the image of controlled experimentation being particularly central – its 'findings' seemed to offer strong confirmation of popular assumptions and anxieties. These, in turn, were anchored in a deep-rooted formation of fear about the precarious balance between anarchy and order in the modern age.

As nineteenth-century observers knew very well, the dynamics of modernity called all pre-existing moral and social relations into question. As Marx put it in 1848, in one of his most lyrical passages, there was an 'uninterrupted disturbance of all social conditions . . . all fixed, fast-frozen relations are swept away . . . All that is solid melts into air, all that is holy is profaned' (Marx and Engels, 1968, p. 38). What Marx celebrated as a liberation others mourned as a loss. They saw established social restraints crumbling away. They were haunted by the spectre of moral decline amidst material plenty. Many worried about the loosening grip of religious faith, and drives to 'purify' popular entertainment were often linked to campaigns to re-Christianise society.

As Andrew Neil's piece illustrates, anxieties about the moral and spiritual costs of social and cultural change remain central to present debates. They establish potent connections between concern about media violence and more general fears for the future. If we are to develop a more comprehensive analysis of the interplay between popular media and everyday thinking, feeling and behaviour, and to argue convincingly for expressive diversity in film, television and the new media, we need to challenge popular fears. Retracing the intellectual and political history that has formed them is a necessary first step. This is a substantial task. What follows is simply a very bald sketch of an embedded structure of feeling which will, hopefully, suggest some lines for future inquiry.

Dangerous associations

The civic culture of high modernity was increasingly based around the social contract of citizenship. Every adult was entitled to participate fully in social and political life. In return they were expected to behave responsibly. Citizens were model Enlightenment individuals. They made rational choices on the basis of careful reflection and disinterested evidence. But the fact that the French Enlightenment had also produced the French Revolution and the Terror left an indelible impression on contemporary observers. As the great British constitutionalist Walter Bagehot warned in 1876: 'Such scenes of cruelty and horror as happened in the great French Revolution . . . we now see . . . were the outbreak of inherited passions long repressed by fixed custom, but starting into life as soon as that repression was catastrophically removed' (quoted in McClelland, 1989, p. 162). From the outset, the imagination of citizenship was shadowed by the fear of the elemental power of the crowd and the mob waiting to be detonated just below the surface of routine social life. As the journalist Charles Mackay put it in his highly successful book *Extraordinary Popular Delusions and the Madness of Crowds*, first published in 1841, men 'go mad in herds, while they only recover their sense slowly, and one by one' (Mackay, 1956, p. xx).

The packed tenements and slums of the major cities offered the most visible image of the crowd, and depictions of the 'mass' as a physically dense body continually on the edge of unpredictable motion played a central role in the formation of respectable fears. They constituted what Matthew Arnold called, in a memorable passage written after a crowd broke down the railings around Hyde Park during a demonstration protesting at the defeat of the Reform Bill of 1866, a 'vast residuum', a murky mass left at the bottom of the decanter after the drinkable wine had been poured off (Arnold, 1966, p. 105). This notion of a population at the bottom of the pile, disconnected from the mainstream, finds powerful contemporary expression in the notion of an urban 'underclass'. Mackay, however, was careful to stress that 'the madness of crowds' was a psychological rather than a physical phenomenon, and he set out to explore a variety of 'moral epidemics which have been excited, sometimes by one cause and sometimes by another, and to show how easily the masses have been led astray, and how imitative men are, even in their infatuations and crimes' (Mackay, 1956, p. xvii). These ranged from the fashion for beards to the craze for magnetism and a spate of slow poisonings.

The idea of the 'psychological crowd', physically separated but united by shared experiences, regularly surfaced in debates throughout the second half of the century and, by the time the Chicago sociologist and former journalist Robert Park came to write on the subject in 1904, the view that 'it is the psychological conditions rather than the spatial relationships of individuals which forms the essential content of the concept of the crowd' (Park, 1972, p. 12) was widely accepted. It found its most forceful and widely quoted formulation in Gustave Le Bon's massively influential 1895 book, *The Crowd*.

Crowds were the beast within, the absolute antithesis of a public composed of citizens. As Le Bon argued, 'by the mere fact that he forms part of a crowd, a man descends several rungs in the ladder of civilisation. Isolated he may be a cultivated individual, in a crowd he is a barbarian – a creature acting by instinct' (Le Bon, 1960, p. 32).

Where citizenship relied on rational debate and respect for evidence, psychological crowds, Le Bon argued, were formed by images. They worked with emotional associations rather than sequential arguments:

> Crowds being only capable of thinking in images are only to be impressed by images. It is only images that attract them and become motives for action . . . Nothing has a greater effect on the imagination of crowds than theatrical representations . . . Sometimes the

sentiments suggested by the images are so strong that they tend, like habitual suggestions, to transform themselves into acts.

(Le Bon, 1960, p. 68)

This argument appeared eminently plausible since it coincided with a major shift towards a more visually oriented popular culture. The Lumière Brothers' first film performance in Paris in 1895 ushered in the age of commercial cinema, and the rising generation of press enterpreneurs (such as Alfred Harmsworth who launched his *Daily Mail* in 1896) were pioneering new styles of popular journalism in which visual illustrations had a much more central role to play.

It was almost universally assumed that the seductions of imagery operated particularly powerfully among groups who were either pre-literate or semi-literate. Children were seen as particularly vulnerable to suggestion and exploitation. In a fierce attack on the 'penny dreadfuls', James Greenwood, one of the leading muck-raking Victorian journalists, pictured the publishers as vampires preying on the innocent, and urged 'careful parents' to beware: 'already he may have bitten your little rosy-cheeked son, Jack. He may be lurking at this very moment in that young gentleman's private chamber, polluting his mind and smoothing the way that leads to swift destruction' (Greenwood, 1874, p. 168). Children were vulnerable but they were not regarded as a threat to social order. Dangerousness lay with adolescents. They were not only suggestible, but capable of acting out what they had seen.

The new psychology of adolescence, pioneered by writers like Stanley Hall, argued that, because puberty unleashed physical and emotional potentials which young people did not have the moral and mental maturity to cope with, they were in constant danger of 'descending the ladder of civilisation'. As Frank Lydston, a professor of medicine in Illinois, put it in 1904:

> The pubescent is in the greatest danger . . . the emotions are keyed to the highest pitch; centres of ideation are plastic. As the psychic twig is bent at this time, the cererbral tree is indeed inclined. Many a life has been ruined by psychic wounds – wounds from infected and infective ideas at this critical period.
>
> (Lydston, 1904, p. 101)

Working-class adolescent boys were a particular focus of respectable fears. They were highly visible on the streets of the cities, they regularly featured in press reporting, and they figured prominently in the official crime statistics. Moral entrepreneurs believed that they were locked in an uphill battle for young hearts and minds. As one prominent expert on 'Boy Life' put it:

> The boy's mind is in many respects a blank sheet at fourteen, and the writing that will be engraved upon it is dependent on the influences

through which the boy passes. The senses of the adolescent, now open at their widest, are opened not to Art, but to cheap and tawdry pantomime, his emotions are fed, not with gracious and elevating influences, but with unnatural excitements.

(Freeman, 1914, p. 151)

These 'excitements', many observers believed, had turned young men into 'hooligans'. As *The Times* complained in 1900:

Our 'Hooligans' go from bad to worse . . . they hustle and waylay solitary old gentlemen with gold watches; they hunt in packs too large for a single policeman to cope with . . . At best they will be bad citizens. They are an ugly growth on the body politic . . . a hideous excrescence on our civilisation.

(Quoted in Schwarz, 1996, p. 104)

The figure of the hooligan (and the parade of later folk devils) comprehensively undermined the idealised image of the citizen and condensed 'with great power a cluster of anxieties . . . around masculinity and youth, read through the lens of class' (Schwarz, 1996, p. 119).

Within this framework of concern, censoring 'infective ideas' or trying to keep them out of adolescents' reach (as in systems of film classification) was not simply an expression of aesthetic judgement but a social duty designed to repair the rents in the body politic. However, because these measures cut across two of the most cherished values of capitalist democracy, freedom of artistic expression and freedom of consumer choice, their supporters were obliged to look for plausible proofs to support their demands for action.

Persuasions and panics

Some commentators seized upon the substantial sums of money being spent on advertising by the turn of the century to argue that, since marketing seemed to work in the world of goods, as shown by sales figures, images of crime and violence probably promoted anti-social behaviour in the same way. They saw the sensationalist popular press as a potent agent of both kinds of persuasion. As W. I. Thomas, the Chicago sociologist, argued in 1908:

[A]n article in commerce – a food, a luxury, a medicine or a stimulant – can always be sold in immense quantities if it be persistently and largely advertised. In the same way the yellow journal by an advertisement of crime . . . in a way that amounts to approval and even applause, becomes one of the forces making for immorality.

(Thomas, 1908, p. 496)

This argument still features regularly in contemporary comment, as in the editorial carried in the *Independent on Sunday* after the Dunblane shootings:

> The modern, liberal mind is strangely resistent to cause and effect . . . Yet millions of pounds are spent annually on advertising and the entire media industry strains over presentation, using music, visual effects, camera, lighting, to put audiences in the right mood. How can we possibly believe that the film shoot-out never has an effect?
>
> (*Independent on Sunday*, 1996, p. 20)

At first sight, this is an attractive argument, but it ignores the fact that popular representations of crime organise pleasures, fears and excitements in complex combinations that can be responded to at a number of levels. Some readers may be attracted to the aggressor but many more are likely to identify with the victim and to support calls for tougher policing and sentencing.

As *The Times* leader quoted earlier illustrates, by the turn of the century 'hooligan' had become a handy popular label that was liberally applied by the press to all kinds of youthful street disorder. And, as one London magistrate of the period remembered, this continual labelling prompted a response out of all proportion to the threat.

> Southwark and Bermondsey were famous for some years as the headquarters of hooliganism . . . the press had so boosted the heroes of it that it was quite dangerous at one time for a group of youths to walk together down a street. They were sure to be charged with insulting behaviour and to be reported with the words 'more hooliganism in the Borough'.
>
> (Chapman, 1925, pp. 11 – 12)

As a number of commentators observed at the time, the popular press had played a leading role in orchestrating concern. The educationalist John Trevarthen, for example, was quick to castigate sensationalist reporting for prompting an over-reaction:

> Gangs of young roughs and thieves are no new thing in London and other large towns . . . though something like a scare has been produced by paragraphs in popular newspapers . . . The result has been numerous leading articles in various papers, with reports of speeches and sermons on the subject, followed as usual by letters from people, some of whom are evidently very imperfectly informed on the subject.
>
> (Trevarthen, 1901, p. 84)

This argument was pursued more systematically in one of the pioneering works of critical criminology, an inquiry into the workings of the criminal justice system in Cleveland, Ohio, published in the early 1920s. The authors noted that 345 crimes were reported in the city's newspapers in the first half of January 1919, and 363 in the second half, but that the amount of news space devoted to issues of crime and justice jumped dramatically over the same period, from 925 column inches to 6,642. As they argued, although there had been no appreciable change in the situation on the ground, the press had set in motion an escalating cycle of public fear, leading to calls for tough action that placed order above law or civil liberties. They went on to provide a very clear outline of the main stages in this cycle of response:

> News treatment tends to create . . . the belief that all crimes commit-ted at such a time are part of some phenomenon that constitutes a 'crime wave' and can be cured by some quick panaceas [and stimu-lates] a tendency to demand summary action and quick reportable 'results' on the part of police, prosecutors, and judges . . . Officials responsive to popular whims will, at least unconsciously, care more to satisfy popular demands than to be observant of the tried process of law.
>
> (Pound and Frankfurter, 1922, pp. 545–6)

This pioneering anatomy fits the career of later 'moral panics' about the possible links between popular media and social violence almost exactly.

Unreliable accounts

As public reactions to the Hungerford killings, the James Bulger murder and the Dunblane shootings illustrate, moral panics are often sparked off by one particularly dramatic and newsworthy event that crystallises and distils a range of latent social fears and concerns. The practice of generalising from single cases has a long history; but, as sceptics were quick to point out in the nineteenth century, miscreants hoping to appeal to notions of diminished responsibility had every reason to try to blame their actions on allegedly corrupting influences from outside. As one commentator observed at the height of the nineteenth-century panic over 'penny dreadfuls':

> It often happens, we are aware, that some juvenile till-robber is found to be a reader of 'penny dreadfuls'. Nevertheless, we cannot agree with the conclusion usually taken for granted in these cases, that the reading and the robbery stand in the relation of cause and effect. Young gentlemen 'in trouble' are ready enough to avail themselves of this plea when it is put into their mouth.
>
> (Wright, 1881, p. 35)

The problem of putting convenient words into young men's mouths surfaced again and again. In their eagerness to establish a secure link between mis-directed reading and subsequent misdeeds, interviewers often asked leading questions designed to elicit the response they were looking for.

In the spring of 1875 the American publisher James T. Fields visited the adolescent murderer Jesse Pomeroy in prison. The case, which had involved the killing of children, had received enormous publicity, and Fields was concerned to discover what had prompted Pomeroy's actions. As his memoir records, in the course of their conversation he asked him about what he liked to read:

> *Fields* 'Were there any pictures in the books?'
> *Pomeroy* 'Yes, Sir, plenty of them, blood and thunder pictures, toma-hawking and scalping.'
> *Fields* 'Do you think these books were an injury to you, and excited you, and excited you to commit the acts you have done?'
> *Pomeroy* 'Yes, Sir, I have thought it all over, and it seems to me now they did.'

Unfortunately for Fields, the reliability of Pomeroy's testimony is immedi-ately undermined by his next remark: 'I can't say certainly of course, and perhaps if I should think it over again, I should say it was something else' (quoted in Hawes, 1971, p. 112).

Diseased imaginings

One response to the unreliability of individual witnesses was to assemble a large number of cases, on the grounds that there might be safety in numbers. Doctors, lawyers and other professionals working in the prolifer-ating institutions set up to maintain surveillance and control over the urban poor and the youthful population could draw on their practical experience and invest their hunches and prejudices with claims to an expertise won in the rough-and-tumble of investigation.

Hence William Wadsworth could in 1911 write to the American Academy of Medicine claiming that:

> After years of observation of a stream of crime, in one of the largest centres of population in our country, and a careful professional study of the details of a very large number of cases of crimes, I have no hesitation in pointing out the fact that newspaper accounts of crimes influence those who commit crimes.
> (Wadsworth, 1911, p. 316)

Wadsworth, who practised as a coroner's physician in Philadelphia, worked with a medical model which presented media influence as a contagious disease attacking the mentally and morally unfit. This powerful meta-phor was deeply attractive to many commentators. As Frank Lydston, a professor of genito-urinary surgery, argued in his book *The Diseases of Society*:

> There is a moral or psychic contagium in certain books that is as definite and disastrous as that of the plague. The germs of mental ill-health are as potent in their way and, as things go nowadays, as far-reaching in evil effects as syphilis or leprosy.
>
> (Lydston, 1904, p. 101)

From this vantage point, the new popular media appeared as open sewers of the imagination, carrying a continuous flow of infection. The sensationalist newspapers were seen as a 'gutter press'. As the Italian criminologist Corre put it: 'Infectious epidemics spread with the air or the wind; epidemics of crime follow the line of the telegraph' (quoted in Tarde, 1912, pp. 340–1). The metaphors changed later, the image of a hypodermic needle injecting drugs into an unresisting body being a particular favourite, but the basic elements of the medical model remained remarkably stable.

But the new professionals were by no means unanimous. Those with other claims to expertise frequently rejected the medical model's argument for direct effects and emphasised more tangible environmental causes. As Newcastle's Director of Education, Percival Sharp, told a British inquiry into the influence of cinema in 1917:

> I have not during the last three years of investigation (covering 186 cases of committal) had a single case brought to my notice in respect of which it has been alleged or even suggested by police, school attendance officer or head-teacher that the genesis of the wrong-doing was to be found in the cinema show, EITHER IMMEDIATELY OR REMOTELY.
>
> (National Council of Public Morals, 1917, p. 284; emphasis in the original)

Other critics, like the American author Horace Kallen, went further, insisting that

> Investigation discovers no ground for the belief that any one of the arts . . . has in and by itself any important influence at all on conduct . . . The fact is that crowded slums, machine labour . . . barren lives, starved emotions . . . are far more dangerous to morals, property and life than . . . any motion picture.

On the contrary, he argued, in a version of what later came to be called the catharsis theory, films 'are substitutes for more elaborate and more serious overt actions, not inciters to them' (Kallen, 1930, pp. 50–1)

Faced with their critics, supporters of imitative effects could appeal to one further source of evidence: they could try to establish strong correlations between the details of well-publicised court cases and subsequent 'copy-cat' crimes. Gabriel Tarde, one of the leading early criminologists, was happy to support his case for contagious imitation by drawing on Corre's argument about the effects of press reporting of the notorious Whitechapel murders:

> What more striking example of suggesto-imitative assault could there be . . . The newspapers were filled with the exploits of Jack the Ripper and, in less than a year, as many as eight absolutely identical crimes were committed in various crowded streets of the great city. This is not all; there followed a repetition of these same deeds outside of the capital and very soon there was even a spreading of them abroad . . . the Hamburg murder accompanied by disembowelling of a little girl; in the United States disembowelling of four negroes.
>
> (Quoted in Tarde, 1912, p. 340)

Leaving aside the view, widely held at the time and since, that Jack the Ripper was a serial killer, this argument rests on a classic conflation of correlation and causality. It is possible to see the cases cited as similar only by removing them from their contexts and ignoring all other possible situational causes. At a time when racist attacks were a constant feature of black life in America and the 'bitter fruits' of lynchings hung from trees across the South, there were many more obvious places than London's East End to look for an explanation of a mass murder in Alabama.

Despite the obvious flaws in Corre's case, and in other similar forms of anecdotal and impressionistic evidence, the argument that there was a direct, cause-and-effect relationship between images and actions continued to dominate common-sense thinking. Much of the work undertaken by university-based researchers, from the turn of the century onwards, simply took over this agenda. It was a marriage of convenience. Academics seeking to establish new disciplines could bolster their claims to utility, relevance and research grants. In return, commentators and politicians could draw on seemingly 'scientific' evidence to support their calls for greater controls over popular entertainment.

Banal science

The search for factual support took two main forms. First, there were content-analysis studies which set out to provide statistics on the prevalence of violent imagery by painstakingly counting the space taken up by stories or incidents featuring violence. Second, there were studies designed to

161

isolate direct links between imagery and behaviour. Some of these relied on experiments conducted under laboratory conditions. Others used quasi-experiential designs in real-life settings or applied statistical controls to the results of questionnaire surveys in an effort to eliminate other possible causes. The 'findings' of these inquiries over the years have provided the 'scientific' evidence that is ritually cited in support of claims for direct 'effects'.

Although commentators had been attacking representations of violence in popular literature and journalism more or less continually since the 1850s, it was not until the century's turn that researchers set about calibrating sensationalism more precisely. Delos Wilcox's extensive content study of American newspapers, published in 1900, was a pioneering effort. He used his calculations to show that newspapers defined by critics as 'yellow' tended to feature materials thought likely to activate the mob spirit – advertisements, illustrations, and news of crime and vice (Wilcox, 1900, pp. 77–8). But, unlike most commentators, he was reluctant to draw firm conclusions about effects, arguing that 'the great mass of information we get in reading the papers affects our action only vaguely and remotely, if at all' (Wilcox, 1900, p. 87). Other writers, like Frederick Peterson, writing in 1906, were rather less restrained, however:

> It is not overstating it to say . . . these newspapers represent in the domain of culture and enlightenment the mob spirit, a vast, impersonal, delirious, anarchic, degenerating and disintegrating force. And it is this force which, acting upon the minds of the masses, sways them irresistibly in its own direction, making chaos where there should be order.
>
> (Peterson, 1906, p. 13)

This same basic argument was pursued in another important early study, Frances Fenton's 'The influence of newspaper presentations upon the growth of crime and other anti-social activity', which appeared in 1910–11. This combined a content analysis and a close reading of selected news stories with a model of influence which drew heavily on current writings on imitation and suggestion. After reviewing the evidence, Fenton concluded that 'On the basis of the psychology of suggestion . . . a direct causal connection may be established between the newspaper and crime and other anti-social activities' (Fenton, 1910–11, p. 370).

Gabriel Tarde had already assigned a central place to imitative effects in his influential work on crime. In *Penal Philosophy*, which first appeared in 1890, he had no hesitation in arguing that:

> All the important acts of social life are carried out under the domination of example . . . One kills or does not kill, because of

imitation . . . One kills oneself or one does not kill oneself, because of imitation. How can we doubt that one steals or does not steal, one assassinates or does not assassinate, because of imitation.

(Tarde, 1912, p. 322)

But how did imitation work? In searching for an answer Fenton and a number of other analysts turned to fashionable theories of subconscious suggestion. These shared a number of the overlapping oppositions which made up the structure of respectable fear: rationality versus emotion, progress versus degeneracy and the crowd versus the citizen. As Boris Sidis put it in 1898, in his book *The Psychology of Suggestion*: 'the subpersonal, uncritical social self, the mob self, and the suggestible subconscious self are identical' (Sidis, 1927, p. 364).

Sidis' book carried a foreword by William James, one of the influential central figures in the struggle to establish psychology as an independent discipline in America. But the theory, though attractive, presented formidable problems of evidence. As Fenton pointed out, because people are unaware of 'unconscious suggestion', cases cannot be analysed by getting them to reconstruct their experiences and motivations through introspection (the standard procedure in psychology at the time) and, as a result, 'it is not possible to measure this influence quantitatively' (Fenton, 1910–11, p. 61, p. 370).

This presented a serious problem for a fledgling science attempting to establish its ability to produce firm factual evidence on pressing social issues. One solution was to build on Freud's techniques for unlocking the dynamics of the unconscious mind. The other was to reject the notion of the subconscious altogether and to focus on what people actually did rather than on what they claimed or thought had happened. This line of inquiry was pursued with great vigour by John Watson in his enormously influential theory of behaviourism.

Freud's central ideas first became widely available in America in 1910 when the talks he had given at Clark University were published as *Five Lectures on Psycho-analysis*. Watson, who had been working with his notion of behaviourism since 1903, dismissed them out of hand, claiming that they could 'never serve as a support for a scientific formulation' (Watson, 1924, p. vii). He not only rejected the idea of the unconscious but also set out to make 'a clean break with the whole concept of consciousness' and the prevailing methods of introspection (Watson, 1924, p. viii). He argued that if psychology was to become a true 'science' and to contribute to 'the prediction and control of human action' (ibid., p. xiii) it had to focus on observed behaviour. He claimed that, providing the relevant stimuli were correctly identified, it was possible to explain all forms of behaviour 'from jumping at a sound' to 'having babies, writing books, and the like' as simple, predictable responses (Watson, 1930, p. 6). Unlike Freud, who argued that experiences (particularly in childhood) may only affect action years later, Watson insisted that the relations between stimulus and response were immediate and direct. This made them eminently suitable for investigation by laboratory experimentation, or by studies that followed the basic logic of experimentation.

Laboratories commanded pride of place in popular conceptions of 'science'. They were the spaces where important discoveries were made and conjectures subjected to rigorous testing. Hence any discipline claiming to be a 'science' had to have laboratories. Even so, Watson initially had strong reservations about their relevance to social issues. In the first edition of his major work on behaviourism, published in 1924, he conceded that 'certain important psychological undertakings probably can never be brought under laboratory control. Reference here, of course, is made to the social problems which psychology sometimes has to study. There are many problems of this character that yield only a little at the hands of a laboratory man' because key influences in the outside environment are 'not under the immediate control of the observer' (Watson, 1924, p. 28). By the time the revised edition of the book came out in 1930, however, he had become more assertive, arguing that behaviourism 'is basal to the organisation of society' and expressing the hope that 'sociology may accept its principles and re-envisage its own problems in a more concrete way' (Watson, 1930, p. 44).

By then sociological researchers were themselves deeply divided, however. Some shared Watson's enthusiasm for hard-nosed empiricism and set out to gather 'social facts' using large-scale, relatively impersonal sample surveys. But others argued that the human sciences should be concerned with understanding the close-grained textures of everyday experience and not with prediction and control. They saw them not as 'an experimental science in search of law but an interpretive one in search of meaning' (Geertz, 1973, p. 5).

These divergent traditions of inquiry produced two major research literatures on the possible relations between popular imagery and social violence. One followed the general model of experimentation and attempted to isolate the impact of screen violence, using an array of physical and statistical procedures designed to rule out 'all extraneous influences that might produce the observed effect' (Eysenck and Nias, 1978, p. 66). This approach has produced research practices which single-mindedly neglect 'questions about the social construction of meaning', relegating them to 'on the one hand, technical problems in Content Analysis and, on the other, taken-for-granted views of the general cultural context' (Tudor, 1995, p. 87). The concerted search for statistical proofs of strong effects has led its enthusiasts to make some odd claims. In January 1995, for example, the respected Swedish researcher Karl-Erik Rosengren wrote an article for *Dagens Nyheter*, one of the country's most influential newspapers. In it he claimed that 'one can say that 10–20% of all kicks and smacks in our school yards, and also with time, on our streets and squares, can be explained as direct or indirect effects of media violence' (quoted in Linné, 1995, p. 8). As critics were quick to point out, there was absolutely no way that he could make these calculations on the basis of the evidence he had collected. They were pure guesswork masquerading as 'scientific' precision.

In opposition to this euphoric dream of certainty, the interpretive tradition has developed a range of qualitative techniques – depth interviewing, focus groups, ethnographic observations of everyday life – designed to explore the myriad ways in which the experience of violence (as a reader, viewer, witness, victim or aggressor) is woven into personal identities and everyday thinking and action. Where empiricist approaches depend on a 'transportation' model of media, which sees popular forms as simple vehicles for moving meaning from one place to another, interpretive studies work with a 'translation' model (Murdock, 1994). This views popular representations as complex ensembles of meaning that can be interpreted and responded to in a variety of ways and, in its more critical variant, insists that people's relations with them can be properly understood only in the context of the networks of social relations and forces that envelop and shape them (Murdock, 1989).

Interestingly, Watson's own research experience had presented him with a perfect illustration of the dynamics of 'translation' and the limits of behaviourism. In 1919 he was asked to assess the effect of an anti-VD film on the sexual behaviour of young people. The film, a modified version of *Fit to Win* which had originally been shown as a warning against the dangers of loose living and venereal disease to American troops being shipped to the Western Front, was released for general viewing against the background of a rising tide of concern about the 'loose' morals of 'Flaming Youth'. Watson and his team observed screenings around the country, and attempted to measure any subsequent changes in the sexual behaviour of members of the audience over a period of up to three months. After sifting through the results, Watson reluctantly concluded that 'no lasting effects were found' and that 'there is no indication that behaviour is modified significantly' (Lashley and Watson, 1922, p. 216). However, he did note that observations made during screenings of the film suggested that 'the manner in which the picture presents prostitution and other material tends to break down the sense of reserve, modesty or shame' (ibid., p. 203). He was particularly concerned about the responses that greeted the appearance on the screen of captions such as 'I wouldn't touch a whore with a ten foot pole' and 'Ain't yous afraid you'll have a wet dream tonight?' (ibid., p. 209), warning that flippant banter 'readily slips to the indecent, and the step from indecent in word to indecent in act is short' (ibid., p. 203). He had inadvertently discovered a classic 'boomerang' effect.

The instability of anti-VD propaganda films as bearers of meaning was recognised by a number of social purity campaigners at the time. They applauded their message, but saw problems in the way they spoke to popular audiences through the conventions of narrative cinema. They viewed the pleasures of the screen as, themselves, intrinsically erotic. As one campaigner complained: 'instead of affecting the mind [film dramas] affect the nerves and, above all, the sexual instincts . . . In that lies the mysterious secret of the astonishing success of the cinemas' (quoted in Kuhn, 1985, p. 127).

Ironically, in the year that the report on *Fit to Win* was published, Watson was accused of misbehaviour with a female student and forced to leave his professorship at Johns Hopkins. He moved to the country's leading advertising agency, J. Walter Thompson, where he rose to become vice-president, a position that provided the perfect platform from which to sell his behaviourist theories and to experiment with the promotional stimuli that might prompt a swift purchasing response.

Although Watson has long since fallen from intellectual favour, his single-minded search for simple, direct links between stimulus and response has continued to underpin almost all later work on violent imagery in the effects tradition. This represents an unbroken line of banal science that succeeds in its own terms only because it fails to acknowledge that the making and taking of meaning in everyday life is never as straightforward as it first appears. Before we can understand how popular representations are woven into popular thinking and action, we need to restore a proper sense of complexity and context.

Addressing exclusion

As I have sought to show, the dominant 'effects' tradition has proved so resilient partly because it chimes with a deeply rooted formation of social fear which presents the vulnerable, suggestible and dangerous as living outside the stockade of maturity and reasonableness that the 'rest of us' take for granted. 'They' are the 'others', the ones 'we' must shield or protect ourselves against. As Horace Kallen noted when the new censorship began to bite in Hollywood at the beginning of the 1930s: 'When a censor proclaims that a state of danger has been created by . . . a motion picture . . . whose is the danger? His own? Never. Ostensibly, he is secure, he is beyond the reach of any subversive influence, an untouchable' (Kallen, 1930, p. 30). He was thinking of commentators like William Wadsworth, who was careful to stress that he was calling for tighter controls over popular entertainment not

> for the better care of the smug lawns and pretty garden plots, but for . . . a very real and deadly mischief lurking in our waste places . . . It is for the protection of those accidentally potential ones and for the help of those congenitally defective ones that we plead for methods of prevention.
>
> (Wadsworth, 1911, p. 321)

This bifocal vision remains at the centre of contemporary debate. As *Independent* columnist Bryan Appleyard argued, Tarantino's *Reservoir Dogs* might well be a 'brilliant' film but 'I would prefer [it] not to be seen by the criminal classes or the mentally unstable or by inadequately supervised children with little else in their lives' (Appleyard, 1993, p. 33).

The easy exclusions of these cavalier common-sense labels signal not simply a failure of the respectable imagination. They also have a hard material edge. If we are to understand and respond constructively to social violence in contemporary Britain we need to place it in the context of the massive social and psychic disruptions set in motion by mass unemployment, the decay of communal life and public space, and the evaporation of hope. It is unreasonable to expect 'hooligans' to become upright citizens unless they are offered the full range of resources required for social participation. These include not only jobs, decent living standards and a stake in the future, but also access to the information, arguments and representations that enable people to understand their situation and to recognise and respect the claims of others. Diversity of expression and debate is a precondition for dismantling exclusion. Increased censorship is a precondition for its reinforcement and for the reproduction of the violence it generates.

British controls over the content of films, television programmes and videos are already among the most restrictive of any advanced society. There is no reliable research evidence to suggest that they should be tightened further and, indeed, there are good arguments for encouraging greater openness. The justifications are not to do with the rights of media professionals but with the rights of citizenship.

NOTE

I first used this title for an earlier version of the present paper, presented to a seminar on 'Expression and Censorship' organised by the Institute for Public Policy Research. It was later used by the organisers (with due acknowledgement) as the title for the seminar's published proceedings (see Collins and Purnell, 1996, p. 1).

REFERENCES

Appleyard, Bryan (1993), 'Making a killing in videos', *Independent*, 1 December, p. 33.

Arnold, Matthew (1966), *Culture and Anarchy*, ed. with introduction by J. Dover Wilson, Cambridge: Cambridge University Press.

Chapman, Cecil (1925), *The Poor Man's Court of Justice: Twenty-Five Years as a Metropolitan Magistrate*, London: Hodder & Stoughton.

Collins, Richard and Purnell, James (1996), *Reservoirs of Dogma*, London: Institute for Public Policy Research.

Cumberbatch, Guy and Howitt, Dennis (1989), *A Measure of Uncertainty: The Effects of Mass Media*, London: John Libbey.

Edinburgh Review (1851), 'Juvenile delinquency', 94, October, pp. 403–30.

Eysenck, H. J. and Nias, D. K. B. (1978), *Sex, Violence and the Media*, London: Maurice Temple Smith.

Fenton, Frances (1910–11), 'The influence of newspaper presentations upon the growth of crime and other anti-social activity', *American Journal of Sociology*, 16, pp. 342–71, 538–64.

Freeman, A. (1914), *Boy Life and Labour*, London: P. S. King & Son.

Gauntlett, David (1995), *Moving Experiences: Understanding Television's Influences and Effects*, London: John Libbey.

Geertz, Clifford (1973), *The Interpretation of Cultures: Selected Essays*, New York: Basic Books.

Greenwood, James (1874), *The Wilds of London*, London: Chatto & Windus.

Hawes, Joseph M. (1971), *Children in Urban Society: Juvenile Delinquency in Nineteenth-century America*, New York: Oxford University Press.

Independent on Sunday (1996), 'They deserve our answers', 17 March, p. 20.

Kallen, Horace (1930), *Indecency and the Seven Arts: And Other Adventures of a Pragmatist in Aesthetics*, New York: Horace Liverlight.

Kuhn, Annette (1985), *The Power of the Image: Essays on Representation and Sexuality*, London: Routledge & Kegan Paul.

Lashley, Karl S. and Watson, John B. (1922), *A Psychological Study of Motion Pictures in Relation to Venereal Disease*, Washington, DC: Interdepartmental Social Hygiene Board.

Le Bon, Gustave (1960), *The Crowd: A Study of the Popular Mind*, New York: Viking Press.

Linne, Olga (1995), 'Media violence research in Scandinavia', *The Mordicom Review of Nordic Research on Media and Communication*, 2, pp. 1–11.

Lydston, G. Frank (1904), *The Diseases of Society (The Vice and Crime Problem)*, Philadelphia, Pa: J. B. Lippincott Company.

McClelland, J. S. (1989), *The Crowd and the Mob: From Plato to Canetti*, London: Unwin Hyman.

Mackay, Charles (1956), *Extraordinary Popular Delusions and the Madness of Crowds*, London: George Harrap.

Marx, Karl and Engels, Frederick (1968), *Selected Works in One Volume*, London: Lawrence & Wishart.

Murdock, Graham (1989), 'Critical inquiry and audience activity', in Brenda Dervin *et al.*, eds, *Rethinking Communication, Vol. 2, Paradigm Exemplars*, London: Sage Publications, pp. 226–49.

Murdock, Graham (1994), 'Visualising violence: television and the discourse of disorder', in Cees J. Hamelink and Olga Linne, eds, *Mass Communication Research: On Problems and Policies*, Norwood, NJ: Ablex Publishing Corporation, pp. 171–87.

Murdock, Graham and McCron, Robin (1979), 'The television and delinquency debate', *Screen Education*, 30, Spring, pp. 51–67.

National Council of Public Morals (1917), *The Cinema: Its Present Position and Future Possibilities*, London: Williams & Norgate.

Neil, Andrew (1996), 'Shots straight to the heart of our sick society', *Sunday Times News Review*, 17 March, p. 5.

Park, Robert (1972), *The Crowd and the Public and Other Essays*, Chicago, IL: University of Chicago Press.

Pearson, Geoffrey (1983), *Hooligan: A History of Respectable Fears*, London: Macmillan.

Peterson, Frederick (1906), 'The newspaper peril: a diagnosis of a malady of the modern mind', *Collier*'s, 1 September, pp. 12–13.

Phillips, Melanie (1994), 'Mediocrity's fight against violent truth', *Observer*, 17 April, p. 25.

Pound, Roscoe and Felix Frankfurter (1922), *Criminal Justice in Cleveland*, Cleveland: The Cleveland Foundation.

Schwarz, Bill (1996), 'Night battles: hooligan and citizen', in Mica Nava and Alan O'Shea, eds, *Modern Times: Reflections on a Century of English Modernity*, London: Routledge, pp. 101–28.

Sidis, Boris (1927), *The Psychology of Suggestion: A Research into the Subconscious Nature of Man and Society*, New York: D. Appleton.

Tarde, Gabriel (1912), *Penal Philosophy*, London: William Heinemann.

Thomas, W. I. (1908), 'The psychology of the Yellow Journal', *American Magazine*, March, pp. 491–6.

Trevarthen, J. (1901), 'Hooliganism', *The Nineteenth Century*, 49, pp. 84–9.

Tudor, Andrew (1995), 'Culture, mass communication and social agency', *Theory, Culture and Society*, 12:1, pp. 81–107.

Wadsworth, William S. (1911), 'The newspapers and crime', *American Academy of Medicine Bulletin*, 12:5, pp. 316–24.

Watson, John B. (1924), *Psychology from the Standpoint of a Behaviourist*, Philadelphia, PA: J. B. Lippincott Company.

Watson, John B. (1930), *Behaviourism*, Chicago, IL: University of Chicago Press.

Wilcox, Delos F. (1900), 'The American newspaper: a study in social psychology', *Annals of the American Academy of Political and Social Science*, 16, July, pp. 56–92.

Wright, Thomas (1881), 'On a possible popular culture', *Contemporary Review*, July, pp. 25–44.

10

US AND THEM

Julian Petley

Debates about media effects tend to focus on how children and young people are supposedly affected – usually for the worse. But lurking behind these fears about the 'corruption of innocent minds' one finds, time and again, implicit or explicit, a potent strain of class dislike and fear. The object is often the spectre of the working class in general – at other times it is more specifically defined as an 'underclass', an ideologically loaded version of what used to be called (equally ideologically) the redundant population, the relative surplus, the residuum, the *lumpenproletariat*, the social problem group, the dangerous classes, the undeserving poor and so on.

There is nothing new about such fears and dislikes, and nothing new about attempts to locate the causes of working-class 'hooliganism' in the allegedly malign effects of various forms of popular entertainment. As Orwell put it: 'the genuinely popular culture of England is something that goes on beneath the surface, unofficially and more or less frowned on by the authorities' (Orwell, 1968a, p. 78). Geoffrey Pearson (1983) has made a seminal study of the history of middle-class disapproval of working-class culture, in which he concludes that:

> popular entertainments of all kinds have been blamed for dragging down public morals in a gathering pattern of accusation which remains essentially the same even though it is attached to radically different forms of amusement: pre-modern feasts and festivals; eighteenth-century theatres and bawdy houses; mid-nineteenth-century penny gaffs; the Music Halls of the 'Gay' Nineties; the first flickering danger signs from the silent movies; the Hollywood picture palaces between the wars; and then television viewing in our own historical time. Each, in its own time, has been accused of encouraging a moral debauch; each has been said to encourage imitative crime among the young.
>
> (Pearson, 1983, p. 208)

Nor are such attitudes unique to Britain. Herbert Gans (1974) has argued that dislike of popular culture frequently stems from 'a marked disdain for ordinary people and their aesthetic capacities'. He also quotes with approval the conservative sociologist Edward Shils to the effect that 'fictions about the empirical consequences of mass culture' are based partly on a dislike of those that consume it, and also stem from the fact that 'the objects of mass culture are repulsive to us' (Gans, 1974, p. 61).

Chief amongst these 'repulsive objects' are films, whether on cinema or television screens. From its inception the cinema has been regarded by moral entrepreneurs as a cause of decline and deterioration, and as a veritable textbook of bad examples to the young, the easily influenced, the working class. Nowhere was this more clearly the case than in Britain which, consequently, had by the 1920s and 1930s built up one of the most strict and elaborate systems of film censorship in Europe. Although cinema-going was hugely popular by then, 'highly educated people saw in it only vulgarity and the end of old England' (Taylor, 1970, p. 392). Indeed, Rachel Low, the leading historian of the early British cinema, has suggested that this snobbish and fearful attitude hampered British cinema's development as an industry, making it unable to attract the necessary talent and capital. She concludes that

> in Britain the film had to overcome the resistance of a particularly inelastic social and intellectual pattern. In France and Italy the film might be a younger sister of the arts, in America art itself. In England it was a poor relation, and, moreover, not a very respectable one.
>
> (Low, 1949, pp. 137–8)

Evidence for this view is not hard to find. Pearson (1983, p. 32) quotes H. A. Secretan's 1931 account of youth work, *London Below Bridges*, to the effect that 'every boy's sympathy goes out to the lithe and resourceful crook ... Occasionally a weak-minded youth may be urged by the exploits of a Chicago gangster to essay a feeble imitation'. Meanwhile Hugh Redwood's *God in the Slums* (1932) infantilises the working class thus:

> the boys of the slums are wonderful training material for good or evil. They are children in their love of pictures and music. Hollywood's worst in the movie line has recruited hundreds of them for the gangs of race-course roughs, motor-bandits, and smash-and-grab thieves.
>
> (Pearson, 1983, p. 32)

The Second World War brought its quotient of fears about 'spivs' and 'Blitz kids', and the arrival of the Americans in Britain in large numbers served only to fuel the anti-Americanism which was to become an increasingly prominent feature of attacks on working-class popular culture. Thus, for example, George Orwell in his essay 'Raffles and Miss Blandish', comparing English and American crime fiction:

> the common people, on the whole, are still living in the world of absolute good and evil from which the intellectuals have long since escaped. But the popularity of *No Orchids* and the American books and magazines to which it is akin shows how rapidly the doctrine of 'realism' is gaining ground.

This was something which Orwell viewed with alarm:

> in Mr Chase's books there are no gentlemen and no taboos. Emancipation is complete, Freud and Machiavelli have reached the outer suburbs. Comparing the schoolboy atmosphere of the one book [*Raffles*] with the cruelty and corruption of the other, one is driven to feel that snobbishness, like hypocrisy, is a check upon behaviour whose value from a social point of view has been underrated.
>
> (Orwell, 1968b, pp. 259–60)

By the late 1940s, in spite of the efforts of the British Board of Film Censors (BBFC), the American style had found its way not only into British crime novels but into British crime films, too, such as *Noose, They Made Me a Fugitive, Brighton Rock*, the Diana Dors vehicle *Good Time Girl*, and a version of the aforementioned *No Orchids for Miss Blandish*. These 'spiv' films, with their working-class settings, then rather unusual in the overwhelmingly middle-class British cinema, aroused considerable concern on the part of society's self-appointed moral guardians, including the film critics of the national press. Thus we find Fred Majdalany of the *Daily Mail* complaining of *They Made Me a Fugitive* in the same terms that nineteenth-century critics had lambasted stories about Dick Turpin:

> I deplore the picturesque legend that is being created round that petty criminal fashionably known as the spiv. The spiv as stylised by the writers and caricatured by the actors seems to be a mixture of delightful Cockney comedian and pathetic victim of social conditions. For myself, I find the activities of sewer rats – in or out of a sewer – of strictly limited interest.
>
> (Quoted in Murphy, 1986, pp. 294–5)

Meanwhile *Miss Blandish*, even though heavily interfered with by the British Board of Film Censors, was the object of a quite extraordinarily hysterical campaign of vilification by the press, which led MPs to allege that it would 'pervert the minds of the British people', local councils to ban it and, eventually, the President of the BBFC, Sir Sidney Harris, to apologise to the Home Office for having 'failed to protect the public'!

By the early 1950s the first of the major working-class folk devils of the post-war period had appeared – the Teddy Boy. Inevitably the media were blamed, in this case music (the newly emergent rock 'n' roll) and the cinema. An early victim of this particular panic was the Marlon Brando film *The Wild One* which, it was thought, would encourage anti-social behaviour among the young, and specifically the working-class young. Thus the BBFC told the film's distributor, Columbia, that

> having regard to the present widespread concern about the increase in juvenile crime, the Board is not prepared to pass any film dealing with this subject unless the compensating moral values are so firmly presented as to justify its exhibition to audiences likely to contain (even with an 'X' certificate) a large number of young and immature persons.
>
> (Quoted in Mathews, 1994, p. 128)

This attitude was to persist. In 1959, on the occasion of one of the film's periodic rejections by the BBFC, its then Secretary John Trevelyan stated that

> the behaviour of Brando and the two gangs to authority and adults generally is of the kind that provides a dangerous example to those wretched young people who take every opportunity of throwing their weight about . . . Once again we have made the decision with reluctance because we think it is a splendid picture. I only hope the time will come, and come soon, when we do not have to worry about this kind of thing.
>
> (Quoted in ibid., p. 130)

In other words, the film is fine for us middle-class intellectuals who will judge it on 'aesthetic' grounds, but it can't be shown to the plebs in case it gets them worked up.

The Board were equally worried about the potential effects on the young of the film *The Blackboard Jungle*, which they rejected out of hand when it was first submitted, complaining, as in the case of *The Wild One*, that 'the moral values stressed by the film' were not

> sufficiently strong and powerful to counteract the harm that may be done by the spectacle of youth out of control . . . We are quite certain that *Blackboard Jungle*, filled as it is with scenes of unbridled, revolting hooliganism, would, if shown in this country, provoke the

strongest criticism from parents and all citizens concerned with the welfare of our young people and would also have the most damaging and harmful effect on such young people.

(Quoted in Robertson, 1989, p. 114)

In the event the film was passed with heavy cuts; the occasional trouble in the audience was not because of the effects of the scenes of 'unbridled, revolting hooliganism' but because the soundtrack contained Bill Haley's 'Rock Around the Clock' and teenagers, long denied proper access to rock 'n' roll by a censorious and nannyish BBC, got over-excited!

The alleged ill effects of rock 'n' roll, whether on film, record or in clubs, filled acres of column space in the press. According to a 1956 edition of the *Daily Sketch* 'rhythm-crazed teenagers terrorised a city last night', and in the same year the *Daily Mail* actually printed a front-page editorial entitled 'Rock 'n' roll Babies' in which it claimed that the music is 'often known now as rock, roll and riot' and has 'led to outbreaks of rowdyism'. It links this 'music of delinquents' with the picket-line troubles which, then as ever, were obsessing the British press, concluding that both were 'manifestations of the primitive herd instinct'. But at least the pickets were British, whilst the music 'has something of the African tomtom and the voodoo dance . . . We sometimes wonder whether this is the negro's revenge' (quoted in Pearson, 1983, p. 24). Nor were such sentiments confined to the Conservative daily press. The same year, the *Melody Maker* described rock 'n' roll as 'one of the most terrifying things to have happened to popular music' and featured a review by Steve Race of Elvis Presley's 'Hound Dog' which concluded that 'I fear for the country which ought to have had the good taste and the good sense to reject music so decadent' (quoted in Chambers, 1985, pp. 19, 30).

By the late 1950s fears about disaffected working-class youth, media effects, Americanisation, crime and national decline had become thoroughly sedimented in British 'common sense' and had formed a pervasive mythology which could routinely be wheeled out to 'explain' each and every new object of panic. In 1957 these feelings found their most comprehensive expression, up until that time, in Richard Hoggart's celebrated *The Uses of Literacy*. Whilst it needs to be stressed that Hoggart does not draw a causal connection between crime and the consumption of popular culture, his strictures on the negative effects on working-class consumers of 'Americanised' culture are unremitting. An important section of the book is devoted to the 'juke-box boys'. According to Hoggart, these are particularly symptomatic of the general trend whereby the working class has been 'culturally robbed' and fed on an ersatz diet which

is surely likely to help render its consumers less capable of responding openly and responsibly to life, is likely to induce an underlying sense of purposelessness in existence outside the limited range of a few immediate appetites. Souls which may have had little opportunity to open will be kept hard-gripped, turned in on themselves, looking out 'with odd dark eyes like windows' upon a world which is largely a phantasmagoria of passing shows and vicarious simulations.

Thus the juke-box boys, 'living to a large extent in a myth-world compounded of a few simple elements which they take to be those of American life'. Furthermore (and this is particularly important in the present context), although the whole of the working class is exposed to the 'debilitating mass-trends of the day', certain sections are more prone than others to surrender to their blandishments. Hoggart notes that if the juke-box boys

> seem to consist so far chiefly of those of poorer intelligence or from homes subject to special strains, that is probably due to the strength of a moral fibre which most cultural providers for working-class people are helping to de-nature. The hedonistic but passive barbarian who rides in a fifty-horsepower bus for threepence to see a five-million dollar film for one-and-eightpence, is not simply a social oddity; he is a portent.
>
> (Hoggart, 1957, pp. 246–50)

In the 1960s the debate about the effects of the media, especially upon the young (implicitly or explicitly working class) tended to shift its focus on to the television, and it would take a book in itself to map the features of this particular, and on-going, debate. Such a book urgently needs to be written; but, for the moment, I want to cite a couple of other cinematic instances which illustrate the class basis of many fears about media effects before going on to a more detailed study of two key 'moments' in the history of domestic video in the UK which prove the point only too clearly.

Both examples come from 1972. That was the year that the British Board of Film Censors looked as if it were going to ban the Warhol/Morrissey film *Trash* and thus confine it, like its predecessor *Flesh*, to the limbo of the specialist film club. In the end the film was passed with cuts, but not before the furore had elicited the immortal remark from a BBFC chief censor to the *Guardian*'s film critic, Derek Malcolm, to the effect that 'it is all very well for sophisticated, educated people like you to go to the ICA cinema and see Warhol's *Trash*. But think of its effect on your average factory worker in Manchester' (quoted in Malcolm, 1984). (I myself was present at a National Film Theatre screening of *The Texas Chainsaw Massacre* in the late 1970s when the then BBFC Director, James Ferman, made a similar remark, except that the 'average factory worker in Manchester' became the 'car-worker in Birmingham'.)

Nineteen seventy-two was also the year that *A Clockwork Orange* was released. Even before it had appeared, the Labour MP Maurice Edelman was writing in the *Evening News* that 'when *Clockwork Orange* is generally released it will lead to a clockwork cult which will magnify teenage violence' (27 January 1972). Needless to say, within weeks of the film's release the press was full of stories about 'copy-cat crimes' and wild denunciations of both Kubrick and his creation. The *Evening News* dug out a former chaplain to Pinewood Studios to denounce this 'celluloid cesspool' and allege that 'it is the weak, the impressionable and the immature which such a film helps to destroy' (4 July 1973). Needless to say, the stories of 'copy-cat crimes' don't bear up to investigation, but this hasn't stopped them passing into effects mythology (see Martin, 1995; Petley, 1995; Wistrich, 1978, pp. 129–30).

As Tom Dewe Mathews has argued (1994, p. 2), in Britain censorship is governed by the 'long-serving, silently spoken rubric: the larger the audience, the lower the moral mass resistance to suggestion'. In other words, the more popular the cultural form, the more likely it is to be seen by members of the working class, the more heavily its content is likely to be regulated and, if necessary, censored. The whole attitude is perfectly summed up by the prosecution's famous question at the start of the *Lady Chatterley* trial in 1960 – 'Is it a book that you would even wish your wife or your servants to read?' – but it is often overlooked that an important part of the prosecution's closing speech rested on a quite explicit contrast between the way in which the defence's academic and literary experts would read the book and the way in which 'the ordinary man in the street' would do so. Thus, for example, the film critic Dilys Powell's reading is explicitly contrasted with how 'the young men and boys leaving school . . . at the age of 15, going into their first jobs this last September' would supposedly read it; the Bishop of Woolwich with 'the girls working in the factory'; Rebecca West with 'the average reader'; and all of these witnesses with the 'ordinary, common men and women' (Rolph, 1961, pp. 214–19).

No one should be in the least surprised, therefore, given the prevalence of such attitudes, that the prospect of unregulated, uncensored videos being freely available to the British public at the start of the 1980s was greeted with such horror and dismay from certain quarters, and that draconian censorship was soon imposed (for the full story of this process see Barker, 1984; Petley, 1984; Martin, 1997). What concerns us here are the threads of class dislike and fear that weave their way through this particular saga. Admittedly, most of the concern expressed about the original so-called 'video nasties' was about their supposed effects on children and young people, but from time to time the class dimension of the perceived problem rose visibly to the surface.

For example, in the *Mail* on 28 June 1983, Lynda Lee Potter complained of 'the impact that this sick, beastly, money-making corruption is having on illiterate minds', whilst in the *Telegraph* of 2 November 1983 the Prime Minister's daughter Carol Thatcher quoted the NSPCC's director Dr Alan Gilmour as describing the experience of a senior social worker in a deprived area of Greater Manchester who, making a call on a family at 9.30 a.m., had to wait until the whole family had finished watching the rape scene in *I Spit on Your Grave*.

Mathews (1994, p. 250) also quotes a revealing remark by Ken Penry, the deputy director of the BBFC, about one of the most notorious 'nasties', *Driller Killer*:

> now and again, you get clever dicks who say, 'Ah, this is art. This is bigger than it seems'. But I think of Joe Bloggs who's going to the Odeon on Saturday night who's not on that wavelength. He's going along seeing it literally and I always keep that in mind. Joe Bloggs is the majority and film censorship is for the majority.

The issue of class also crops up in the *Video Violence and Children* report which played such a major role in the passing of the 1984 Video Recordings Act. This is not the place to recount the story of the report (see Barker, 1984) but it is important to note what it has to say about social class and exposure to 'video nasties'.

Thus, for example, apropos children's alleged exposure to 'nasties', the report says that 'social class seems to be a relevant variable . . . working-class children, especially those from large families, appear most at risk in watching the "nasties"' (Hill, 1983, p. 15). There's a suggestion that this remark is based on a questionnaire sent out to parents, but the only problem is that this had not been analysed at the time the report was published. The remark appears in the section entitled 'Reactions of Children', but the report itself makes clear that this is not based directly on answers to questionnaires which were handed out to schoolchildren but was 'compiled from data supplied to us by teachers who conducted the survey and subsequently led discussions and had conversations with individual children' (Hill, 1983, p. 14). In a later document (Barlow and Hill, 1985, p. 14) it is explained that the purpose of these discussions was

> to provide additional data relating to the children's viewing patterns and to act as a check upon the accuracy of the answers provided in the questionnaires . . . Further data was obtained from head teachers who often gave an overview of the situation in their school with age groups other than those included in the sample obtained from their school. Hence a dossier of anecdotal data was produced to go alongside the statistical data derived from the analysis of questionnaire returns.

Clearly, then, a good deal of the report is based on teachers' *perceptions* of their pupils' viewing habits. In responding to criticisms of the report's methodology, Hill (1983, p. 164) offers a rather unfortunate hostage to fortune by stating that 'children are notoriously unreliable respondents. But so are adults!' In this respect it is extremely difficult to take seriously those sections of the report which seem to have been strained through a sieve of intense teacherly disdain for popular culture – not to mention for their pupils as well. For example, this is a teacher in a South London comprehensive with a mixed fourth-year class of boys and girls:

> this is quite a 'nice' class by this school's standards. In discussion afterwards I was quite surprised. They nearly all prefer the horror films. They like the blood and they didn't think that 'video nasties' should be banned. For most there was no parental control over television or video viewing. Most parents would allow younger children to watch violent videos.
>
> (ibid., p. 143)

In the earlier document we find that:

> One headmaster of a school in the Surrey commuter belt said that even those children who come from home backgrounds where they are highly protected and where parents take them and fetch them from school are nevertheless being affected by the values of violence and horror that are being transmitted in the playground from children from less protected home backgrounds.
>
> (Hill, 1983, p. 15)

Nor were such attitudes confined to the Home Counties:

> the headmaster of a primary school in a mixed social class London suburb said that the reaction of middle class children to hearing the playground stories of those who were allowed to watch violent videos was often one of 'suppressed envy'. He spoke of the great danger facing the children through the permissive attitude of the playground that reinforces the values of violence and impresses them upon the children despite the values they derive from their home and family backgrounds.
>
> (ibid., p. 16)

Teachers' observations also led them to conclude that

> among many boys, especially from working class backgrounds, watching the 'nasties' has become a test of manliness ... For working class boys, especially those who are unable to achieve

educationally, knowledge of the most intimate details of violent video films carries with it a kind of 'butch kudos'.

(ibid., p. 16)

As Michael Tracey put it at the time: 'it is very difficult to see what can be claimed for such information, which of its nature can have no real social scientific significance' (Tracey, 1984) – except as, one might add, a depressing indicator of the degree of paedophobia and snobbery amongst teachers. To be asked to regard such people as reliable rapporteurs of young people's viewing habits – particularly in the midst of a lurid press blitz on 'video nasties' – is quite frankly preposterous.

Such sentiments would matter less if they had remained firmly in the staff room; but, unfortunately, if entirely predictably, they were massively amplified by the way in which the report was treated by the press – often as the lead story on the front page, no less. Such stories build on the already-existing repertoire of class dislike which, as we have seen, has a long history. They, in turn, then enter the mythology: witness Harry Greenway, the Conservative MP for Ealing North, in a debate on the Video Recordings Bill on 16 March 1984, who argued that videos 'are often a higher priority in the homes of people who are not particularly articulate, and who do not read books or listen to music very much. In some homes videos even take priority over food and furniture'. Clearly, the Sturdy Beggar was alive and well and stalking the streets of West London in 1984.

By the time of the next most significant 'moment' in the seemingly never-ending 'video nasty' débâcle in Britain – the aftermath of the murder of James Bulger, and the efforts of the press to blame it on the effects of *Child's Play III* on his killers (see Petley, 1993) – the discourse of class had become even more evident in the 'debate' (and this in spite of John Major's rhetorical evocations of the 'classless' society). More specifically, the 'video nasty' issue was deliberately and explicitly used as an illustration of the dangers of the so-called 'underclass'.

Broadly speaking, there are two versions of 'underclass' theory. The liberal version, of which Frank Field's *Losing Out: The Emergence of the British Underclass* is a clear example, holds that increasingly uneven economic growth, the restructuring (or destruction) of manufacturing industry, poor education, poor childcare facilities and the general failure of the 'flexible' economy to create a sufficient number of decently paid jobs have detached a growing number of people from society and from citizenship. The Conservative version of this theory, best represented by Charles Murray's *Losing Ground* and *The Emerging British Underclass*, and L. M. Mead's *Beyond Entitlement: The Social Obligations of Citizenship*, is really little more than an updating of the notion of the 'undeserving poor'. Its more recent antecedents can be traced at least as far back as the 'Cycles of Deprivation' project initiated by Sir Keith Joseph when he was Secretary of State for

179

Education, to the 'moment of the mugger' (Hall *et al.*, 1978), and above all to the great 'scrounger-phobia' outbreak of 1976 so brilliantly analysed by Golding and Middleton (1982).

In the Conservative version of 'underclass' theory 'the term has acquired a sense both pejorative and threatening', as Lydia Morris (1994, p. 1) has put it. Here the 'underclass' is represented as a sub-section of the poor, living off mainstream society (either via welfare benefits or crime) whilst not only refusing to participate in it but actively rejecting its dominant norms and values. The real problem, according to this point of view, is that benefits have created a 'dependency culture' or 'culture of poverty', in which no stigma or disadvantage is attached to being unemployed and/or a single mother. Indeed, since the State will provide, either or both may well have distinct advantages. If members of the 'underclass' are unemployed it is because their attitudes exclude them from the labour market, not because there are no jobs. An absence of proper role models (that is, the two-parent family), parental irresponsibility, early school leaving and poor socialisation have combined to produce entirely unemployable people trapped in a 'cycle of dependency'.

Such a theory obviously has enormous attraction to the Right, and there are no prizes for guessing which version of the theory has been overwhelmingly favoured by the British press, especially *The Times, Sunday Times* and *Mail*, which have regularly provided a highly uncritical platform for the ideas of Murray and his followers. Let me conclude by illustrating this by reference to press coverage of the aftermath of the murders of James Bulger and Suzanne Capper (another young person whose murder was pinned by the press, without a shred of justification, on *Child's Play III*).

The link between videos, violence and the 'underclass' during this particular 'moment' was first made, interestingly, not in a Conservative paper but in the *Independent*, by Brian Appleyard on 1 December 1993, in which he asked rhetorically: 'Would you allow an ill-educated, culturally deprived, unemployable underclass unlimited access to violent pornography?' Ignoring the inconvenient fact that *no one* in Britain has unlimited access to such material anyway, he blithely continues that if you abolish censorship (which most certainly has *not* happened in the UK)

> you don't just get Mapplethorpe for the connoisseur, you also get vicious drivel for the masses. More painfully, you also get unarguably fine films such as *Taxi Driver* and *Goodfellas*, which, if you are honest, you would rather were not watched by certain types of people.

Reservoir Dogs is also singled out as a 'brilliant, bloody film that I would prefer not to be seen by the criminal classes or the mentally unstable or by inadequately supervised children with little else in their lives'.

Even more up-front was an editorial in the *Mail* on 18 December in the wake of the just-concluded trial of the murderers of Suzanne Capper. Noting that the police had commented on the murderers' 'ordinariness' the paper went into ideological overdrive, proclaiming that

> they are the product of a society which tolerates petty crime, the break-up of families and feckless spending. It subsidises and, in many cases, encourages them. It is interesting to note that most of Suzanne's tormentors were on social security. But then those in society who are genuinely out of work but who have savings, do not receive income support. Thus are the prudent penalised while the negligent are nurtured . . . All this reflects a society showing reckless disregard for the survival of its own decency. An underclass is being created today which is a grave threat to Britain's future. If it is not countered, then we will continue a decline towards lawlessness and degeneracy.

What kind of mind makes ideological capital out of a particularly brutal murder? One that is so demented that it appears to think that sadistic killers are created, if not by 'video nasties', then by what's left of the welfare state.

In the *Telegraph*, 20 February 1984, the inner-city GP and Fleet Street regular Theodore Dalrymple also bemoans the condition of a section of the population, although not from the *Mail*'s grotesque viewpoint nor with any direct reference to the 'underclass'. However, it is clear to whom he is referring. This is a terrible sphere in which 'children are growing up without any spiritual or cultural framework whatever', a world of 'degraded rootlessness and desolate isolation', in which mothers appear not to know that parental control is either 'desirable or necessary' and 'fathers, except in the biological sense, are generally unknown or, if known, are violent, arbitrary, abusive and uncouth'. In this void of 'quotidian savagery' 'there are no positive moral influences [but] there are plenty of negative ones, chief among which are those of television and, worse still, of video'. Whilst 'liberals in Hampstead' and the 'intellectual classes' pooh-pooh the effects of video, from which they are anyway immune, 'the effect on minds which are entirely empty of a moral framework' is likely to be devastating.

Entirely unsurprisingly, the connection between the 'underclass' and 'video nasties' came very much to the fore at the time of the Alton amendment to the Criminal Justice Bill, aimed at tightening video censorship still further. Thus in the *Sunday Times* of 3 April 1994 we find one Margaret Driscoll arguing that 'the children most likely to be damaged are those being brought up in sink estates where family values no longer hold sway – the products of the "anything goes" society', whilst a *Times* editorial of 11 April 1994 held forth that 'horror-video addiction is part of a socially-disadvantaged sink culture in which lack of parental supervision is endemic'.

Meanwhile, two days later the inevitable Lynda Lee Potter in her *Mail* column shrieked that

> there are thousands of children in this country with fathers they never see and mothers who are lazy sluts. They are allowed to do what they want, when they want. They sniff glue on building sites, scavenge for food and, until now, they were free to watch increasingly horrific videos. By 16 they are disturbed and dangerous.

Again, it's worth pointing out that such views are not confined to the Conservative press. In the *Guardian* of 16 April, Edward Pearce argues that, as far as the sale and renting of videos is concerned,

> it won't do just to restrict juveniles. Let's be plain. In an underclass family where books are unknown, where dynastic unemployment has brought all restraints to a base level, who do we suppose buys the nasty – uncontrolled kids or indifferent father? The law must aim at all sales of injurious goods to anyone.

And in the following day's *Observer* Melanie Phillips, in the course of a polemic against media researchers who have the temerity to disagree with her, confidently states that 'video violence is merely a part of that culture of material and emotional disadvantage which gives rise to young delinquents'.

The most sustained attempt to link 'video nasties' to the 'underclass', however, is to be found in Barbara Amiel's column in that day's *Sunday Times*. Curiously, the article takes an anti-censorship line, arguing that 'while much ails the nation, it is not the viewing of *Child's Play III*, no matter how wretched that video' and that 'time and again we enact cosmetic legislation rather than deal with the real issues'. Quite. However, it rapidly becomes clear that what Amiel means by this is knocking the hell out of what she revealingly calls the 'residium' (sic). This entails that we 'revise immigration policies' and 'stop further reform of our divorce laws'. In more general terms we have to stop trying to create an 'inclusive culture', and

> we can segregate the underclass and forget about egalitarian prin-ciples. We should try to reintroduce the best of our values while getting rid of the worst. We must stop ruining our free society by enacting rules appropriate for a zoo. Just because some of the rooms in our house have been taken over by pigs and donkeys does not mean that we should turn the entire kingdom into a place appropri-ate for the housing of animals – which is what we do when enacting blanket legislation for everyone, such as the new censorship rules . . . We cannot even console ourselves that we are doing something useless that is at least not injurious. We are injuring everything.

In other words, thanks to the presence of the 'underclass', who can't be entrusted to watch violent videos without running amok, the freedom of the middle class to do what it wants has been unreasonably curtailed.

This chapter has attempted to demonstrate, across a wide time-scale and range of media, the remarkable prevalence and persistence of certain quite specific views of the effects of the media on members of the working class. We started off in the pre-modern era and ended up in 1994, though readers of Barbara Amiel may have thought it was 1794. It's depressing how little has changed in the way of attitudes, both to popular culture and to the working class. Of course, it could be argued that these are not the attitudes of ordinary people but, for the most part, of the moral entrepreneurs and of a notoriously conservative (and Conservative) press. None the less, it *is* disturbing that, in the on-going controversy about 'video nasties', the tone of class dislike and, in some cases, hatred should be so much more pronounced, unashamed and *naked* in 1993/4 than in 1983/4.

It could also be argued that these attitudes have remained so constant for so long because they are rooted in actuality and based on fact. In other words, people believe that working-class people are more likely than middle-class ones to be adversely affected by media messages because it's true, they are! The answer to that, however, is: prove it. Anybody who tries to read through the literature on this subject will encounter a great deal of confident assertion and bluff 'common sense', but precious little in the way of social scientific research. *Video Violence and Children* attempted to penetrate this particular thicket but, as we have seen, its assertions about the links between social class and video viewing are really little more than that. Other than that, what are we left with – except the huffings and puffings of a few Fleet Street pundits, a hideously reactionary bunch at the best of times, and hardly an informed or authoritative source of reliable knowledge on this or any other matter. Of course, to lay bare the lengthy history of a particular claim or belief is not sufficient to expose it as a myth, but it does begin to look dangerously threadbare when no reliable evidence can be adduced with which to back it up.

Our main concern in this chapter has been with how films, television and videos have been regarded as affecting working-class people 'worse' than middle-class ones. In our discussion of the 'underclass', however, and of the way in which ultra-Conservative versions of the theory have been assiduously pedalled by sections of the British press, we have ended up by touching on one of the most poisonous legacies of the Thatcher–Major years – the deliberate exclusion of a growing number of people from being considered as members of society. But then, of course, there was no such thing.

REFERENCES

Barker, M. (ed.) (1984), *The Video Nasties: Freedom and Censorship in the Media*, London: Pluto Press.

Barlow, G. and Hill, A. (eds) (1985), *Video Violence and Children*, London: Hodder & Stoughton.

Chambers, I. (1985), *Urban Rhythms: Pop Music and Popular Culture*, London: Macmillan.

Field, F. (1989), *Losing Out: The Emergence of the British Underclass*, Oxford: Basil Blackwell.

Gans, H. (1974), *Popular Culture and High Culture: An Analysis and Evaluation of Taste*, New York: Basic Books.

Golding, P. and Middleton, S. (1982), *Images of Welfare: Press and Public Attitudes to Welfare*, Oxford: Martin Robertson.

Hall, S., Critcher, C., Jefferson, T., Clarke, J. and Roberts, B. (1978), *Policing the Crisis: Mugging, the State and Law and Order*, London: Macmillan.

Hill, C. (1983), *Video Violence and Children: Children's Viewing Patterns in England and Wales*, London: Oasis Projects.

Hoggart, R. (1957), *The Uses of Literacy*, London: Chatto & Windus.

Low, R. (1949), *The History of the British Film, 1906–1914*, London: Allen & Unwin.

Malcolm, D. (1984), 'Stand up to the new censorship', in the *Guardian*, 15 March.

Martin, J. (1997), *The Seduction of the Gullible: The Curious History of the British 'Video Nasty' Phenomenon*, Nottingham: Procrustes Press.

Martin, J. (1995), 'Curse of the copycat people', in *The Dark Side*, 50, October.

Mathews, T. D. (1994), *Censored: What They Didn't Allow YOU to See and Why: The Story of Film Censorship in Britain*, London: Chatto & Windus.

Mead, L. M. (1986), *Beyond Entitlement: The Social Obligations of Citizenship*, New York: Free Press.

Morris, L. (1994), *Dangerous Classes: The Underclass and Social Citizenship*, London: Routledge.

Murphy, R. (1986), 'Riff-raff: British cinema and the underworld', in C. Barr, ed., *All Our Yesterdays: 90 Years of British Cinema*, London: British Film Institute.

Murray, C. (1984), *Losing Ground*, New York: Basic Books

Murray, C. (1990), *The Emerging British Underclass*, London: Institute of Economic Affairs.

Orwell, G. (1968a), *The Collected Essays, Journalism and Letters of George Orwell, Vol. 2, My Country Right or Left*, London: Secker & Warburg.

Orwell, G. (1968b), *The Collected Essays, Journalism and Letters of George Orwell, Vol. 3, As I Please*, London: Secker & Warburg.

Pearson, G. (1983), *Hooligan: A History of Respectable Fears*, London: Macmillan.

Petley, J. (1984), 'A nasty story', *Screen*, 25:2, pp. 68–74.

Petley, J. (1993), 'In defence of "video nasties"', *British Journalism Review*, 5:3, pp. 52–7.

Petley, J. (1995), 'Clockwork crimes', *Index on Censorship*, 24:6, pp. 48–52.

Robertson, J. C. (1989), *The Hidden Cinema: British Film Censorship in Action, 1913–1975*, London: Routledge.

Rolph, C. H. (ed.) (1961), *The Trial of Lady Chatterley: Regina v. Penguin Books Limited*, London: Penguin.

Taylor, A. J. P. (1970), *English History 1914–1945*, London: Penguin.

Tracey, M. (1984), 'Casting cold water on the ketchup', *The Times*, 25 February.

Wistrich, E. (1978), '*I Don't Mind the Sex It's the Violence': Film Censorship Explored*, London: Marion Boyars.

11

INVASION OF THE INTERNET ABUSERS

Marketing fears about the information superhighway

Thomas Craig and Julian Petley

When video games first appeared around the beginning of the 1980s, people who played them regarded them simply as harmless fun. But, as with any new form of popular entertainment, voices of concern began increasingly to make themselves heard both within academic research and via the mainstream media. Unsurprisingly, given the history of fears about the popular media, a common theme was the level of violence within some of these games, and the worry was increasingly voiced that playing video games containing high levels of violence would lead to the stimulation of violent behaviour by the player. Although relatively little research had been carried out up until this point, in 1991 Eugene Provenzo felt confident enough to assert that 'concern about the games is in fact justified' (Provenzo, 1991: 50), and that 'there does seem to be a significant relationship between aggressive behaviour on the part of the subjects and the playing of video games' (ibid.: 69). However, it needs to be understood that Provenzo (a Professor of Education at the University of Miami) relied almost exclusively on work conducted within the kind of psychological paradigm criticised elsewhere in this book, and seems simply unaware of any form of media studies research – which might, for instance, have undone his naïve categorisations of games by 'levels of violence' and by 'stereotypes'.

By the early 1990s, in Britain at least, some parents were already beginning to demand refunds on games containing violence which they felt was not only inappropriate for their children, but just plain inappropriate. An increasing number of pundits had already begun to voice concerns not simply about violence but also about 'keyboard-junkies', the neglect of more 'worthwhile' activities and various other allegedly negative consequences of playing video games. Thus, for example, in 1993 the *Sun* reported that a boy had choked to death after an epileptic fit induced by playing video games, whilst on 25 October 1993 a story appeared in the *Daily Telegraph* under the headline 'Children "act out video violence"' which began:

> Children who regularly play video games admit they can be addictive and lead to them acting out the violent scenes that are an intrinsic part of many games, according to a survey by researchers at Aston University. Many described violent scenes 'with relish', they found. Almost 60 per cent had witnessed other children mimicking violent games.

The *Telegraph*'s negative slant becomes all the more apparent if we compare it with the way the *New Scientist* reviewed the report on 4 December 1993. Under the headline 'How kids cope with video games', it began:

> Video games can make children lose their temper and act violently, but they are not a root cause of bad behaviour, say psychologists who have investigated the way children respond to games. Children play video games essentially to fill in time, to relieve boredom on rainy days, and also to make friends. Parents misinterpret their effects because they cannot understand the technology or the attraction, say the psychologists.

Needless to say, it was to be the former style of reporting which would dominate the coverage of video games in the years to come.

Equally predictably, the fears about video which found such momentous expression in the press following the death of James Bulger had a knock-on effect in the field of computer games. In April 1994 a report entitled *The Street of the Pied Piper* was published by the Professional Association of Teachers (PAT) and caught the attention of sections of the press. In particular, the *Daily Express* (18 April 1994) published a long article entitled 'Videos turn a generation of children into violent louts'. Here 'violent videos and computer games' are lumped together as having a 'devastating impact' on 'the vast majority of children'; three quarters of the 'more than 1,000 teachers' questioned are reported as saying that pupils were being 'adversely affected' by video games, and 'more than half claimed that the games are destroying pupils' ability to concentrate. Some children are so hooked that they are unwilling to talk about anything else'. According to the article: 'computer games cause tiredness and inattention in class. Among other effects are: aggression, addiction, slow academic progress, acting out fantasies, withdrawn behaviour and epileptic seizures'. The report also received a good deal of uncritical coverage in the same day's *Telegraph*, *Independent*, *The Times* and *Guardian*.

The report itself, however, barely begins to substantiate these lurid claims in a remotely convincing fashion. Exactly like the notorious *Video Violence and Children*, this work is based solely on a survey of teachers' *perceptions* of the effects of new entertainment technologies on children, and as a result tells us a great deal more about teachers than about their pupils (see Barker, 1984: 68–87 and the previous chapter of this book).[1] The PAT report is nothing more than a mass of anecdotal evidence. It attempts to substantiate its conclusions simply by anonymously reprinting teachers' comments, many of which are speculative, alarmingly over-simplistic, or simply betray a striking dislike of their pupils. Although questionnaires were sent to 35,000 members of the Association, the findings of the report were based on an analysis of only 833 replies (not the 'more than 1,000' alleged by the *Express*). Despite such a poor response (which suggests that many members may not have perceived the new media as such a pressing problem), the Association argued that this sample constituted a 'solid body of opinion' (ibid.: 2). Just as likely is that, since 48 per cent of respondents had been teaching for over twenty years, many of these teachers were themselves very uncomfortable with new communications technologies and therefore more inclined towards technophobia. A *Guardian*/ICM opinion poll conducted at the end of 1999 showed that, even five years after the PAT survey was carried out, only 35 per cent of 35 to 64-year-olds had access to the Internet, compared with 60 per cent of the 18 to 24 age group.

As stories such as these continued to circulate in the press, demands soon followed in Parliament for tighter external regulation and control of video games, and for games to be subject to a ratings system similar to that applied to videos. Moreover, the increasingly shrill condemnations of certain items of software seemed to be spilling over into a condemnation of the *technology itself*.

These claims did not go unchallenged, even among those inclined towards standard psychological researches, even if the challenges went largely unreported in the press. Thus, for example, the psychologist Mark Griffiths has argued that assertions that children become more aggressive after playing video games 'have been made without the backup of empirical evidence. Despite the continuing controversy for over 15 years, there has been relatively little systematic research' (1997: 397). He concludes that what research there has been has concentrated only on short-term effects, that 'correlations may not be directly causal at all but may result from mediating factors (e.g. low educational attainment, low socio-economic status etc.) that may themselves be causally related both to video game playing and to aggressive behaviour' (ibid.: 399), that 'there is much speculation as to whether the procedures to measure aggression levels are valid and reliable' (ibid.: 400), and finally that 'there are also problems concerning the definition of "violent" and "aggressive"' (ibid.: 400) as applied to individual computer games. Two years later Griffiths was still concluding that 'research into the effects of long-term exposure to video games on subsequent aggressive behaviour is noticeably lacking and at present remains speculative' (1999: 210). Similarly, Barrie Gunter (1998), summarising all the research to that point, concludes that such fear and loathing within the media has yet to be substantiated by any conclusive research into the negative effects of video games. As he says, 'as yet there is insufficient research to support strong causal statements about the impact of playing violent electronic games' (1998: 94), and

> so far, however, the research evidence on the effects of violent video games has been equivocal. Whether or not playing such games displays any manifest link with players' subsequent behavioural tendencies seems to vary with the type of research methodology deployed to investigate this question (ibid.: 108–9).

The point here is that, as so often, the conclusions are 'known' before the research is even attempted.

Worse even than 'violence'

As the new communications technologies spread and grew, so the papers began to broaden their concerns. The alleged dangers of video games continued still to be reported, *Carmageddon II*, *Postal* and *Grand Theft Auto* all coming under sustained attack – along with the non-existent *Scum*, a spoof game (motto: 'if it breathes, it's toast') invented one April Fool's Day by the magazine *Playstation Plus* to demonstrate just how gullible the papers were about video games. But the 1990s also saw the arrival of a new and infinitely more seductive enemy in town: computer porn, especially when found on the Internet. In February 1994 the Home Affairs Committee published its first report on computer pornography, which opened with the words 'computer pornography is a new horror' (1994: v), noted that 'we have been told that pornographic disks have been swapped in school playgrounds' (ibid.) and that 'we have been told of developments such as interactive computerised pornography and eventually Virtual Reality, which will result in pornography which has a much greater tendency to deprave and corrupt, and on a much wider scale' (ibid.: xv), and concluded with the recommendation that the Government 'remains vigilant towards the threat to the innocence and decency of our children posed by computer pornography' (ibid.). As the *Guardian* helpfully put it on 16 April 1994: 'forget the video nasty: the latest moral panic is computer porn'. Allegations about the availability of computer pornography in British schools soon began to become widespread. For example, that year it was widely reported that a police officer in Luton had infiltrated a school exchange network and seized approximately 700 floppy disks containing computer pornography. After all the publicity surrounding this incident, it later emerged, quietly, that the seized disks were in fact clean.

As in the case of the PAT outcry over computer games, the computer porn story was given a significant boost in the press by a piece of 'research' which claimed a great deal more than it could actually substantiate. A survey carried out by Vicki Merchant, Harassment Officer at the University of Central Lancashire, claimed that computer pornography has been seen by pupils at one in ten secondary schools in Britain and in 2 per cent of primaries. The survey was based on a questionnaire sent to 28,000 schools, of which 27 per cent responded. However, only a quarter of these were from secondary schools, and only 1.4 per cent of the total came from all-male secondary schools, suggesting a low level of concern about the problem in the educational sector in which one might have expected it to be strongest. Furthermore, even Merchant herself had to admit that the 'vast majority' of respondents did not report any computer pornography at all in their schools. But the most important point is that the survey, just like *The Street of the Pied Piper*, is based simply on teachers' *impressions*, and these, as any researcher knows, are far from reliable. Furthermore, it's difficult to avoid the conclusion that a certain kind of agenda is being peddled here. Thus in a piece entitled 'Computer porn "at 1 in 10 schools"' in the *Guardian*, 16 June 1994, Merchant is quoted as describing the hard-core discs reported by teachers as containing images of 'real people being abused, raped and tortured. They are not actors and nothing is simulated',[2] whilst in a piece in Sainsbury's *The Magazine*, September 1994, Merchant puts forward another highly questionable view, namely that 'because it [computer pornography] demands intense interaction with the screen, it has a more addictive and isolating effect. It enables a young male to manipulate, use force against and control a woman. If on screen, why not in reality?' What Merchant's rhetoric does here is something which is documented elsewhere in this book: making a case that *this time* it is different, *this* technology is uniquely 'dangerous'.

Although the Internet, as it is recognised today, has yet to reach its tenth anniversary, public interest in cyberspace has escalated at an extraordinary rate since the Internet's inception. Not all of this interest has been positive, however, and the press in particular have frequently concentrated on the 'dark side' of the Internet, utilising their tried and tested scare stories about 'video nasties' and video games as a partial blueprint. As John Naughton felt the need to point out as far back as 1996 in an article 'Monsters from cyberspace' in the *Observer* (9 June): 'to judge from British coverage of the subject, there are basically only three Internet stories': 'Cyberporn invades Britain', 'Police crack Internet sex pervert ring', and 'Net addicts lead sad virtual lives'. An apt summary. A pity, then, that the *Observer* itself was far from immune from the temptation to demonise the Internet. Indeed, as many of the quotations in this chapter clearly demonstrate, the broadsheet press has been just as adept as the tabloids, and arguably *more* so, at playing this particular game. And as time has gone on, the papers have come to develop an approach to the issue that increasingly, and quite bizarrely, intermingles condemnation of this new technology for bringing pornography into the home with the most uncritical hype about it changing all our lives for ever.

The increasing demonisation of the Internet was given a substantial boost by Senator Charles E. Grassley's 1995 announcement that '83.5 per cent of all computerised photographs available on the Internet are pornographic' (Hoffman and Novak, 1997). His statement was based on a recently published report by Marty Rimm of the Carnegie-Mellon University of Pittsburgh entitled *Marketing Pornography on the Information Superhighway*. This claimed that pornography was 'one of the biggest, if not the biggest, recreational applications of users of computer networks', and that 15 of the top 40 (as measured by traffic volume) Usenet newsgroups distribute pornography. Rimm's report was later heavily criticised for, amongst other things, misrepresentation (the report deals neither with 'marketing' nor 'the information superhighway'), manipulation (the study was not subject to peer-review), lack of objectivity (it makes a number of unsupported causal statements), confusion (mixing up the World Wide Web, Usenet and bulletin board services) and methodological flaws (for further discussion of the problems with the report see Hoffman and Novak, 1995).

However, nothing daunted, on 25 June 1995, under the headline 'On a screen near you: cyberporn', *Time* magazine used this same report to persuade its readership that computer monitors across the world were on the verge of being invaded by the most graphic depictions of rape, paedophilia, bestiality and other unmentionable acts. Furthermore, it suggested that you did not even have to bother to go looking for such material: 'it' would find you, whether you liked it or not. Inevitably, this lurid report soon became the basis for a media game of Chinese Whispers. Thus on the American television show *Nightline*, Ralph Reed of the conservative Christian Coalition 'quoted' from *Time* to the effect that 'one-quarter of all the images [on the Internet] involve the torture of women', an allegation which appears neither in the magazine nor in Rimm's original.

It was not long before similar sorts of stories were appearing in the British press. On 13 September 1995, two months after *Time* had run its story, the *Daily Telegraph* declared in a story headlined 'Electronic porn floods network' that 'paedophiles and pornographers are becoming the biggest users of the Internet', adding for good measure that 'half the non-academic material in the "global village" is pornographic', whilst the *Evening Standard*, 11 October 1995, called the Internet 'a heavily used red-light district, sending pornography into millions of homes'.

Today, reports relating to the pornographic invasion of cyberspace still appear in the press with monotonous regularity, and 'pornography' and 'violence' still remain key words in many newspaper stories and features about cyberspace. Furthermore, spreading pornography is by no means the only sin laid at the Internet's door. Not untypical was an article on 23 June 1999 in the *Guardian* which gave considerable uncontested space to a study by the

National Criminal Intelligence Service which argued that 'hacking, viruses, child pornography are already well-known problems [on the Internet], but others are emerging such as cyber-stalking, blackmail by email, hate sites, work rage and gambling'. However, the study appears to be largely a pretext for arguing for the creation of a national computer crime unit. And it was 'hate sites' which attracted a great deal of media attention in the wake of the Columbine high school massacre a few months later. Thus in a lengthy *Guardian* piece on 26 August 1999 with the sub-heading 'The dream of using the net to promote global harmony has been shattered by neo-Nazis and white supremacists who are using it to beat bans on racial hatred', Nick Ryan rehearsed an already over-familiar litany: 'if you believe the scare stories, the net is a hive of hate, from anti-abortionists promoting hitlists to an international trade in white power music CDs – and even a British far right with an increasingly active web presence'. In recent times the Internet has also been regularly blamed for helping soccer hooligans to plan their campaigns of violence and (especially in the *Sunday Times*) anti-globalisation protestors to organise demonstrations against the World Trade Organisation and similar institutions of global capitalism.

The discovery of 'kiddie porn'

1999 saw the publication of over 200 stories centred on the distribution of child pornography alone via the Internet. Nonetheless, it cannot be stressed too strongly that there is less pornographic material *in general* on the Internet, and it is more difficult to access, than is often claimed. Even the *Time* article cited above had to admit, albeit buried deeply in the text, that 'pornographic image files, despite their evident popularity, represent only about 3 per cent of all the messages on the Usenet newsgroups, while the Usenet itself represents only 11.5 per cent of traffic on the Internet'. Meanwhile, an article by Mike Holderness, entitled 'In search of a sea of sex' (*Guardian* 3 August 1995) revealed that:

> The Lycos search engine at Carnegie-Mellon University in Pittsburgh had, by July 25, indexed the text of 5,535,148 World-Wide Web pages. Searching on the word 'sex' produced 7,814 documents. Of the top hundred, 22 led to 'safer sex' information at the University of California, San Francisco. Only one of the 100 had pictures. The odds against finding a random pornographic image thus seem to be worse than 70,000:1.

Holderness also took up the Usenet theme, arguing that:

> Much is made of the percentage of Usenet 'traffic' which is porn – and indeed in June, 15 of the top 40 newsgroups, measured by

megabytes of messages, were such. But the busiest of these groups had only 6,736 messages in 205 megabytes, compared to 33,891 messages in 50 megabytes for a group listing job openings.

More recently, Yaman Akdeniz (1997) has estimated that of the 14,000 Usenet discussion groups all around the world, only 200 are sex-related, of which a number are dedicated to serious discussion of issues such as sexual abuse, whilst Angus Hamilton (in Liberty, 1999: 170) suggests that only about 0.002 per cent of newsgroups contain sexual images, concluding that, in cyberspace in general:

> Pornography and other 'offensive' material is undoubtedly available
> – although you have to look reasonably hard to find it. Contrary to
> some popular conceptions a pornographic image does not pop up
> on to the screen the moment you log on. Communications over the
> Internet do not invade an individual's home or appear on one's
> computer screen unbidden. Users seldom encounter content by acci-
> dent: a title or description of a document usually appears before the
> user takes the steps necessary to view it.

Furthermore, pornographers, even of a mild kind, are hardly likely to give away their wares free: there are very few porn sites today which, apart from a few soft tempter images at the front end, are anything other than pay-per-view, thus necessitating a credit card transaction before anything remotely pornographic can actually be seen. (For a useful discussion of the issues raised by the 'darker' side of the Internet see Gauntlett (1999) and O'Toole (1999). The civil rights aspects of the Internet are thoroughly treated in Liberty (1999) and on the *Cyber-Rights and Cyber-Liberties (UK)* website at http://www.cyber-rights.org).

However, the undoubted appeal of this new form of media for those who *do* have an interest in pornography has granted a certain degree of authority to negative press depictions of cyberspace. For the first time in Britain, a supply of pornographic images catering to every imaginable taste is indeed available for viewing in the comfort of your own home – providing you know where to look for it and have a credit card. The threat to the ordinary porn-ography buyer of public censure, embarrassment and even arrest in one of the few countries in the 'free world' where hard-core pornography is still heavily restricted has, to some degree, been averted by technological means. Privacy, safety and user-friendliness have become central to the consumption of pornography, which might be regarded by many as a positive develop-ment. But because pornography is largely illegal in Britain, and because the Internet undoubtedly carries pornography, it not only becomes guilty by association but is accused of undermining the existing legal constraints on pornography. That the Internet demonstrates that these constraints are now well past their sell-by date, if indeed they ever had any justification in the first place, are obviously not questions that can be treated sensibly within the narrow ideological parameters with which most of the British press operates.

As John Naughton argued in his *Observer* article on cyberfears stories in the press: 'their constant retailing has prejudiced millions of British citizens against the most astonishing development of the age'. These negative perceptions do indeed exist, and stories about cyberporn have clearly played their part here. For example, in 1998 a survey by *Which? Online,* entitled *Conspiracy, Controversy or Control: Are We Ready for the E-Nation?*, found that 72 per cent of respondents felt that the Internet should be regulated; 58 per cent believed that it undermined public morality; and 22 per cent suggested that it spawned unsociable 'anoraks' in danger of losing their grip on reality, and that it represented a grave threat to traditional family life. Both *Which? Online*'s editor Alan Stevens, and the above-mentioned Mark Griffiths, are quoted as attributing this negative image at least partly to media scare stories.

Strong support for their views can be found in a recent piece of research carried out by the Independent Television Commission and the Broadcasting Standards Council. This consisted of establishing a citizens' forum in order to investigate people's attitudes towards the regulation of Internet content. Predictably, before the forum the largest number of people (30 per cent of participants) expressed fear at the possibility of children being exposed to unsuitable material, followed by 24 per cent who worried about the general accessibility of offensive material. Afterwards the former dropped to 21 per cent, the latter remained the same, but the largest group was now the 30 per cent (as opposed to 18 per cent beforehand) worried about credit card fraud. Another significant finding was that before the forum only 56 per cent of the participants felt that the Internet had more advantages than disadvantages; by the end this had risen to 67 per cent. As the report based on the forum notes: 'as participants grew more knowledgeable about the Internet, their concerns about it tended to lessen. They became more confident that individual users could and should control Internet access for themselves and on behalf of their children, provided that the appropriate information and tools were available' (Hanley, 2000: 5).

Regulating the Internet

Policing a global medium is clearly an incredibly complex task (for a useful discussion of this issue see Akdeniz (1997)). But it is important to understand that a number of measures have been put in place in recent years. Any discussion about possible 'dangers' of inadvertently accessing material which some people might find unacceptable has to take account of these. Firstly, the Obscene Publications Act 1959 and 1964 and Telecommunications Act

1974 (Section 43) already make it an offence to send 'by means of a public telecommunications system, a message or other matter that is grossly offensive or of an indecent, obscene or menacing character'. Of course such legislation is difficult to apply to the massive volume of Internet traffic, and so, in 1996, the Internet Watch Foundation (IWF) was established. This London-based assembly, set up by Peter Dawe, founder of one of Britain's largest ISPs, has pursued two specific avenues in their approach to monitoring the Internet. Firstly, with assistance from both Government and the police, the IWF has established a telephone hot-line allowing members of the public to report material which could be perceived as 'damaging', 'unacceptable' or in contravention of the Obscene Publications Act. If the IWF agrees with the complainant, then it will take steps to deny access to the site. Secondly, the group has begun to investigate the possibility of establishing a rating and filtering system to help regulate what can and cannot be downloaded from the Net. This response has developed specifically from the success of commercially available rating and filtering packages such as *SafeSurf* and *Net-Nanny* which, while crude, enable users to block access to any sites which they might feel to be unacceptable. There are therefore a number of ways in which those who feel uncomfortable with what may – or may not – be available in cyberspace can ensure that they never stray into unfamiliar territory. (For a detailed account of the surveillance and control issues surrounding the Internet see Loader (1997) and Liberty (1999).)

But while for some people pornography of any description is offensive, the most powerful way of attacking the Internet is, as we have already seen, to raise the spectre of child pornography. Indeed, newspapers' passion for demonising the Internet has been built largely on this subject. However, a closer examination of the issue reveals that, as well as making critical mistakes about the actual availability of child pornography on the Internet, the media, as well as the police and the judiciary, are also extremely confused over what actually constitutes 'child pornography' in the first place, whether or not on the Internet. At present, there appears to be a clear tendency for all nude images involving children to be lumped together by the police and prosecuting authorities under the term 'child pornography'. As O'Toole puts it:

> In Britain during the nineties the suspicion has grown that in the absence of sufficient prosecutions for actual child pornography, and the lack of more successful seizures of child-porn materials, other innocent individuals and innocent materials are being required to fill in. It is widely thought that a shortage of results for the police, Customs and Crown Prosecution Service, during an era of anxiety over the existence of child sex abuse, has led these authorities to become what a representative of Liberty has called 'moral entrepreneurs' – in the business of creating crimes and to make arrests and secure convictions.

This clumsy approach can alarmingly easily make something as innocent as photographing one of your children naked at the beach or in the bath a criminal activity. That this is by no means a paranoid fantasy is demonstrated by, inter alia, the arrest of Lawrence Chard in June 1989 and the rather higher profile arrest of television newsreader Julia Somerville and her partner Jeremy Dixon in November 1995 for doing exactly that. One might also cite the case of the professional photographer Ron Oliver, who has on occasion photographed children naked, but solely at their parents' request, and who, in January 1993, was raided by the police and had 16 years' worth of work seized under the Protection of Children Act. The officers told him that that they were operating on the assumption that any photograph of a naked child under the age of 16 taken in the United Kingdom is illegal, an assertion later repeated to his solicitor by the officer leading the case. However, nothing in the law implies that this is so. Oliver was never charged, and left Britain in disgust. The police also investigated the families of the children depicted in Oliver's pictures for evidence of child abuse. (For an extended account of this case see Preston (1993) and also O'Toole (1999): 239–45. For further discussion of the admittedly thorny issue of what actually constitute pornographic pictures of children see also Holland (1992) and Higonnet (1998).)

It's also worth pointing out that many of the sites that the media would have us associate with child pornography contain nothing more than scanned images of photographs taken by celebrated photographers such as Jock Sturgis and David Hamilton. That both artists have made successful careers out of photographing child nudity, and that their books can be bought freely from any British bookshop, are clearly inconvenient facts which the press has chosen simply to ignore.

It's also extremely important to recognise that, while new technological advances may indeed facilitate the distribution of child pornography, very little has changed in terms of the way in which the making of such pornography, which of course involves the actual committing of sexual offences against real children, is carried out. The creation of child pornography is a clandestine and above all *illegal* activity which cannot be simply lumped together with the up-front (except in Britain) hyper-commercial business of producing hard core pornography both with and for adults. There was in fact a brief period in the 1970s when the Netherlands and Denmark tolerated a limited amount of production of child pornography, but those days are long gone. Interestingly, O'Toole (1999: 222) cites a 1992 study by two Dutch academics which suggested that a considerable amount of child pornography in circulation at the start of the 1990s dated from that era (and images from that era undoubtedly still circulate). Furthermore, there is little real difference between a copy of a privately produced paedophile magazine being posted to a paedophile under plain cover from an underground paedophile ring, and a paedophile downloading a scanned-in version of exactly the same publication onto a home computer – and both acts are equally illegal. As Gauntlett (1999: 117) points out: 'paedophiles have traditionally distributed photographic contraband through the surface mail. If they now choose to do so by e-mail, little has changed and they may still be brought to justice'. Indeed, the ability to apply electronic checks and filters to e-mail traffic in order to identify suspect cargo would appear to be much more efficient than utilising Customs officers to wade through surface mail looking for illegal material. And, certainly, the difficulties inherent in remaining anonymous when posting material on the Internet (there is almost always a digital 'trail' left behind whenever one enters cyberspace) means that if anyone is distributing child pornography then they are probably *more* easy to find and to prosecute than if they are posting it in the conventional sense.

More significantly, the lack of any reliable research into the availability of child pornography in cyberspace (discounting methodologically flawed reports such as *Marketing Pornography on the Information Superhighway*) has, as we have seen, allowed the media to establish a number of myths about the subject which remain, as yet, largely unchallenged. Given the problems surrounding the way in which the media (as well as the police, as we have seen) actually define child pornography, it's hard to disagree with O'Toole (1999: 223) when he argues that 'statements about the content and prevalence of [such] material are speculative or provisional at best'. Certainly, little research has been done into the availability of child pornography on the Net compared with the availability of child pornography delivered by more traditional means. Furthermore, the media frequently neglect to make a comparison between arrests made for accessing or posting child pornography on the Internet and arrests for accessing it in other forms.

Moreover, if one investigates the ways in which the relevant web sites market themselves, it is possible to claim that, despite recent arrests by the police and attendant speculation by the media, there is simply no child pornography *commercially* available on the Internet. Although any search on a key-word like 'Lolita', 'child-porn' or one of their derivatives will produce an apparent wealth of pages seeming to contain child pornography, such results cannot be viewed as accurately reflecting what is actually available, commercially and openly, on the Net. While the following sample of website listings, taken from a site advertising itself as *The LolitaWorld Top 100*, would appear to be both self-explanatory and deeply disturbing:

Lolita girls (4–9 yrs): see yung girlz fuck cock

Lolita rape site (visit before we are closed down!): youngest girls on the net. Little girls forced to fuck for first time

Neither these, nor any of the other sites advertising child pornography will supply the content which they advertise. Instead, these sites misleadingly advertise a content that they are unable or unwilling to deliver to the subscriber. If one pursues such sites past the nauseating hyperbole of the initial website listings, one will inevitably arrive at a page offering to supply the most appalling material imaginable on the understanding that one enters one's credit-card details and pays a monthly subscription to the site. But once this transaction is completed, the most likely outcome is that the disappointed customer will be linked merely to straightforward, commercial, adult web sites offering nothing more controversial than the type of material easily available over the counter in any London sex-shop. Of course, such practices are no more morally acceptable than the base desires to which they pretend to cater. But media reports about the availability of child pornography on the Internet which are based simply on such dubious website marketing practices are hardly likely to be either accurate or reliable. And indeed these sites derive a good deal of their 'appeal' from promising the most illicit thing their authors can dream of – which is the exact opposite of real paedophiles who, notoriously, see nothing at all wrong with having sex with children.

Of course, this is by no means to claim that the Internet is *not* used by paedophiles for the distribution of child pornography. However, such sites are well hidden 'underground' and completely inaccessible to the casual browser. One is as likely to find evidence of the existence of 'snuff' movies as to come across authentic child pornography while browsing the Internet. As with traditional forms of paedophile material, the only way to access such material is to take the obvious risk of attempting to contact and infiltrate a group in possession of such images: access to this sort of material is wholly dependent on being accepted into the right circles. Nevertheless, the myth of easily available child pornography in cyberspace persists, and again it's difficult to disagree with O'Toole (1999: 264) when he states that 'the suspicion remains that the issue of child porn was exploited as part of a bid to gain leverage over this new, unregulated technology, in order to get things under control'.

Evidence to back up O'Toole's claim, and much else in this chapter, can be gleaned from an article in the *Observer*, 25 August 1996, entitled 'These men are not paedophiles: they are the Internet abusers', which was part of a three-page report on child abuse. The men in question are Clive Feather, an associate director of the ISP Demon International, who is described on the front page as 'the school governor who sells access to photos of child rape', and Johan Helsingius, an anonymous-remailer operator from Finland, described as 'the Internet middleman who handles 90 per cent of all child pornography'. The 'story', such as it is, is a textbook example of the cyberfears discussed in this chapter; thus we are told that 'the Internet has created a vile perpetual motion: no longer do paedophiles have to make expensive trips to countries where laws are lax: they can upload and download their sick fantasies from the comfort of their homes, fuelling a demand for more abuse, and a need for more child victims'; we are also treated to the extraordinary (and, one would have thought, actionable) claim that 'for £14 and a further £11 a month, subscribers [to Demon!] are given access to photographs of children as young as eight being subject to harrowing abuse', and so on and on, with inaccuracy piled upon innuendo. What the article omitted to mention was that Helsingius' remailer was non-profit-making and had not handled any image files for more than a year, while the only source given for the extremely dubious figure of 90 per cent is an unsubstantiated quote from Toby Tyler, 'an FBI adviser on child abuse and pornography'. Regarding Demon, the idea that ISPs are no more responsible for the information accessed through their host computers than are British Telecom for the content of phone calls made on their equipment, is never seriously entertained. Instead it is allowed to be introduced by the police themselves simply in order to be then rubbished by them in the shape of Detective Inspector Stephen French, who states that 'This is a fruitless, redundant argument which we do not accept. Morally you cannot adopt this position.'

And here, of course, is a rather large clue as to the article's purpose. For throughout 1996 the Metropolitan Police had been telling the Internet Service Providers Association (ISPA) that the content carried by some of the newsgroups available through their services was illegal, that they considered that the ISPs to be publishers of that material, and that they were therefore breaking the law. During the summer the police sent all ISPs a list of 132 newsgroups which they believed to contain pornographic material: the only problem is that many of them, such as the gay discussion groups, didn't. Indeed, all of this (apart from, of course, the far from illegal nature of many of the newsgroups) can be gleaned from the article itself – as can the fact that Demon regarded the police request as 'unacceptable censorship'. It's also clear from the piece that Demon's attitude had considerably annoyed the ISPA chairman, Shez Hamill, who is quoted as complaining that:

> We are being portrayed as a bunch of porn merchants. This is an image we need to change. Many of our members have already acted to take away the worst of the Internet. But Demon have taken every opportunity to stand alone in this regard. They do not like the concept of our organisation.

It is thus not too fanciful to regard the *Observer* article as at least partly a crude form of pressure, stemming from both the Metropolitan Police and the ISPA, to bring Demon and any other recalcitrant ISPs into line. That such pressure existed is undeniable; indeed, throughout summer and autumn 1996 the police were making it known that they were planning to raid an ISP with the aim of launching a test case over the publication of obscene material on the Internet. The *direct* result of this pressure was the setting up of the Internet Watch Foundation mentioned earlier: self-regulation had begun in earnest. Thus the police and government finally achieved a degree of censorship, albeit of a privatised, self-imposed, commercial kind. What is undeniable, however, is that the twin spectres of both paedophile porn on the

Net *and* of children accessing porn (paedophile or otherwise) through the Net, played a key role in the events leading up to the founding of the IWF, events in which the media, and especially the press, were leading actors. (For further discussion of the setting up of the IWF see Oswell (1998) and (1999).)

Of course, the question *why* negative reports of the Internet achieve such prominence in the media as whole, and in the British press in particular, is a multi-faceted one. In Britain, as the chapters by Murdock and Petley in this book demonstrate, fears about popular culture and new forms of media have a long history, and have been amply exploited by a conservative-minded press. Nor is there anything particularly new in journalists peddling inaccurate, ill-informed and lurid scare stories in the interests of 'good copy'. As John Naughton observed in his *Observer* article cited earlier:

> These stories are, in the main, the products of journalists who are either entirely unfamiliar with the Net or who are hellbent on misrepresenting it in the interests of sensationalism and easy news-bytes. Where there is ignorance, they sow fear; and where there is fear, they sow technophobia.

Of course, since these words were written, many papers have themselves embraced the Net and begun to publish on-line editions. Whether the papers' ever-increasing involvement in the whole e-world will lead to a decline in the kind of journalism cited by Naughton or, alternatively, and as many now fear, it will actually spread onto the Net itself the kind of sensational, inaccurate, commercially-motivated pap for which the British press is so notorious, remains to be seen.

NOTES

1   In this respect, it's not insignificant that *The Street of the Pied Piper* is cited approvingly at some considerable length in a report entitled *Violence, Pornography and the Media*, which was submitted in 1996 to the Parliamentary All Party Family and Child Protection Group, and 'co-ordinated' by none other than Dr Clifford Hill, of *Video Violence and Children* fame.
2   Disregard the point that equivalent claims have been made over many years about the existence of 'snuff' movies, and none has *ever* emerged. Instead, just ask: how could she know? What sort of research would she have to have done to know whether something was real or acted?

REFERENCES

Akdeniz, Y. (1997), 'Governance of pornography and child pornography on the global Internet: a multi-layered approach', in L. Edwards and C. Waelde, eds, *Law and the Internet: Regulating Cyberspace*, Oxford: Hart Publishing, pp. 223–41.
Barker, Martin (1984), *The Video Nasties: Freedom and Censorship in the Arts*, London: Pluto Press.

Cyber-Rights and Cyber-Liberties (UK) website (available at http://www.cyber-rights.org.

Gauntlett, A. (1999), *Net Spies: Who's Watching You on the Web?*, London: Vision Paperbacks.

Griffiths, M. (1997), 'Video games and aggression', *The Psychologist*, 10: 9, pp. 397–401.

Griffiths, M. (1999), 'Violent video games and aggression: a review of the literature', *Aggression and Violent Behaviour*, 4: 2, pp. 203–12.

Gunter, B. (1998), *The Effects of Video Games on Children: The Myth Unmasked*, Sheffield: Sheffield Academic Press.

Hanley, P. (2000), *Internet Regulation: The Way Forward?*, London: Independent Television Commission.

Higonnet, A. (1998), *Pictures of Innocence: The History and Crisis of Ideal Childhood*, London: Thames and Hudson.

Hoffman, D. and Novak, T. (1995), *A Detailed Analysis of the Conceptual, Logical and Methodological Flaws in the Article: 'Marketing Pornography on the Information Superhighway'*, http://www.2000.ogsm.vanderbilt.edu/novak/rimm.review.html.

Hoffman, D. and Novak, T. (1997), *The Cyberporn Debate*, http://www.2000.ogsm.-vanderbilt.edu/cyberporn.debate.html.

Holland, P. (1992), *What is a Child?: Popular Images of Childhood*, London: Virago.

Home Affairs Committee (1994), *Computer Pornography*, London: HMSO.

Liberty (1999), *Liberating Cyberspace: Civil Liberties, Human Rights and The Internet*, London: Pluto Press.

Loader, B. (ed.) (1997), *The Governance of Cyberspace: Politics, Technology and Global Restructuring*, London: Routledge.

Merchant, V. (ed.) (1994), *Computer Pornography in Schools*, Preston: University of Central Lancashire.

Miller, J. and Carver, G. (1994), *The Street Of The Pied Piper*, Derby: Professional Association of Teachers.

Naughton, J. (1996), 'Monsters from cyberspace', *Observer*, 9 June.

Oswell, D. (1998), 'The place of "childhood" in Internet content regulation', *International Journal of Cultural Studies* 1:2, pp. 271–91.

Oswell, D. (1999), 'The dark side of Cyberspace: Internet content regulation and child protection', *Convergence* 5:4, pp. 42–62.

O'Toole, L. (1999, Second edition), *Pornocopia*, London: Serpent's Tail.

Preston, R. (1993), 'A question of taste', *Independent Magazine*, 4 September 1993, pp. 28–32.

Provenzo, E. (1991), *Video Kids: Making Sense of Nintendo*, Cambridge: Harvard University Press.

12

ON THE PROBLEMS OF BEING A 'TRENDY TRAVESTY'

Martin Barker (with Julian Petley)

Among the central arguments of this book is this: that the dull endless-
ness of debates about media 'effects' could be broken with relative ease.
If only journalists, policy-makers, politicians and pundits could be shifted
from their deference and devotion to American-style social psychological
research, and persuaded to give a hearing to some of the findings of British
and continental European (and indeed, in some cases, American) media/
cultural studies work on audiences, how different their perspective would
be!

That they won't do so isn't because they have read the research and found
it wanting – I have yet to meet a journalist with even a passing understanding
of audience research from the media/cultural studies tradition. That they
won't is at least partly down to the strong tradition of denigrating media and
cultural studies in the UK. And although there is not the hard data to prove
it, most of us within the field sense that the tempo of those attacks has
increased considerably in recent years – now including, for instance,
reporters doing 'inside jobs' on particular courses and publishing their
'irrefutable proofs' of the stupidity and harm of what people like me do. The
parodic version of these attacks is that all we do is to 'teach our students to
deconstruct *Neighbours* and then expect them to go off and get jobs as TV
producers and film directors'. The background claim is that we are the site of
serious damage to British culture.

What is it with this hostility to our tradition? I ask this question in all
seriousness. If we cannot answer the question, how will we know how to
defend our subject area and its achievements effectively? At this moment, a
new cloud is hanging over our field, a 'passing' proposal by Secretary of
State Chris Smith that perhaps the Government might reinvest more wisely
the money it is currently 'wasting' on media and cultural studies courses.
More recently, Chris Woodhead, at the time head of the Schools Inspector-
ate, agreed with a 'profound scepticism' about whether media studies courses
teach students anything worthwhile. How will we best reply to this, if we

don't understand the basis of these casual but confident assertions that we are wasting the public's time and money?

It is all too easy, unfortunately, to come up with 'explanations' for this hostility without doing any real research. Over the last few years, asking people about this, I have been offered the following 'explanations':

- *Journalists are being self-protective. They don't like the idea of an academic subject that studies them with a critical eye, so they attack us to ward us off. If they can prove that we aren't valid enquirers, then they can dismiss our criticisms of them.* In our field's early days, there is clear empirical evidence for such an account. When the Glasgow University Media Group published their early studies of BBC and ITN news, for instance, we know – from leaked evidence – that hurried committees inside the TV companies formed the view that a good line of response was to belittle the critics. But beyond particular cases such as this, I do not see the evidence for a broader application of this explanation.

- *It is all part of a great fear about the 'death of high culture', a last-gasp reaction by the cultural conservatives.* This is an interesting and potentially fruitful line, but it begs the question of why we haven't, on the whole, been targeted for abuse by the official guardians of 'high culture' – art associations, galleries, museums, perhaps, or by those other fields of traditional academia which feel themselves threatened by our success (say, History, which has suffered a drop in recruitment recently).

- *Media studies is seen as a problem because it really* is *a problem – it is producing unemployable students.* Were the hostility to media studies solely based on this it would very easily refutable by recourse to the employment record of our students. But a slightly different version of this argument, which references the hostility to media studies shown by organisations such as SkillSet, argues that there is something of a conspiracy by the media employers, who would like to take control of our field through processes such as 'benchmarking'. Attacking the 'uselessness' of our graduates then becomes a political tactic in pursuance of that goal. If this were indeed the motive, it would require significantly different responses.

- *Media studies is perceived to be politically mischievous, on a par with sociology in the 1960s. Therefore the attack on media studies, albeit only sometimes directed overtly at its 'politics', is in fact a demand that academia not be politically committed.* This explanation is the most self-serving for our field – it confirms us in our own righteousness. Here we are, daring to ask the critical questions that no-one else will ask, maintaining the reservoirs of critical thinking against the dark forces of reactionary ideology and media mystification, as it were. Their attacks on us simply prove how important and necessary we are.

Any or all of these might be true, or a contribution to the truth, but the fact is that, as they stand, they are all guesses. In this essay, I am attempting to put some empirical meat on their putative bones. My tactic is to turn on our attackers those exact tools which they have frequently derided: by conducting a textual analysis of their attacks I will attempt to uncover the *motivating ideological position(s)* that lurk, largely undeclared, behind their innocent-seeming masks. Using a mix of simple content analytic and discourse analytic devices, I have looked to see if there is evidence of one single point, or multiple points, from which the attacks stem.

I have drawn here on fifty press reports from the period 1993–99, garnered from the collections of five people. In at least two cases, university publicity departments contributed. Given that these draw on professional cuttings services, there is reason to think that not too much will have passed us all by. Still, I have no way of knowing for certain exactly how representative the cuttings are. They contain, for instance, very few from local papers. My intuition tells me that that is not surprising, since this is not a topic likely to emerge with much regularity at local level. But it could be that, simply, such as there are have not come my way, or the way of any of my colleagues. These caveats aside, the exercise still seems to me to have been worthwhile, for it reveals some striking things about the patterns within the press coverage of our field over the last six years.

Classification procedures

My analysis begins by classifying the materials from which I was working under a number of headings: date/year; publication (individual and kind); genre of article. This found:

1993	1994	1995	1996	1997	1998	1999	
1	0	7	21	10	6	5	= 50

Local/regional	National	
4[1]	46	= 50

National materials break down as follows:

Tabloid	Broadsheet	Other[2]	
2[3]	33	11	= 46

As can be seen, the first really interesting thing to note is the predominance of the national broadsheets, which subdivide as follows:

Guardian	15
Independent	6
Sunday Times	4
The Times	3
Observer	1
Independent on Sunday	1
Daily Telegraph	1
Sunday Telegraph	1
Financial Times	1
	= 33

Again, it is necessary to treat these with caution, since the size of the *Guardian* sample is at least partly occasioned by its willingness to allow space for replies (in letters or, in one case, an article) in response to attacks on media studies. Even so, the proportions are striking.

A notable absence here is the *Daily Mail*, that epicentre of Thatcherite thinking. It is possible, of course, that they have never in this period joined the attacks on media studies, but it would be surprising. Simply, then, I have to say that if they did go for us, then we all missed their attacks, and I don't know how they conducted them.[4]

Types of article

Although I was well aware that there are areas of overlap between the classifications below (the British press is especially notorious for intertwining fact and opinion), it still seemed worth taking the risk of classifying all the published pieces into the following categories:

- *news* (understood as onward reporting, however mediated, of information, ideas and events sourced outside the newspaper),
- *editorials* (those columns distinctively marked as the opinion of the newspaper itself),
- *features* (more-or-less researched pieces, not necessarily based on a current event, in which a variety of sources are accessed to present an investigation or argument),
- *opinion columns* (authored pieces, usually by 'star names', presenting an opinion which may or may not be that of the newspaper itself),
- *letters* (a space for readers, usually – but not always – enabling them to respond to previously published material)
- *responses* (a rare space granting a reply to someone who has been attacked in the newspaper concerned).

News	Editorials	Features	Opinion	Letters	Responses	
9	3	19	18	6	1	= 56[5]

Again, these figures are striking in themselves. They show a predominance of journalist-generated material, rather than responses to already-existing external events. It is worth stressing at this juncture that these figures become all the more pointed if we note that of the nine news items, seven concern only one issue: the employability of media studies graduates (on which more below). And the other two are introductions to feature articles carried elsewhere by the newspaper.

On the basis of just this initial examination, then, we can already say that the archetypal attack on media studies came in an opinion column or a feature article in the *Guardian*, *Independent*, or *Sunday Times*, with a clear date epicentre. Or in *Sun/Cluedo* terms, it was the liberal broadsheets wot did it, in 1996 with a number of opinion pieces . . . What is more, and what is more curious, is that the heart of the attack coincides – and, in terms of editorial input, contains some small overlap – with the rise of these papers' fascination with the media. In the case of the *Guardian* this period saw the creation of its weekly 'Media' section, along with more recently the emergence of its 'On-Line' supplement within which an almost devotional attitude is displayed towards digital media.

Examining discursive elements of the attack

There is a problem, let it be noted immediately, in analysing these attacks. And the problem is that in a good number of cases their judgements, though strongly negative, are also deeply buried. Consider, for example, this recent piece. On 23 April 1999, the *Times Higher Educational Supplement* carried an opinion piece by David Blunkett on the general topic of the relation of university courses to work experience. In the course of his article, Blunkett made the following observation:

> I have a deep love of history and believe it is vital that our universities continue to provide world-class academic study of subjects with less obvious practical application. Students who take such subjects often have a greater creative capacity than those who opt for narrower subjects. Many rightly see a history degree as more valuable than some media studies courses. Yet many students choose the latter because, rightly or wrongly, they see a clearer link to future work.

Spit as we might at the gratuitous differentiation between an old 'high' subject and our own, and its unproven implication that history students are more 'creative' than ours, that is surely not the most relevant point. The point – and the difficulty, discursively – is that Blunkett doesn't even bother to 'name' his problem with media studies; and his use of the word 'rightly' clearly marks his belief that his readers will share his intuition. This problem recurred in a number of other pieces, but is perhaps best illustrated in a column by 'Bel Littlejohn' in the *Guardian*, 2 February 1996, headed 'Let me spel out why eggheads crack me up'. 'Bel Littlejohn' is of course a device used by journalist Craig Brown to parody various contemporary fads and fancies but, of course, the whole point about parodies is that they work *only* if their intended audience is extremely familiar with what is actually being parodied. Think, then, what shared 'knowledges' are here assumed:

> For the past two years, I've been proud to call myself Visiting Professer of Culture and Civilisation at the University of Dorking. And for these past six years I've slogged my guts out with at least two full-length lectures a term in order to enthuze and – yes, let's go for it, it's not a dirty word – educate a helluva lot of students in the swings and roundabouts of contemporary culture. In that time, I've disquisitioned them on such diverse subjects as 'Like a Virgin: Madonna and The Semiology of Semiology', 'Interpreting Vivienne Westwood', and 'From Rin-Tin-Tin via Tintin and Ten-Pin to Tampax, Tintax and Tarantino: Studies in Cultural Relativism', as well as making a major contribution to the two-year art-history course at the neighbouring University of Abinger Hammer on 'The Complete Works on Video of Depeche Mode 1983–88'.

Compare lists: we're lazy; we're ill-educated but don't know it; we suffer from a kind of mental flatulence; and we're self-important. It seems that journalists feel that the ground for sneering at media studies is already well-tilled.

Because of this tendency to implicitness, I concentrate mainly on analysing articles in which there is at least a semblance of some overt statement of the nature of our 'sins', and in which therefore the sources of the antagonism become more open. It is through these that we can most easily reach back to the positions from which these negative judgements make sense? Consider, therefore, the following quotations:

> Media studies is a trivial, minor field of research, spuriously created for jargon-spinners and academic make-weights. Students learn nothing of value because the subject doesn't know its own purpose, is unimportant, and because most people teaching it don't know what they're talking about.
>
> (Editorial, *Independent*, 31 October 1996)

Many children . . . across the country are being denied the right to better themselves [because of the abolition of grammar schools]. They can, of course, go on to do media studies at university. This is little more than a state-funded, three-year equivalent of pub-chat . . . This is a dumbed-down educational world in which the bright are deprived of their futures, and those who soldier on are tempted into useless university courses. The government should act to improve schools by separating pupils according to ability so they can all thrive, and it should abandon its backdoor campaign against the handful of surviving grammar schools. It should then take a stick to universities that waste taxpayers' money and demand they meet sensible standards.

(Editorial, *Sunday Times*, 12 December 1998)

Pseudo-science is menace enough to growing minds, but pseudo-social science is something new in the pantheon of puffed-up non-sense masquerading as academic discipline . . . Media studies is an outgrowth of the 'relevance' boom . . . [It] rose to its current status as the great cop-out subject from early teenage onwards for kids and teachers (alarmingly, often media wannabees themselves) who want to spend all the time, not just rainy end-of-term days, bathing in glorious relevance and holding animated discussions on *EastEnders* . . . What may be needed for an understanding of how the world turns . . . is to be taught not the difference between good and bad telly, but that between specious and valid academic disciplines.

(Jonathan Margolis, *Guardian*, 17 July 1999)[6]

Media studies reek not only of trendiness – the history of Holly-wood, for example – but of political correctness. The myriad courses on cultural identity and on racial and sexual stereotyping, the modish textbooks with titles such as *The Gendering of a Leisure Technology* (women's use of the domestic video recorder), smack of an in-built message ready to be preached. Even more, I dislike how media studies emphasise the here-and-now. Even physics or engin-eering carry some trace of history. 'Media' are simply too bound to the 20th century to classify as today's classics. The young people flocking to them seem to be what Yeats deplored as 'unremembering hearts and heads' – utterly unconcerned with the past.

(Brenda Maddox, *Daily Telegraph*, 3 April 1996)

A number of discursive features need pointing to here. First, and perhaps most importantly, these are not so much arguments about the rightness or wrongness of media studies, as about the *motivations* of those involved in it. *We* are judged, not just our subject. We are spurious . . . specious . . . make-weights . . . masquerading . . . trendy . . . playing at 'relevance' . . . and all the time doing nothing more than indulging in 'animated discussions on *EastEnders*'. In short, we are effectively *pretending* to be academics and researchers.

There is a certain assuredness about these attacks, which also bears comment. Re-read that sentence by Margolis: 'What may be needed for an understanding of how the world turns . . . is to be taught the difference between specious and valid academic disciplines'. This is worldly-wise, self-consciously 'educated' commentary. Here speaks a man who knows how to be more 'academic' than those who themselves claim to be academics. The pretty writing ('how the world turns') marks not only his distance from 'us' but also his right to speak: he speaks for the *genuinely* educated.

Note, next, that media studies is never, in these quotations, a problem simply in itself. It is a *symptom* of wider cultural or political failings. There is an *excess* in these attacks which reveals a depth to the antagonism far outrunning any worries about the usefulness or not of media studies. And the key terms seem repeatedly to concern *confusions over 'quality' and 'standards'*.

What exactly is the name of the problem? In a recent conference presentation, Larry Grossberg of the University of North Carolina talked about the considerable hostility in the USA which has been directed towards 'cultural studies'. He made clear, furthermore, that the bulk of the attack came from within academia: from individuals in other disciplines who are hostile to the intellectual procedures and claims of 'cultural studies'. This is, for the most part, *not* the case in Britain Here, the problem's 'name' is definitely 'media studies' – or, in press-speak, 'meejah studies' (although sometimes the boundaries of cultural and media studies do become blurred in the course of the attack – as in the *Guardian* article by Henry Porter noted below). A small but revealing indicator points up just how precise this designation is. The Chris Smith who warned about the 'waste' involved in media studies courses is in fact the selfsame Chris Smith who warmly welcomed a report prepared at his behest by the British Film Institute. Entitled *Making Movies Matter*, it made a powerful case for the development and diversification of film education at every level of the education system. So, clearly, film is not seen, officially, as part of the 'media studies' problem.

From another angle, consider one of the very few tabloid attacks. On 21 August 1996 the *Express* carried a front page lead article, with supporting feature and editorial inside, whose headline denounced the 'Farce of useless degrees'. What is striking about this piece is the complete *absence* of media studies from its initial charge sheet. Instead, the attack there is directed at 'crazy subjects such as knitwear, brewing, and floor covering'. True, on an inside feature page we find a section devoted to media studies. But this is given over almost entirely to a discussion of whether there are enough jobs in the media for the rising numbers of media students. Or, as the headline puts it, 'Slim chance for 30,000 hopefuls'. Again, mark the difference. For the 'liberal' broadsheets, our main opponents, our crime is ideological. For a conservative tabloid, on a rare mention, the crime is waste.

What the above emphasise is the distinctiveness both of the definition of the 'problem' and of the source of the attacks. 'Media studies' seems genuinely to *offend* those who think of themselves as the *real* intellectuals.

Examining a complete article again reveals some striking things. Consider Figure 12.1 reproduced from the *Independent on Sunday*. The headline alone warrants considerable attention. '***Dons.***' Who are these? This word has long been a synonym, with occasionally slightly mocking overtones, for academics: roughly, the equivalent of 'boffins' but without the scientific connotations. Who gets included in this 'community'? Clearly not media studies lecturers or researchers – our exclusion from this community marks our failure to be *real* academics. '***Despair.***' An entire community of scholars experiences frissons of fear at 'our' illegitimate incursion into their world. 'We' are harming their prospects, undermining their aspirations. How? Because students '***spurn***' their subjects. Picture the wretched scene: students, armed presumably with the appropriate A Levels, are eagerly offered places on biochemistry or electrical engineering courses, but the ingrates turn scornfully away from real study towards . . . '"***media studies***"'. The quote-marks tell the story on their own: unlike science, which needs no qualifying punctuation, 'media studies' immediately proclaims itself as a fake subject. So, the body politic of academia (not, of course, including us) sees our subject for what it is, a bogus intrusion, and sees its own students tempted away from serious subjects which otherwise they would surely take. The headline actually makes no sense at all unless we recognise these suggestions contained within it well enough to navigate their implications. The fact that these implicit claims, once spelt out, appear ludicrous does not, of course, weaken the headline's persuasiveness.

But the article as a whole reveals more than this. It demonstrates many of the broadsheets' strategies. At first sight, a simple classification might suggest that the article takes a relative neutral attitude to media studies. Broadly classifying paragraphs as *neutral* (primarily reporting facts and situations), *anti* (primarily citing or supporting critical positions on media studies) or *pro* (primarily citing or supporting defences of media studies), the 29 paragraphs divide as follows: neutral = 7, pro = 12, anti = 10. Yet there is no question but that the overall attitude of the article towards media studies is one of hostility – not least because of the dominating headline which puts a negative spin on the entire subject. But in addition, the article manages to locate one insider, Brian Winston[7] who is made to *appear* to be attacking media studies from within, as it were, by being quoted (no doubt highly selectively) to the effect that 'I'm concerned that good teachers are forced to offer courses which do not provide the vocational training students need if they are going to get jobs'. In short, the whole article is a classic example of the

INDEPENDENT ON SUNDAY, 20 JUNE 1995

Education/ fashionable courses

Dons despair as students spurn science in favour of 'media studies'

By Nick Cohen

MEDIA studies – a subject either mocked or ignored by conventional academics 20 years ago – is sweeping British universities. Nearly 35,000 sixth-formers finishing their A-levels this week have applied for degree courses that they hope will get them into television or the press – far more than have applied for maths, physics or chemistry.

To scientists, the success of universities offering to introduce students to everything from music videos to quantitative methods of media analysis is a symbol of the country's change and perhaps its decline.

"I wonder if watching the telly stretches the mind", said Peter Saunders, professor of mathematics at King's College, London, whose department has been at the centre of attempts to raise standards of numeracy in Britain. "And I wonder if we should treat students as if they're customers and give them what they want to study.

"The real customer is society. If we forget that we might as well offer students courses in beer-drinking. I'm sure they would be popular."

Media studies academics regard such lamentations as cries from the past. They are convinced that study of the media is not just "relevant", to use one of their favourite words, but serious.

Their conviction is bolstered by the remarkable popularity of their courses.

In 1990, 5,855 people applied for degree courses in media studies, according to the Universities and Colleges Admissions Service. Last year, 21,277 applied. This year the numbers have rocketed. There are 32,862 media studies applicants and a further 12,039 for communication studies courses.

Pupils wanting to take traditional science courses have remained unchanged, however, despite the expansion of higher education. A mere 24,416 want to study mathematics this year; physics and chemistry attracted 21,422 and 30,290 applicants respectively.

The popularity of media studies allows departments to be very choosy. At Loughborough University, where 600 have applied for 34 places, the department demands the equivalent of two Bs and a C at A-level, grades that would applicants into many law faculties.

The Westminster University school of communications is so oversubscribed that it is moving out of the city and building a £30m department, the "biggest media studies cen-

tre in Europe", in suburban Harrow.

Its academics look slightly confused when asked what the point of it all is. Their practical courses offer students vocational training in video, radio, periodicals, public relations – every conceivable branch, in fact, of the media. About three-quarters of students find work.

Theoretical courses are served with dollops of Marx, Weber, Brecht, feminism, psychoanalysis and postmodernism. When asked how such learned techniques are used to analyse something as apparently insubstantial as the modern media, David Cardiff, principal lecturer at the school, said: "Well, you can analyse why *Dallas* was watched round the world and how different cultures interpreted it".

Does it matter how *Dallas* was interpreted?

> ## 'Questions of what it's all in aid of seem to evade them. There's a terrible silence'

"It matters a great deal if you are concerned with American cultural imperialism. Look, I simply do not have a problem about the intellectual relevance of media studies. They are just as important as English literature and probably more directly important in the modern world."

Away from the classroom, others are not so sure.

The intellectual ancestor of today's lecturers, and a man to whom they constantly refer, is Richard Hoggart, whose 1957 book *The Uses of Literacy* was the first study to take popular culture seriously. He went on to Birmingham University to found what was in effect the first media studies department.

Like many parents, he is disappointed by the way his children have turned out. The section on media studies in his new book, *The Way We Live Now*, which will be published in the autumn, complains about the "moral cretins" who are frightened of making judgements.

"I never suggested that the ephemeral and the serious were of equal worth", he said last

week. "Too many people in media studies are simply fascinated by the media, especially TV. All the questions of what it's all in aid of seem to evade them. There is a terrible silence."

Some of Mr Hoggart's younger contemporaries have more worldly concerns. Brian Winston is director of the centre for journalism studies at Cardiff University. His postgraduate courses, providing intensive training for aspiring journalists and broadcasters, are very successful. But he worries about the undergraduates on media studies degrees and wonders if they will find work.

"I'm concerned that good teachers are forced to offer courses which do not provide the vocational training students need if they are going to get jobs", he said.

Professor Winston estimates that a course that ensures that a student is properly trained costs about £5,000 per student per year. But most undergraduate media studies courses spend about £3,000.

"It's not enough," Professor Winston said. "The fact is that the concentrated training you need for a job in the real world is very expensive."

To get the training requires to have a hope of a job in broadcasting or print journalism, students have to go on to postgraduate courses. Most have to find the fees themselves because the Government will not pay and the media will not finance training directly.

The result is an increasing gentrification of the media, as graduates with access to money flood the market. Working-class accents in most "serious" newspaper offices are as hard to find as small egos, and a recent National Union of Journalists survey discovered that only one in 100 journalism students and one in 200 national newspaper journalists were black.

"I call it the Lucinda syndrome", said Professor Winston. "We have wonderful postgraduates who are eminently employable, but, boy, are they posh!"

Posh or not, the students keep on coming. Professor Winston is not always sure why.

"I suppose to people brought up on videos and television it seems relevant and glamorous," he said.

"And when all's said and done, at least there are jobs in the media, however difficult they are to find. There are no jobs in coal-mining."

Figure 12.1 A 'balanced' assault on media studies . . .
(Courtesy Nick Cohen and *The Independent on Sunday*)

way in which 'quality' journalism maintains an *appearance* of 'neutrality' whilst actually proffering strong value judgements.

How are these judgements expressed and embodied? A useful way in to answering this question is to consider a sample set of headlines. Take, then, the following small sample:

> 'Students "misled" over jobs in the media.'
> 'Media graduates finish up as clerks and cooks.'
> 'A degree of sanity over "meejah" mania.'

Using standard discourse analytic tools on these, we find that there are some striking components here. For instance in the first, who, by implication, has 'misled' the students? Unstated, the clear suggestion is that *we* did. That turns an alleged error into a crime. Consider the second: the assertion that media students end up as clerks and cooks is significant only if (a) this is unusual, and thus not true, for instance, of physics or English students, (b) this is something unexpected – in other words, if they had been led to believe that a director's chair was theirs for the asking on the completion of a media studies degree, and (c) this is something permanent, in that they are only *ever* going to be clerks and cooks. And as for the third, who on earth, other than ironically, ever uses an expression like 'meejah'? In fact no-one, but the idea is clearly established that people who get caught up in this latest 'trendy' (a popular word in these reports) subject can't speak properly and are thus, by extension, not 'properly' educated. Furthermore, any interest in the 'media' (said properly) that we or our students might *claim* to have is simply a symptom of some kind of 'mania', and thus not to be listened to, only diagnosed.

But what all of this tells us is only how silly these attacks are – it does not pin down their origins. So let us try a slightly more systematic approach in order to try to identify the *discursive sources* of these claims. To do this, I approached the fifty press reports with four questions to hand:

- From what discursive position, in each case, is 'media studies' being criticised? If media studies is the sickness or the sin, what, by opposition, counts as health and virtue?
- What wider implications does each position have? Whether acknowledged or implicit, what more general political or cultural understandings are presumed and mobilised as part of these critiques?
- How overt and coherent is each position? How openly and fully does each state its charges and remedies, or are these left implicit, assumed, and fragmentary?
- How differentiated is each position from the others that are available? Or, to what extent does each critique allow itself to merge and run with other, perhaps not wholly compatible, critiques?

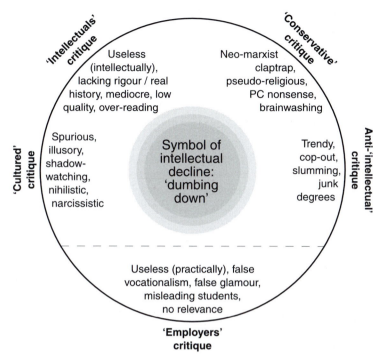

Figure 12.2 Semantic patterning of the attacks on media studies.

From posing the four questions outlined above, five positions come into view; for the sake of clarity I have constructed these into a semantic table. Each position is characterised by an at least semi-coherent language of criticism, as the table indicates. Because so many of the critiques remain at the implicit level, these keywords are sometimes all we have available – although shortly I will give examples of more elaborated critiques using these languages. In brief, then (with *italics* indicating that keywords are taken from among my sample of reports):

The ***Cultured Critique*** comes from a claimed position from which those who inhabit it can, by virtue of their presumed rich sensibility, spot a charlatan. Being genuinely cultured themselves, they can see that 'we' are *shadow-chasers*, *nihilistic*, *specious* and *narcissistic*. 'We' *lack imagination*, and our subject (its questions, methods and conclusions) is *spurious* and *illusory*. Interestingly, we are seen also as having *bad manners*, rather in the style of TV show presenters. Like poodles to their owners, 'we' have become like the thing 'we' study.

The ***Intellectuals Critique*** challenges media studies from a position of high intellectual insight, usually from another academic field. Because its

213

spokespeople count themselves as deep thinkers and proper researchers, they assess our research as lacking in substance, *useless intellectually*, *lacking in rigour*, *mediocre* and *low quality* deriving from *over-reading* the materials we study. Here, to be new is to have cheap novelty value. Unlike, say, computer studies which would surely count as a genuine subject, albeit by necessity new, to this critique the newness of media studies proves that we are insubstantial, a *novelty*, *lacking real history*.

The **Conservative Critique** discovers a politics, fake of course, within the subject – and taints the validity of the whole subject with that. It is not even conceivable that the political claims and values of the field (let us say, concern about how people are represented in and through different media) might be based on the findings of research. The values are rejected, therefore the research has to be fixed. So 'we' talk *neo-marxist clap-trap*, which offers students a kind of *pseudo-religion*, not much short of *brainwashing*. It all comes down to *PC nonsense*.

The **Anti-Intellectual Critique** uses the language of generalised suspicion of idea-mongers to damn 'us'. We are *trendy*, our field is a *cop-out*, we offer *junk degrees*. What is curious about this critical position is how it adopts the language of tabloid journalism in effect to draw a line between real and bogus intellectuals. It is only worth smearing *'junk'* degrees if there are others that are more worthwhile. A *'cop-out'* implies something more worthwhile which is being avoided. But in each case the critique is *expressed* in populist terms. So, this language of criticism, interestingly, is as likely to be found in the broadsheets as in the rarer tabloid materials.

These four sources of attack share a common premise, that in some way media studies amounts to and embodies a 'death of standards'. It is this which allows their combination. Although the 'standards' would be differently conceived by each source, by remaining implicit they can largely agree. 'We' are a threat because we amount to (we teach, we preach, we embody) a *'dumbing down'* of culture. It is in this respect that the **Employers' Critique** seems different. It is (with one exceptional strain, as I shall show) distinct and largely separate from the other four. It asserts that 'our' courses are *useless for practical purposes*, they put a *false glamour* on the media and sell students *false job* hopes, and a *false vocationalism*. We *mislead students*. We are simply *irrelevant*. This critique is the one which invests virtually all the specifically news items, albeit traces of it can be found melanged in with others in feature articles (though much more rarely in opinion pieces). But it bears no trace of that 'critique of standards' which consumes and unites the other positions.

Consider then how this might lead us to answer the third question I posed above, concerning how overt and coherent each position is. Let us look first at the critique from that 'employers' perspective.

The Employment Critique

The main charge here is that media studies courses hold out to students false and unrealistic prospects of a job in the media. A common ploy is to get a well-known media professional to condemn the subject. Thus, for example, in the *Guardian*, 17 February 1997, news presenter John Humphrys is quoted about his career to the effect that 'if I were doing it again I'd go to University. I would *not* do a "media studies" course. Better, surely, to do a more rigorous degree and maybe a post-grad media course later. Better still to get your knees brown on a local paper or radio station'. Meanwhile, an editorial entitled 'How not to be a journalist' which appeared in the *Independent* on the same day as an article about media studies headed 'The trendy travesty' stated that 'this paper regards a degree in media studies as a disqualification for the career of journalism' – which was ever so slightly odd in that the paper had just hired as one of its best-paid star columnists Suzanne Moore, the proud possessor of a degree in media studies. Furthermore, one of the academics interviewed in the 'travesty' article was a former *Independent* journalist.[8]

The claim that media students don't have a good employability record (in the media or elsewhere) was given legitimacy by a report published in 1996 by Alan Smithers and Pamela Robinson of Brunel University, which formed the pretext for the 'travesty' piece. According to the *Independent*, the report showed that 15.2 per cent of media students were still 'casting around' for work six months after receiving their degrees, putting them second (after design students) in the league of unemployed graduates. Smithers himself is quoted to the effect that

> The implication is that media studies will lead to a career writing scripts for *EastEnders* or *Coronation Street*, that you will have the edge over students who have not done such a course. But there isn't a direct connection. By and large the media recruit on talent whatever the background.

Since then, Smithers has become the most regular representative in the press of this particular point of view. The factual inaccuracies, which have been repeatedly pointed out, have more recently underpinned Woodhead's intervention. Woodhead received a good deal of press coverage at the beginning of March 2000 when, in a discussion on lifelong learning on the Radio 4 *Today* programme, he singled out media studies as an example of the kind of courses 'that I do not think are likely to lead to worthwhile employment', adding that

> It might enhance students' lives, but if you embark on a degree course and you drop out – and one in five do – or if you embark

on a degree course, finish, and then find yourself unemployed, is that enhancing your life? I don't think so ... I have talked to enough people in the media to know that there is a profound scepticism as to whether these courses teach the students the skills and understanding that they want.

This standard argument from employment is readily refuted by two simple counters; first, that the great majority of courses which include study of the media make no claim at all to vocational preparation of students – they are based instead on a claim of the central importance of the media in the processes of contemporary life; second, and almost paradoxically, an extraordinarily high proportion of students exiting these courses do in fact enter the 'media world' in a wide sense (covering public relations, marketing, small media companies, etc.).[9] But this vulnerability to factual defeat becomes less important if this approach is synced into a wider political-educational project: to shift the whole basis on which degrees are designed, chosen and evaluated so that they match only what is needed, financially and ideologically by 'the market'. Thus Smithers' final contribution to the *Independent* piece appears to link the attack on media studies to an endorsement of the further marketisation of the university system:

> The question, says Mr Smithers, is whether students would choose to study the new cool subjects if they had real choices. As it is, they know their fees will be paid by the taxpayer, which means that they don't have to think as hard as they would if they were having to contribute. 'I think there is a connection between the development of higher education and the funding of it,' he says.

This is an evaluative argument for redefining the *purposes* of higher education. At this point, questions of 'standards' rear their heads again, and overturn the supposedly empirical claims he has based his complaints on up to this point. What those evaluations might be, became clearer in a quotation in the *Evening Standard*, 14 May 1997, under the headline 'A degree in futility', that 'I can see why reading Shakespeare provides illumination. I don't see how engaging with *Coronation Street* is doing the same thing.' Here Smithers the employment analyst segues into something quite different.

I venture the conclusion that the employment critique lurks as a backdrop, a semi-separate resource to which critics can turn to provide tougher 'ammunition' than soft complaints about 'standards' can provide. What though of the other positions which, as I hoped I have showed, are each marked at least in the press by a blurriness, and a will to merge and find common cause with each other around 'standards'. How far have they been articulated and coherently laid out? It is worth looking, at least in brief, at three cases where the 'case' against media studies has been spelt out: by

Roger Scruton, giving full voice to the conservative critique; by Richard Hoggart, who speaks much of the language of the cultured critique; and by Melanie Phillips, who manages to make a peculiar custard out of combining several positions.

Roger Scruton's Conservative Critique

The conservative attack on media studies in the 1990s is almost identical to the conservative attack on sociology from the late 1960s onwards. To illustrate this one has only to compare Roger Scruton in the *Independent* describing media studies as 'very political with a clapped-out Marxist agenda', or in the *Standard* piece quoted above as 'sub-Marxist gobbledegook' with Roger Scruton over twenty years ago delivering a malediction on sociology in *The Meaning of Conservatism* (1984).

According to Scruton, sociology courses were typical of those degrees 'connected with the rise of humanities departments in polytechnics. Their guiding principle is the principle of "relevance", according to which education is not an end but a means' (ibid.: 149). The first step towards creating 'relevant' courses consists in setting up what he calls 'second-order' subjects or 'meta-disciplines', which is done by 'throwing together rival disciplines and creating links with areas of "relevance" and "social concern"' (ibid.: 150). This project, he argues, is particularly strongly supported by sociology which 'containing no agreed theoretical structure, and having all but eliminated from its content the reflections of those perceptive men who founded it (men like Durkheim and Weber, whose style was the historical style, of elevated critical insight), may exist largely as a vehicle for mindless statistics and political prejudice. There is nothing to which it cannot be applied, and its application is always and inevitably "relevant"'. (ibid.: 150–51).

A clear example linking the critique of both sociology *and* media studies came from the then Education Secretary John Patten, in the Conservative house journal, the *Spectator* ('Must think harder', 2 October 1993). This early attack in many ways raised the banner for later onslaughts. 'What I really want', fulminated Patten, 'is a counter-revolution against the pseudo-religions of radical sociology, the flabbier social sciences, and the apocalyptic diatribes of extreme environmentalism that now pass for serious intellectual activity'. Later in the same piece, media studies is explicitly singled out as a 'pseudo-religion' – along with 'literary theory, feminism or the more radical whores of sociology'. What is apparently wrong with these subjects is their 'woolliness' and 'moral and intellectual softness' as compared to 'the hard objectivity of science, its abstraction from the human and its concern for a truth which is independent of us all'.

Earlier, I quoted Brenda Maddox inveighing against 'political correctness' in media studies. This ties in with Scruton's attack on media studies as exemplifying the increasing number of degree courses which are regarded as means to an end as opposed to ends in themselves. In this sense the Conservative critique differs considerably from the employment critique, for which, logically, media studies might 'redeem' itself if it became vocationally useful. But this would be anathema to the high-minded Scruton, who makes it clear in the *Standard* that 'there's nothing really to learn except by way of an apprenticeship on the job'. Higher education, for Scruton, has to be a sphere of abstracted, disconnected 'learning of good things'. To offend against such a requirement sounds awfully like a great compliment to me.

Richard Hoggart's Liberal *cri de coeur*

Richard Hoggart's articulation of the critique has its roots in a debate which has been raging for some time both *within* cultural studies and, to some extent, *between* media and cultural studies (see in particular Ferguson and Golding, 1997, and Philo and Miller, 1997). It comes from an *ideological* position which is very different from that of the Conservative critique. Hoggart's critique is part of a much broader attack on what he perceives as the damaging trend towards relativism in all areas of British society, a trend which, however, he sees particularly clearly illustrated by recent developments within media and cultural (as well as literary) studies. This argument finds its fullest expression in *The Way We Live Now* (1996), a book which is referenced by both the *Independent* piece above and in an article by Henry Porter, headed 'Trivial pursuit', in the *Guardian*, 1 February 1996.

Briefly summarised, Hoggart's argument goes something like this. Relativism, defined as 'the obsessive avoidance of judgements of quality, or moral judgement' (ibid.: 3), is the 'perfect soil' for the 'endless and ever changing urges' that characterise technologically advanced, consumer-driven, media-saturated, capitalist societies such as our own, in which 'the great body of people are more and more led towards having undifferentiated, shared, but always changing tastes' (ibid.: 6). This is a world in which, whatever its other inequalities, 'all opinions are as good as all others; therefore head-counting will produce the "right" answer on every conceivable issue' (ibid.: 8). Hence populism and the 'manufacture of consent' enter the picture. At the same time, the forces of consumption contribute to a process of homogenisation: 'so as to make economies of scale and enhance profits, consumerism must persuade people to allow themselves to be seen as, to come to see themselves as, a single body with shared tastes, small to large' (ibid.: 8).

Hoggart speaks with the mantle of having helped to 'found' cultural studies in the UK. He easily therefore sounds like a parent admonishing an errant child. We are 'told off' for being too theoretical *and* for refusing to make judgements. So what sorts of judgement does Hoggart himself make, and on what bases? An indicative passage is where he grades popular songs according to whether they are irredeemably 'mass', or whether they have saving elements of the prettily popular. In the latter (A) category come songs such as 'Let's Face The Music And Dance', and 'Jeepers Creepers' ('songs with some life in them'). In the bad (C) category come 'You'll Never Walk Alone' and 'Keep Right On To The End Of The Road'. Why? Apparently the latter are simply 'indefensible, often silly emotions, jingoism, false bucolics, palliness pretending to be the feeling of community' (Ibid: p. 110). This is a cartload of nostalgia spiced with arbitrary judgements. It is a fair sample of what he would put in place of the extensive *debate* that has taken place within cultural and media studies over *how* we should try to find a basis of value-judgements without simply imposing tastes learned by dint of our particular social locations. Perhaps, though, the most offensive part is Hoggart's reduction of the critical work of cultural studies to the 'roar of the crowd':

> Hence, as in so much, the only standard is the echo back. If the roar of the crowd comes back, that is success, and so unanswerably right and good. This is the numbers game, a substitute for judgment, the refusal to tangle with 'better' and so with 'worse'. In this world there can be no 'worse', only failure by numbers; there can be no 'better', only the jingle of the cash registers and the number-crunching of the pollsters. (ibid.: 10)

It is offensive because, crucially and often unpopularly, cultural and media studies have spoken loudly over many years in support of *minority* tastes and cultures. Be it on the basis of class, gender, ethnicity, fan cultures, or whatever, one of the defining marks of my field has been its willingness to voice the marginal. It is plain insulting for Hoggart to impose *his* standards as though the alternative is simply 'mass culture'.

Melanie Phillips' defence of 'civilisation'

That Melanie Phillips is no admirer of media studies is clear from quotations by her elsewhere in this book. To these we can add her attack on Guy Cumberbatch (during the Newson furore) as a 'prominent member of the mediocracy' and as representing 'ivory-tower academics in thrall to an abstract ideology' (*Observer*, 17 April 1994) and her observation in the *Guardian* (12 March 1993) that 'there is no proof that any cultural artefacts civilise society; yet we know they do. The impact of the works of Michelangelo, Shakespeare or Mozart on the human psyche can hardly be measured in statistics by the professor of communications at Penge University. And if we can't quantify the civilising effects of culture, how can we quantify its debasing impact?'

However, the clearest statement of Phillips' antipathy towards media studies is to be found in her book *All Must Have Prizes* (1998). This, like Hoggart's *The Way We Live Now*, utilises media/cultural studies as a symptom of a wider malaise – in this instance, 'liberalism betrayed', by

Left and Right alike – but here the approach is so scatter-shot, the tone so apocalyptic, the generalisations so ill-informed, that it is at times hard to understand the points which the author is trying to make. Indeed, as Colin MacCabe pointed out in his review in the *New Statesman* (13 September 1996) the book itself is actually a damning example of the very process of intellectual degeneration which it so hysterically condemns:

> It says something about the collapse of any hierarchy of authority in knowledge that this farrago of ignorance and inaccuracy can appear under the imprint of a reputable publisher . . . This is a book for our media age, in which opinion is all, knowledge nothing and the niche marketing of prejudice has reached a fine art.

However, there *is* an argument at the heart of this deeply confused and confusing book, and we need to understand what it is if Phillips' attack on media studies is to make any kind of sense.

According to Phillips, since 1979 the Labour and Tory parties have not embodied opposing political philosophies but 'represented two sides of the same individualistic coin'. She continues:

> The left stood for egalitarian individualism in the social sphere, for the doctrine of equality of values and lifestyles; the right stood for libertarian individualism in the economic sphere, for the doctrine that those who could achieve wealth and success should be left alone to do so while those who lost out would have to go to the wall. Neither stood for a culture based on altruism, fuelled by a principled concern for other people. The moral relativism of the left was thus the mirror image of the debased liberalism of the right.
>
> (Phillips 1998: 289)

The manner in which the Tories under Thatcher and Major 'debased' the liberalism of Adam Smith by refurbishing the nineteenth century 'Manchester Liberalism' of Herbert Spencer and others, as well as turning for inspiration to Friedrich Hayek, is actually convincingly argued by Phillips. However, her main concern is to show how the 'moral relativism' of the left and the 'debased liberalism' of the right have combined to produce what she calls the 'de-education of Britain'. But although the brickbats are handed out liberally all round, it's hard to escape the conclusion that it's the 'left', in the form of 'the new orthodoxies of free expression and "relevance"' (ibid.: 104), which is perceived by Phillips as having to shoulder most of the blame for this state of affairs. And although her account of modern educational methods is so caricatural as to be laughable, it has to be outlined, briefly, if we are to understand where her attack on media studies is actually coming from.

According to Phillips, then, back in the 1960s and 1970s the educational orthodoxy began to take hold that 'children could somehow pick up knowledge by their own efforts, and that what they did manage to pick up through their everyday lives was of greater value than anything that might be taught them in the classroom' and, furthermore, that 'nothing should be taught which might cause any child to fail or to feel that others were progressing faster'. Thus rules of spelling, punctuation and grammar 'became a taboo' (ibid.: 105), and all languages and dialects were regarded as good as one another. Furthermore, 'the revolt against teaching the rules of grammar became part of the wider repudiation of all external forms of authority and any discrimination that might flow from them' (ibid.:106). What we have apparently witnessed, in the name of creativity and the primacy of the imagination, is a seismic shift from teacher to pupil, and from adult to child, along with

> The sidelining of objectivity, the retreat from facts, order and evidence into the world of make-believe as a higher order of experience [and] the distrust of teachers, whose influence on their pupils is apparently wholly malign, whose every utterance fetters children's capacity for independent thought and from whom children therefore need to be protected.
>
> (ibid.: 115)

The consequence of this state of affairs is that

> Education, as the primary site for the transmission of a culture, can no longer easily transmit a hierarchy of cultural values because there is no longer general agreement that any mode of expression is better or worse than any other. This is cultural relativism. In the schools, it flows inevitably from the destruction of all external authority and the relocation of that authority within the child ... It is first cousin to that moral relativism by which moral values have also been privatised, so that everyone has become their own individual arbiter of conduct with no-one else permitted to pass judgement. Judgement itself is taboo for an intelligentsia which has declared an egalitarianism of values.
>
> (ibid.: 116)

And this is where media studies enters the picture. We, apparently, are in the business of 'advocating the destruction of literacy and sounding the "retreat from the word"' and promoting the media as 'of equal value to literary texts'.

Anyone who has worked in the fields of media or cultural studies will have real problems recognising themselves in this account, because it is based on such a great deal of sheer ignorance.[10] The great successes of the field have been in the way that, repeatedly, researchers and thinkers have pressed us to *change the questions*. So, for instance, the powerful influence had by the work of Pierre Bourdieu has been to ask us to investigate the *sources* of different groups' judgements – and the ways those judgements occasion judgements of self and others ('Taste classifies the classifier', as Bourdieu tidily puts it.) Unable to conceive the way such reformulations change the questions we need to ask, Phillips can only see this as the abolition of all value-judgements. If we do not *teach her standards*, we must not have any ...

What finally needs noting about Phillips and others like her is the extra-ordinary power they attribute to the likes of us. This of course is how and why media studies signifies – it is always more than just a field of knowledge. Describing the Centre for Contemporary Cultural Studies at Birmingham University after Stuart Hall became its 'leader', she writes:

> The Centre promptly broke with the literary traditions of its founders in favour of a Marxist perspective which saw the literary tradition as a form of ideological domination. Under Hall, the Birmingham Centre became the catalyst for every passing fad in critical theory and significantly helped the culture to implode under the pressures of relativism

> (ibid.: 126)

'Imploding a whole culture' ... that is an attribution of quite awesome power! Its rhetorical clangour is most reminiscent of the kinds of claims made by the evangelically-minded about the 'powers of satan'. What it evidences is the high degree to which the world-view of people such as Phillips has become uncomfortable and unsure. She sure needs a devil to blame.

ENDNOTE

The point of examining these three wider articulations of the 'case against media studies' is not to prove them wrong – if that were seriously needed, this just isn't the place for it. It is to demonstrate how each assault turns on a set of claims about 'values' and 'standards'. 'Media studies' is evidently a blister on the heels of a number of feet. This is not for what we do, at all – the staggering ignorance among our critics soon betrays this. In each case, be it in press coverage or in book-accounts, it is easy to see the caricatures, bedded on a fine tilth of false claims. But that isn't the point, really. It is because we *signify*. We are, media studies is, a symptom of a felt malaise. This conclusion, if correct, doesn't suggest any easy solutions. I began with the problem of the ignoring or marginalising of a powerful, innovative set of researches of the kind that we introduced in our new Introduction. It is now possible to see why. It isn't because they have been found wanting in some way. It is because we insist on asking awkward questions. As that has been the project of this book since its inception, it's not a bad – albeit not an easy – place to end up.

The question that remains, and will remain unanswered here, is this: why 1996? If attacks peaked then, and if those attacks turned on media studies' ability to 'symbolise', what wider developments were peaking then such that we were *needed* as demonstrable enemies? My suspicion is that a much wider set of claims about 'declining standards' were coming to a head at that time: concerns covering education, children, political morals, the media, etc. But I have to say that this is a suspicion, and to test the suspicion is beyond the bounds of this essay.

NOTES

1 Of these four, two were from the London *Evening Standard*, which often claims for itself a sort of national perspective. Indeed one of the articles is partly borrowed from a piece earlier published (by the same individual) in the *Independent*, which re-emphasises its para-national position.

2 **Other** includes: *The Big Issue* (1), *Broadcast* (1), *Spectator* (1), *New Statesman* (1), *20:20* (1), *Times Educational Supplement* (1), *Higher* (3).

3 These were *Sun* (1), *Express* (1) – but we must be aware that much can be hidden here. The *Sun* article was a sneering reference in an opinion column. The *Express* material was a front-page lead, plus feature article, plus editorial.

4 In March 2000, the *Mail* carried a substantial report on Woodhead's critique of media studies ('Woodhead criticises media studies boom'), with a strong response from Brian Fender of HEFCE. If there is a direction to the *Mail*'s report, it is to associate the 'media studies issue' with a general problem of funding HE and the debate about top-up fees. There is no sign of an *intellectual* critique of the subject.

5 Note that this number is higher than that for all published references, because several newspaper editions carried a set of linked articles on the same day: for example the *Sunday Times* (6 December 1998) carried a news report, a feature and an associated editorial on 'media studies'.

6 I should say that choosing these quotations was not easy. Too often, as for instance in Judith O'Reilly's infamous 'exposé' of Coventry University's media studies course (*Sunday Times*, 12 December 1998), the dismissive judgements were so embedded and scattered as to make meaningful quotation nigh on impossible. The quotation from the editorial associated used here does not do full justice to her snide invective.

7 Let me say now that I am not assuming that Brian was accurately quoted – for the purposes of this article, that is not the issue. The issue is the function 'his' words were able to perform for the newspaper.

8 Interesting to note a sharp shift of position. Following the Woodhead intervention the *Independent* carried an editorial ('Mr Woodhead tilts at another trendy windmill') which takes a very different line, which concludes with this virtual panegyric: '[T]he point about the mass communications industry is that it is worth studying in its own right. Understanding the media – newspapers, broadcasting and now the Internet – is increasingly important for a career in business, and certainly in politics. The case for media studies as a proper academic discipline is overwhelming.'

9 Research by the then Standing Conference on Cultural, Communication and

Media Studies in Higher Education in 1996 showed that nationally students from these courses were doing *better* than other sectors of the social sciences and humanities in finding course-related employment.

10 Phillips is guilty of enormous carelessness in her book. At one point, for instance, she complains that media education is harmful because it 'has an explicitly ideological purpose' (ibid.: 118). How does Phillips know this? Because David Buckingham says so. The only problem is, however, that Phillips is quoting others quoting Buckingham. Had she bothered to read Buckingham's original text she would have discovered that he is actually *criticising* such a conception of media studies, and that it is only one among a number of competing paradigms of the subject. This kind of mistake is symptomatic of her simple lack of knowledge and understanding. Or as John Sutherland put it in his review in the *London Review of Books* (3 October 96): 'the whole argument of *All Must Have Prizes* rests on unsubstantiated assertion. Where one has any personal acquaintance with the subject, Phillips is invariably wrong ... It's a nice question as to what is most offensive about this book: the author's ignorance of her subject, the laziness of her methods, or the arrogance of her pronouncements'.

REFERENCES

Ferguson, M. and Golding, P. (1997), *Cultural Studies in Question*, London: Sage.

Hoggart, R. (1996), *The Way We Live Now*, London: Pimlico.

Phillips, M. (1998), *All Must Have Prizes*, Warner Books.

Philo, G. and Miller, D. (1997), *Cultural Compliance*, Glasgow: Glasgow University Media Group.

Scruton, R. (1984), *The Meaning of Conservatism*, Basingstoke: Macmillan.

INDEX

Note: this index does not include references to categories such as 'media effects' and 'violence' as these are central to all the discussions throughout.

Accused, The 3–4
advertising 31, 36–9, 67
Age Green Guide 117
Akdeniz, Yaman 193, 194
Alton, David 27, 28, 30, 181
Amiel, Barbara 182
Americanisation 171–2, 174
Anthropophagous 130
Apocalypse Now 132
Appleyard, Bryan 167
Arnold, Matthew 154
audiences: audience research 2–23, 43, 87, 137–8; fans 126–34, 135–46
Australian, The 118
Australian Broadcasting Tribunal 121

Baby of Macon, The 34
Bacon-Smith, Camille 43
Bad Lieutenant 137, 180
Bad Taste 130
Bagehot, Walter 153
Barker, Martin 35, 38, 40, 89; and Brooks, Kate 8–10
Barlow, G. and Hill A. 135, 177–8
Basic Instinct 4
Basketball Diaries, The 23
BBC 174, 203
Belson, William 40–1, 87
Bill, The (ITV) 44
Blackboard Jungle 44, 173
Blunkett, David 206, 207
Bragg, Sara and Grahame, Jenny 88
Brain Dead 132
Brighton Rock 172
British Board of Film Classification (BBFC) 90, 97–8, 134
Broadcasting Standards Council 194
Brown, Ray 76
Bryant, J. and Anderson D. R. 76

Bryant, Martin 117–18
Buckingham, David 13–14, 18, 43, 76, 89, 97, 98, 103; and Sefton-Green, Julian 98
Bulger, James 28, 29, 30, 32, 66, 69, 79, 80, 84, 117, 123–4, 150, 158, 179, 187

Cameron, Deborah and Frazer, Elizabeth 103
Campbell, Beatrix 123
Cannibal Ferox 132
Cannibal Holocaust 132
Capper, Suzanne 29, 180–1
Carmageddon 189
Carrie 80, 129
cartoons 11–12
Castle of Frankenstein 126, 128, 132
censorship 35, 68, 70, 74–5, 82, 121–2, 152, 166, 171, 172, 180, 181; Obscene Publications Act 131, 194–5; Telecommunications Act 194–5; Video Recordings Act 131, 179, 181
Centre for Child and Media Studies 88–9
Centre for Media Literacy 88–91, 94–6, 98, 105
Chambers, Iain 174
Chapman, Cecil 157
Chard, Lawrence 196
Cherland, M. R. 103
Child's Play (series) 28–30, 32–4, 117, 180, 182
children 27–34, 63–76, 79–81; child experts 152–8; child pornography 192, 195–200; conceptions of childhood 14, 63–76, 78–85; fears over children 68–70, 78–81; Protection of Children Act 196
Cinefantastique 128
Cherry, Brigid 23

225

Christine 132
class 35, 63–4, 73, 113, 115, 154, 155,
    166–7, 170–83
Clockwork Orange 175–6
Closing Ranks (BBC) 3
Clover, Carol 24
Cohen, Nick 211
Collins, Richard and Purnell, James
    167
Columbine High School 23
comics 29
common sense 27–45, 152–67, 183
Considine, D. 90
Coronation Street (ITV) 215, 216
Coveney, Peter 81
Crazies, The 129
Crimewatch UK (BBC) 3–4
Cronos 132
Cumberbatch, Guy and Howitt, Dennis
    39–41, 152
Cunningham, S. 120
Curthoys, L. and Docker, J. 114

Daily Express 187, 209
Daily Mail 137, 155, 172, 174, 176, 180,
    205
Daily Sketch 174
Daily Telegraph 137, 176, 187, 191, 205,
    208
Dalrymple, Theodore 181
Dark Side, The 134
Dawn of the Dead 132
Dead Ringers 132
Die Hard (series) 10–11, 137, 138
Dirty Harry 42
Dixon, Jeremy 196
Docker, J. and Curthoys, L. 114
Doolittle, J. C. 90
Dorr, Aimee 76
Downing, L. 112
Driller Killer 177
Driscoll, Margaret 181
Duel 132
Dunblane 150, 158
Durkin, K. 76

Eagleton, Terry 96
EastEnders (BBC) 3–4, 215
Eastwood, Clint 42
Edinburgh Review 151–2
effects research 64–5, 111, 122, 124,
    152–3, 161–6
Ellsworth, Elizabeth 88

Elton, Ben 135
Eraserhead 129
Eron, L. D. 106
Evening News 176
Evening Standard 191
Evil Dead, The 130–2
Exorcist, The 80, 127–8, 129, 132
Eyeball 134
Eysenck, Hans and Nias, P. 164

Falling Down 15
Famous Monsters 128, 132
Fangface 11
Fangoria 128, 129, 131, 134
Feather, Clive 198
Fenton, Frances 162, 163
Ferenczi, Sander 80
Ferguson, Marjorie and Golding, Peter
    218
Ferman, James 88, 131
Field, Frank 179
Financial Times 205
Fiske, John and Dawson, Robert 10–11,
    15, 16
Fit To Win 165, 166
Flesh 175
Fly, The 129
Ford, Harrison 94
Freeman, A. 155–16
Freud, Sigmund 78, 81, 163–4
Friday The Thirteenth 129

Gabriel, John 15–16
Gans, Herbert 76, 171
Gauntlett, David 152, 193, 197
Geen, R. G. 76
Geertz, Clifford 164
gender 65, 113–14, 115–16
Gerbner, George 90, 91, 100, 106
Ghostwatch (BBC) 71
Ghouri, N. 87
Golding, P. and Middleton, S. 180
Good Son, The 132
Good Time Girl 172
Goode, E. and Ben-Yahuda, N. 97, 98
Goodfellas 180
Gore Zone 129
Grand Auto Theft 189
Grange Hill (BBC) 42, 85
Grassby, Charles E. 190
Greenway, Harry 179
Greenwood, James 155
Griffiths, Mark 188–9, 194

Guardian 175, 182, 187, 188, 189, 190, 191–2, 205, 206, 207, 208, 209, 215, 218, 219
Gunter, Barrie 189

Hall, Stuart *et al.* 180
Halloween 129
Hamilton, Angus 193
Hamilton, David 196
Hamlet 94
harm 1–2, 13, 16, 30–1, 35, 38, 64, 70–1
Hart, L. 103
Haunting, The 132
Hawes, Joseph M. 159
Hellraiser 130
Henry: Portrait of a Serial Killer 135, 137, 132
Herald Sun (Sunday) 111–12
Herz, J. C. 17
Higonnet, Anne 196
Hill, A. C. 177–9
Hill, Annette 7–8, 136, 138
Hill, Clifford 200
Hodge, Robert and Tripp, David 11–13, 76, 93
Hoffman, D. and Novak, T. 191
Hoggart, Richard 174–5, 216, 218–19
Holland, Patricia 78, 84, 196
Hollway, W. 103
Hollywood Chainsaw Hookers 130
Holman, J. C. and Braithwaite, V. A. 76
horror films 30–2, 34, 38, 42, 126–34
Howard, Michael 27
Howard, Sue 16–17
Hungerford 69, 76
Hunt, Darnell 14–15
Hunter, I. 96
Huntley, R. 122

I Spit On Your Grave 177
ideology 170, 203–4, 218
Independent 82, 84, 167, 180, 187, 205, 206, 207, 215
Independent on Sunday 157, 205, 210–12
Independent Television Commission 194
Innocent Blood 132
Internet 189–200
Internet Service Providers Association 199
Internet Watch Foundation 195, 199–200
ITN 203

Jenkins, P. 97
Johnston, C. M. 95
Joint Working Party on Violence on Television 88
Judge Dredd 8, 10
Jurassic Park 42

Kallen, Horace 160–1, 166
Killing Zoe 137
King, Rodney (Los Angeles Riots) 14–15, 42
King of Kings 30
Kristeva, Julia 82
Kuhn, Annette 35, 166

Lashley, Karl S. and Watson, John B. 165
Le Bon, Gustav 154–5
Liebes, T. and Katz, E. 76
Linné, Olga 165
Lion King, The 118
lobby groups 36, 45; Movement for Christian Democracy 27, 30; Parliamentary Group Video Enquiry (*Video Violence and Children*) 177, 183, 188
Look Who's Talking (Channel 4) 85
Lord of the Flies 80
Low, Rachel 171
Lydston, Frank 155, 160

McCabe, Colin 220
Mackay, Charles 154
McLelland, J. S. 153
Maddox, Brenda 208, 217
Mail on Sunday
Malcolm, Derek 175
Man Bites Dog 135, 137, 140, 141
Manhunter 132
Mann, Sally 79, 81
Mannheim, Karl 9–10
Margolis, Jonathan 208–9
Mario Bros (series) 17
Martin, J. 176
Marx, Karl 153
Mary Poppins 73
Mathews, Tom Dewe 35, 176
Mead, L. M. 179
media: coverage of effects issues 27, 28, 29, 79, 84, 150–67, 176–83; education 87–106; literacy 66–7; messages 30–1, 35, 65, 183; studies 35, 43–5, 66, 112–13, 152–3, 209–23

Melody Maker 174
Mercury (Hobart) 118
Merchant, Vicki 190
Mighty Morphin' Power Rangers 82
Miller, Alice 81
Miller, David *et al.* 20–2
Mirror 79
modernity 150–2
Morgan, D. L. 136
Morris, Lydia 180
Morrison, David 43; *et al.* 5–7
Motel Hell 130
Mrs Doubtfire 75
Murdock, Graham 165, 200; and
    McCron, Robin 152
Murphy, R. 172
Murray, Charles 179–80

National Council on Public Morals
    160
Nationwide (BBC) 127
Natural Born Killers 137, 141, 146
Naughton, John 190, 194, 200
Near Dark 132
Neighbours 202
Neil, Andrew 150, 152
New Scientist 187
New Statesman 220
New York Ripper, The 132
News of the World 18
Newson, Elizabeth (*The Newson Report*)
    27–45, 63, 68, 76, 219
Night of the Living Dead, The 129,
    132
Nightmare on Elm Street 67, 72, 73,
    132
No Orchids for Miss Blandish 172
Noose 172

O'Toole, Laurence 193, 195, 196, 197,
    198
Observer 152, 190, 198–200, 205, 219
Oliver, Ron 196
Omen, The 71, 80, 132
Orwell, George 170, 172
Oswell, David 200

Palmer, P. 76
panics 67, 156–8
Park, Robert 154
Parliamentary All-Party Family and
    Child Protection Group 200
Patton, John 217

Pearce, Edward 182
Pearson, Geoffrey 151, 170, 171, 174
Penley, Constance 43
Penny Dreadfuls 31–2, 41, 151, 155, 158,
    170
Petersen, Frederick 162
Petley, Julian 76, 176, 179, 200
Pet Sematary 71
Phillips, M. 88
Phillips, Melanie 152, 182, 219–22
Philo, Greg 19–20, 87, 90, 91, 97, 98; and
    Miller, David 218
Pinedo, Isabel 24
Playstation Plus 189
Policy Studies Institute 44
politicians on media effects 74
Poole, Steven 17
pornography 28, 37, 67, 193–4; computer
    pornography 28, 189–200
Porter, Henry 209, 218
Possession of Joel Delaney, The 129
Postal 189
Potter, Lynda Lee 176, 182
Pound, Roscoe and Frankfurter, Felix
    158
Prisoner: Cell Block H 114, 115
Professional Association of Teachers
    187–8, 189–90, 200
Provenzo, Eugene 186
Pulp Fiction 7, 87, 89, 136, 137, 138, 140,
    141, 145

Quasimodo's Monster Magazine 128

Radio Times 85
Rambo 76, 82
Redwood, Hugh 171
Reed, Ralph 191
Reservoir Dogs 135, 136, 137, 138, 139,
    140, 141, 142, 144, 145, 150, 167,
    180
Richards, C. 105
Rimm, Marty 191
Rock Around The Clock 174
Rolph, C. H. 176
Rose, Jacqueline 83
Rosemary's Baby 129
Rosengren, Karl-Erik 164–5
Ross, Andrew 76

Samhain 134
Sanjek, David 43
Schindler's List 37

Schlesinger, Philip *et al.* 3–5, 7
Schwarz, Bill 156
Schwarzenegger, Arnold 42, 81–2
Sconce, Jeffrey 43, 97, 101
Scream 111, 124
Scruton, Roger 217–18
Scum 35
Secretan, H. A. 171
Shivers 133, 134
Shock Xpress 133, 134
Sidis, Boris 163
SimCity 17
Smith, D. 117
Smithers, Alan and Robinson, Pamela
    215–16
Society 130
Somerville, Julia 196
Sound of Music, The 118
Space Invaders 17
Spectator 217
Spurgeon, C. 121
Stallone, Sylvester 81–2
Steedman, Carolyn 84
Stern, L. 114
Stockwell, S. 119
Sturgis, Jock 196
Sun 79, 186, 206
Sunday Telegraph 205, 206
Sunday Times 150, 180, 181, 182, 192,
    205, 206, 208
Suschitzky, Wolfgang 84

Tarde, Gabriel 160, 161, 162
Taxi Driver 117
technology 28, 31, 63, 72, 74;
    technophobia 63, 186, 200
Terminator (series) 82
Terror in the Night 95
Texas Chainsaw Massacre, The (series)
    130, 133, 134, 175
Thatcher, Carol 176
Theweleit, Klaus 81
They Made Me A Fugitive 172
Thomas, W. I. 156
Thompson, K. 97
This Island Earth 129
Three Stooges, The 131
Time 191, 192
Times, The 32, 156, 157, 180, 187, 205

Times Educational Supplement 87, 90
Times Higher Educational Supplement,
    The 206
Tom & Jerry 42
Tomb Raider (series) 18
Trash 175
Trevarthen, J. 157
Trip Trap (BBC) 4
True Romance 137, 141, 145
Tudor, Andrew 164
Tulloch, John and Jenkins, Henry 23
Turnbull, Sue 117, 123
TV Violence – Will It Change Your Life?
    (Granada) 28

Under Siege 4
Ungawa! 134

Van Damme, Jean-Claude 81
Van Evra, J. 135
Vanishing, The 132
V-chip 42, 85
video: 27–9, 41–2, 72, 83, 131, 175, 178,
    181, 187; video games 16–18, 31, 186–9;
    'video nasties' 70, 72, 79, 81, 176, 177,
    179, 181, 183
Video Watchdog 133
Videodrome 130
Voojis, M. W. and Van der Voort,
    T. H. A. 88–9, 92–3, 98, 105

Wadsworth, William S. 159–60, 166
Watson, John B. 163–4, 165–6
Which? On-line 194
Whoops! Apocalypse 132
Wilcox, Delos 162
Wild Boys of London 35
Wild One, The 173
Williams Report 74
Willis, Paul 113–14, 115
Winnicott, D. W. 82
Wistrich, Enid 176
Witness 94–5
Woodhead, Chris 202, 215

Young, A. 117
Young, R. 76

Zombie Flesh Eaters 132